RHYMING HOPE AND HISTORY

Social Movements, Protest, and Contention

Series Editor: Bert Klandermans, Free University, Amsterdam

Associate Editors: Ron R. Aminzade, University of Minnesota
David S. Meyer, University of California, Irvine
Verta A. Taylor, University of California, Santa Barbara

For more books in the series, see page 297.

RHYMING HOPE AND HISTORY

Activists, Academics, and Social Movement Scholarship

David Croteau, William Hoynes, and Charlotte Ryan, Editors

Afterword by William A. Gamson

Social Movements, Protest, and Contention
Volume 24

University of Minnesota Press
Minneapolis • London

Published by the University of Minnesota Press
111 Third Avenue South, Suite 290
Minneapolis, MN 55401-2520
http://www.upress.umn.edu

Library of Congress Cataloging-in-Publication Data

Rhyming hope and history : activists, academics, and social movement
scholarship / David Croteau, William Hoynes, and Charlotte Ryan, editors ;
afterword by William A. Gamson.
     p.   cm. — (Social movements, protest, and contention ; v. 24)
Includes bibliographical references and index.
ISBN 0-8166-4620-1 (alk. paper) — ISBN 0-8166-4621-X (pbk. : alk. paper)
1. Social movements. 2. Social movements—Study and teaching. 3. Social
action. I. Croteau, David. II. Hoynes, William. III. Ryan, Charlotte, 1949–
IV. Series.
HM881.R59 2005
303.48'4—dc22
                                                                    2005003715

Printed in the United States of America on acid-free paper

The University of Minnesota is an equal-opportunity educator and employer.

12 11 10 09 08 07 06 05   10 9 8 7 6 5 4 3 2 1

History says, *Don't hope
On this side of the grave.*
But then, once in a lifetime
The longed-for tidal wave
Of justice can rise up,
And hope and history rhyme.

—Seamus Heaney, "The Cure at Troy"

Contents

Acknowledgments

This book is dedicated to William A. Gamson, honoring him for expanding social movement theory and practice. He personifies the effort to bridge the work of academics and activists. While making significant theoretical contributions, his scholarship has targeted key issues of relevance to activists, such as movement strategies and media framing. He also has used his institutional position to carve out space for activists and academics to work together; nowhere is this more evident than in the Media Research and Action Project (MRAP) at Boston College. Bill Gamson's impact as both a colleague and mentor is evident throughout this volume. He has always supported students to work not in his footsteps but in their own way, whether through scholarly research, teaching in any form, or public life, including organizing. We could think of no better way to honor his legacy than to demonstrate that in many distinct venues we continue to do what he does so well.

We thank the American Sociological Association's Fund for the Advancement of the Discipline, particularly Roberta Spalter Roth, and the Graduate School of Arts and Sciences at Boston College. Their support enabled us to bring together these contributors and others to explore the tenuous relationship between social movement scholarship and activism. Zelda Gamson, Sharon Kurtz, Jeff Langstraat, and Stephen Pfohl offered critical support during the project's infancy and evolution. Additionally, we thank the following people for their ongoing support of the project: Eitan Alimi, Mike Anastario, Julie Childers, Joe Christiani, Annette Duke, Jess Geier, Jess Littenberg, Louise Lymperis, Jorge Martinez, Aldon Morris, David Satterwaite, Leah Schmalzbauer, and Matt Williamson.

We especially remember two colleagues who worked to strengthen the connections between theory and practice, Italian sociologist Paolo Donati and artist-activist Alice Trimiew, who both died before this volume was finished.

We are grateful to our editor at the University of Minnesota Press, Carrie Mullen, who provided valuable advice on this project at every stage. We also thank Jason Weidemann for his assistance preparing the manuscript. Finally, we would like to thank the anonymous reviewer for the University of Minnesota Press for a helpful and supportive review and the editors of the Social Movements, Protest, and Contention series—Bert Klandermans, Ron Aminzade, David Meyer, and Verta Taylor—for their support of this project.

Introduction

Integrating Social Movement Theory and Practice

David Croteau, William Hoynes, and Charlotte Ryan

Modern social movement scholarship began in the 1970s when resource mobilization theory broke with many of the underlying assumptions that animated earlier collective behavior theories. Rather than seeing social movement activism as aberrant behavior best explained psychologically, the new theorizing saw activists as rational actors pursuing political goals. Thus began a revolution in movement scholarship, the effects of which are still very much felt today.

Interestingly, this seismic change in scholarship resulted in large measure from close interaction between scholars and movement activists. University campuses were the home base of many people active in the civil rights, student, antiwar, and women's movements. As this volume shows, some movement scholars of this period were themselves politically active in the teach-ins, demonstrations, and debates of the day. Scholarship benefited directly from its close association with activism, and presumably social movement efforts benefited from the participation of social movement students and scholars.

Times have changed. For more than a quarter century, not only has activism on college campuses waned (with some notable exceptions), but also the links between movement scholars and movement activists have dramatically weakened. Ironically, during this same period, social movement scholarship has become more abundant and sophisticated, and the field's legitimacy has become firmly established within the academy. In the process of establishing this legitimacy, however, the scholar-activist connections that fueled previous movement scholarship's development have been largely lost.

Considering both the promise and perils of engaged social movement scholarship, *Rhyming Hope and History* examines the barriers to meaningful collaboration between academics and activists. More important, it explores the potential benefits that result from successful collaborative efforts.

Theory and Practice

The issues raised in the following chapters relate to a much broader issue with which people have long struggled: the creative tension between thinking and action, between theory and practice. In the contemporary academy, this tension troubles a number of disciplines that seek to advance the boundaries of knowledge as well as contribute to pragmatic ameliorative efforts. Women's studies, African-American studies, and gay and lesbian studies, among others, continue to grapple with an often-unstated tension between theorizing and action.

This tension is of particular concern to those who study social movement activism, the focus of this collection. In recent decades, a significant chasm has grown between social movement activists and those who produce formal theories about social movements. Movement theorists usually speak to themselves, rarely reaching beyond the narrow confines of specialized academic journals and conferences. As a result, movement activists generally do not know or use social movement theorists' work. If they are familiar with some of it, they often think it trivial.

For the most part, movement theorists do not seem particularly concerned by this state of affairs. They continue to focus on debates within their theoretical paradigms, rather than on issues of prominent concern for activists. They continue to write in language and in forums geared toward other academics, rather than try to engage activists. Sometimes, they explicitly embrace this inward orientation, calling for a sharp demarcation between study and practice. And some scholars view detachment and distance from the phenomenon under study as methodologically preferable, a measure of rigorous scholarship.

The development of social movement scholarship has certainly led to greater understanding of movement dynamics. But, especially in its abstract development of theory, the field often produces work that is distant from, and irrelevant to, the very struggles it purports to examine. Theorizing is usually done with real-world referents in mind, and activism is usually predicated on some implicit model of social change—thought and action are never completely separate—but generally speaking, the field of social movement studies is isolated from movement efforts, and movement activists often undervalue reflection in the face of more immediate pressing concerns. The result is an artificial divide between the practice of social change and the study of such efforts.

We believe there is a price to be paid for the disconnect that now exists between scholars and activists. Both activism and theory, we contend, are diminished by the failure to integrate the two. Activism uninformed by broader theories of power and social change is more likely to fall prey to common pitfalls and less likely to maximize the potential for change. Social movements without access to routine reflection on practice are prisoners of their present conditions. Theory uninformed by and isolated from social movement struggles is more likely to be sterile and less likely to capture the vibrant heart and subtle nuances of movement efforts. Theorists without significant connections to social movements can end up constructing elegant abstractions with little real insight or utility. Cautioning that social movement theorists are looking inward while social movements and their publics look forward, social movement theorist Mario Diani suggests that social movement theorists

> have forgotten that the broader public's main interest in social movements has to do with their basic goals and key ideas. . . . In the last analysis, lay people are more interested in what movements have to say on broad political and philosophical issues than in the technicalities of mobilization [which] will not facilitate a broader dialogue between the social movement research community and the general public. (2000, 18)

Beyond the general public, social movement activists seek more in-depth dialogues with social movement theorists. Activist-writer-teacher Cynthia Peters says:

> Frankly, I'm tired of these little corners that we all work in. The [U.S.] empire is wreaking terrible havoc around the world and among our own people. I would love to find writing and help and reflection to find out how we can talk to people and develop strategy. Does social movement theory have a public agenda? If it does, I want to read and think about it and have opportunities to talk to you more. . . . I want to hear those ideas and stop spinning my wheels, going from crisis to crisis. (2002)

How might social movement scholarship be different if it took seriously the issues with which activists like Peters grapple? What are the hurdles that must be overcome in trying to produce such work? What lessons can we learn from existing efforts to bridge the academic-activist divide? Such questions have often been ignored by much of the mainstream of social movement studies, but they are the center of attention in this volume. If theorists and practitioners can establish mutually beneficial collaborative relationships, better theory and stronger movements may result.

Structure

The book is organized into three parts. Part I introduces a set of fundamental questions about the value of, and obstacles to, academic-activist collaboration. Part II provides a series of reflective case studies of collaborative work among scholars and activists. Part III explores the implications of such collaboration for social movement theory.

In Part I, writing from the perspective of academics, Richard Flacks examines the price paid by not pursuing more engaged scholarship, and David Croteau considers the structural barriers that perpetuate the academic-activist divide. The subsequent two chapters present activist perspectives on these issues. Cynthia Peters explores what activists could use from academic research, while Richard Healey and Sandra Hinson describe their efforts to encourage activism more informed by theory and strategy.

Part II consists of case studies in which researchers describe their efforts to pursue collaborative work with social movements and reflect on the lessons of these efforts. Kevin Carragee focuses on his role in a local housing struggle where he was both resident activist and academic researcher. William Hoynes reflects on a series of research projects done in collaboration with the media watchdog group FAIR (Fairness and Accuracy In Reporting). Charlotte Ryan draws lessons from a long-term collaboration around media work with a statewide anti–domestic violence coalition. Myra Marx Ferree, Valerie Sperling, and Barbara Risman describe the challenges of joining research and activism in a cross-national setting, in this case, a collaboration between American and Russian feminists. Cassie Schwerner considers the lessons learned from a statewide campaign for educational equity. Finally, Robert Ross tells about the challenges of trying to contribute knowledge to a campaign when the scholar is not fully integrated with the activist effort.

Part III explores implications of the debates set forth in the previous section. Building on past involvements and current concerns, David Meyer considers possibilities for "activism-oriented scholarship." Adria Goodson suggests the need for movement scholars to integrate the insights of other theoretical traditions, particularly from feminists of color. David Snow and Catherine Corrigall-Brown suggest the value of reflection on failure, using framing theory to distill lessons from unsuccessful movement framing experiments. Verta Taylor and Leila Rupp present the theoretical implications of their collaborative research effort with drag queens elaborating on participatory research's value for theory building.

Finally, reflecting on his own life as a collaborative work in progress, William Gamson provides an afterword connecting some of the themes raised in the volume to his own efforts to bridge theorizing and activism. His reminiscences suggest how historical circumstances, social locations, and serendipity all play a role in determining how theorists or activists can challenge structural barriers to collaboration.

Themes

The contributors to this volume have all, in some way, confronted the gulf between theory and practice. Some of the chapters are from activists who are familiar with movement theorizing and who search for more useful ways to integrate theory and practice. But most of the volume's contributors are academics writing about their perspectives and experiences. These academics represent considerable variation, spanning the gamut from those well embedded within the mainstream tradition of social movement scholarship to some working on the edges of academia, to former social movement scholars now working in social change environments.

The authors' distinctive voices and approaches reinforce our belief that there is no single solution, no simple fix for the disconnections between social movement activists and theorists. The authors tailor their responses, building on their existing relationships, their social locations, and their identities and interests, strengths, and weaknesses. Regardless of perspective, each of these chapters sheds a ray of light on our central conundrum. What emerges from these efforts is a multifaceted dialogue among the authors about the complex relationship between theorizing and participating in social movements.

One recurrent theme revolves around how we define and measure the value of academic and activist work. Since academics and activists generally operate in very different institutional contexts, there is often little opportunity for any meaningful discussion among scholars and activists about their distinct understandings of what it means to make a contribution. This is a result, in large part, of the specific ways that these two arenas—the academic and activist worlds—identify goals and define success. As a general rule, academics and activists have a clear understanding of the different worlds within which they operate. But it is surprisingly rare for academics and activists to talk explicitly about these different locations in ways that might suggest both the possibilities and pitfalls of collaborative work.

Recognizing the importance of structural context is an important first step for identifying opportunities to bridge the academic-activist divide. Both social movement theorists and movement activists are located in structural systems that create constraints on our efforts as well as provide possibilities for action. The tension between theory and practice needs to be understood in relation to larger structural forces rather than being individualized as the problem or vision of a single academic or activist.

In addition, we need to recognize how power and inequality shape context. The themes of power and inequality are central to the study of social movements, yet social movement scholars rarely grapple with the fact that they inhabit a social space that shapes their perceptions of reality. In particular, scholars' distance from social movements and scholars' own social locations, interests, and ideology affect how they perceive social movements. Academics situated within powerful institutions are inevitably implicated in the social inequalities that result. Even when aware of resource and status differentials, scholars cannot always avoid their impact.

Another recurrent issue is the variety of roles for academics and activists in collaborative work. Rather than seeing social movements as simply a field site for research and theorizing, social movement scholars can build more participatory and mutually beneficial relationships with movements. This will require both academics and activists to challenge the often-severe barriers to building such collaborative efforts. Many of the authors in this volume describe cultural, structural, and ideological obstacles to building scholar-activist relationships that serve the needs and goals of both parties. Such hurdles cannot be ignored, since they pose considerable challenges to anyone wishing to pursue collaborative work.

But the case studies in this volume show that the obstacles that make collaborative work difficult—especially professional and political norms that emphasize the differences between scholarly and activist methods and goals—can be overcome. This is particularly likely when academics and activists think creatively about their roles when they build partnerships. Academics who study movements can provide valuable insight to those movements about such contentious issues as organizational structure or tactical repertoires, helping movements to gain a broader context for their goals and strategies. Similarly, scholars can benefit from the experiences and wisdom of activists, who often have substantial insight about both their own activist work and the issues central to social movement theory. The difficulty, however, is in bridging a divide often so wide that neither academics nor activists can see how to expand their roles to create genuinely mutually beneficial partnerships. The saying "You can't get there from here" captures their experience.

In exploring how to "get there from here," the various case studies in this volume highlight the importance for academics of establishing standing with the activists with whom they work. In collaborative work, the role of academics in relation to a social movement—their "standing"—is not fixed in the traditional researcher role. Some academics may build relationships with movements as fellow activists, downplaying—but not entirely erasing—their academic status. Other academics may work with movements as issue-oriented experts, with specific knowledge or skills that activists find valuable. Still others may develop research partnerships with movements that are flexible enough to meet both movement and scholarly needs.

Whatever the role of the academic and however it is established, careful reflection on this relationship is essential if both parties are to avoid the pitfalls associated with miscommunication and misunderstanding. For activists, partnerships with academics may provide significant new resources. For academics, such partnerships may provide an opportunity to connect with the "real world" outside the academy and may raise challenging methodological questions. In every case, respect and mutuality must serve as lodestones, grounding principles.

Perhaps the clearest issue that cuts across the chapters in this volume is the complex meaning of theory at the intersection of social movement research and social movement activism. Academic social movement theorizing, the kind that is published in scholarly journals, is often a bundle of contradictions. It can be full of valuable insight about activist conduct and cognition while, at the same time, paying little attention to whether activists have access to, or interest in, such insights. Social movement theory can be remarkably inward looking, paying attention to questions and articulating problems that only other theorists find important. At the same time, social movement theorists can explore issues that activists are too immersed to see, understanding common challenges for different movements or conceptualizing dynamics that are broadly applicable to a range of movements. Working together, each party can help the other see both the forest and the trees.

The problem is not with theory per se. Rather, we need to focus on how academics and activists each conceptualize the role of theory. Successful collaboration between academics and activists need not require the abandonment of theory, but probably will require that theorizing be democratized. Indeed, movement activists often have sophisticated theories about social change (not to mention their often complex theories about the academic world), which are rarely defined as theory by academics. Part of bridging the academic divide is the process of acknowledging the useful knowledge—not just practical experience but theories of change—that is part of the activist tool kit. In this kind of collaborative context, theory is no longer the abstract thinking of distant intellectuals but a central part of the critical, reflective exchange among scholars and activists. To accomplish this, many authors in this book urge scholars and activists to overcome their "relational deficit" (Diani 2000).

Ultimately, the chapters in this volume speak to a continued interest in pursuing collaborative efforts for the mutual benefits they provide. Despite the obstacles, collaborative work can potentially lead to benefits for both scholars and activists. Authors in this volume describe California's labor-theorist collaborations, the Grassroots Policy Project in Washington, DC, and the Highlander Center operating since the 1930s. But there are other examples, such as Oakland's Applied Research Center focusing on race and inequality and the Center for Research on Women (CROW) at the University of Memphis.

Many of the chapters in this volume originated from a conference sponsored by Boston College in the summer of 2002, organized to explore the relationship between social movement scholarship and activism as a working tribute to the legacy of social movement scholar and activist William A. Gamson. Aldon Morris (2002) reflected aloud at the "Hope and History" conference:

> I was listening to the activists talk about the importance of strategy. What social movements teach us—to some extent—is that one must experiment with strategies and tactics to see what works because, in many ways, it is a political process. Maybe we could bring social movement theorists into the real world of social movements—to struggle and experiment with different tactics and strategies, to collect data on strategies, to analyze them, and think it all through [while] out in the field, in the actual heat of the struggle. Maybe the activists should say [to the theorists], "Come out here and let's see what we can learn together."

In the spirit of Gamson's work, we hope this volume will encourage students of social movements both in and out of academia to begin from wherever they find themselves to explore the value added by collaborative reflection on practice.

References

Diani, Mario. 2000. "The Relational Deficit of Ideologically Structured Action." *Mobilization* 5, no. 1: 18.

Morris, Aldon. 2002. Remarks at the "Hope and History" conference, Boston College, June 13.

Peters, Cynthia. 2002. Remarks at the "Hope and History" conference, Boston College, June 13.

I
Activism and Research

1

The Question of Relevance in Social Movement Studies

Richard Flacks

It is nearly fifty years since the publication of C. Wright Mills's *Sociological Imagination* ([1959] 2000). In this work, Mills certainly honored intellectual work for its own sake, but he wanted intellectuals to understand their moral calling: nothing less than to defend human beings' capacities for reason and freedom. Sociologists' contribution to this defense was to help people understand their apparently private troubles as potentially social issues, to enable people to understand their own lives and their local milieus as embedded in social structures and in history.

Social inquiry, therefore, should be driven not mainly by the need to test and refine theories, but by the human need to know and to act:

> Within an individual's biography and within a society's history, the social task of reason is to formulate choices, to enlarge the scope of human decisions in the making of history. The future of human affairs is not merely some web of variables to be predicted. The future is what is to be decided— within the limits, to be sure, of historical possibility. But this possibility is not fixed. . . . Under what conditions do men want to be free and capable of acting freely? Under what conditions are they willing and able to bear the burdens freedom does impose and to see these less as burdens then as gladly undertaken self-transformations? (Mills [1959] 2000, 174–75)

If Mills Were Alive Today, He'd Be Turning Over in His Grave

I read *The Sociological Imagination* as a young graduate student in social psychology in Ann Arbor in 1960. Two years later, I found myself in Port Huron, Michigan, as part of a group of several dozen young people, many of whom had come there from the front lines of the southern civil rights struggle, to write a manifesto for a new generation and found an organization called Students for a Democratic Society (SDS) to represent an emerging New Left. Mills's vision and language powerfully influenced what became the "Port Huron Statement." That statement embodied a hope and demand that the activists of the emerging movements be able to link to the intellectual resources and free space of the university. It saw the university as a new center of social power in the emerging political economy. The university's growing social relevance, its centrality in the creation of knowledge, and its relative openness to free political debate, the statement declared, "together make the university a potential base and agency in a movement of social change."

For one imbued with the spirit and vision of C. Wright Mills and Port Huron, one who has remained within the university all these years since, I've become increasingly dismayed with the prevailing state of social movement studies in American sociology. I think that compared with the 1960s there is far more involvement by sociologists in social movement scenes and activist organizations and networks. Many of us try to be active on campus and off, and many are providing service to projects, making use of our skills and resources to facilitate movement work. Rather than emphasizing the ivory tower isolation of social movement scholars, I want to ask whether the substance of our systematic theorizing and research connects with the work of activists.

To study social movements is, in Mills's terms, to ask about the conditions under which human beings become capable of wanting freedom and acting freely. The effort to study and theoretically illuminate such matters is essential for those engaged in social struggle, helping to provide them with the theoretical and practical knowledge needed for effective action.

There has been an explosion of research and theorizing about social movements in the last twenty years. Much of that work, especially the work that is now regarded as defining the field, does not, it seems to me, provide such illumination. Instead, the field is coming to resemble that mix of inflated theorizing and abstracted empiricism that Mills thought was dominating sociology as a whole in the late 1950s.

The Dominant Paradigm

The big news in social movement studies in the United States in the last few years has been the concerted effort, led by Charles Tilly, Doug McAdam, and Sidney Tarrow, to formulate a conceptual structure for the field. With foundation funding and a base at the Palo Alto Center for Advanced Study in Behavioral Science, they have succeeded in identifying a network of scholars and a conceptual scheme that now define the main thrust of social movement studies. Their work has resulted in a series of research compilations that are intended to exemplify and set the direction for appropriate lines of inquiry. The three leaders recently published a book that lays out a theoretical structure for the domain of what they call "contentious politics." That phrase itself alludes to one of the main goals of their overall project: to integrate theory and research on a wide range of social dynamics, including, for example, social movements, revolutions, ethnic and religious conflicts, and industrial conflict, within a single theoretical framework.

The goal of achieving such integration seems quite worthy. It is strange that studies of movements and of revolution have evolved as separate lines of inquiry with little cross-fertilization and that efforts to understand religious nationalisms and ethnic rivalries seem intellectually distant from studies of other kinds of popular mobilization. So their project of aiming to integrate theoretical analysis of these forms of collective action makes sense, as does their related intention to "challenge the boundary between institutionalized and non-institutionalized politics" (McAdam, Tarrow, and Tilly 2001, 2).

Their overall aim is to find regularities and systematic variations among all kinds of contentious politics, defined as "episodic, collective interaction among makers of claims and their opponents when (a) at least one government is a claimant, an object of claims or a party to the claims, and (b) the claims would, if realized, affect the interests of at least one of the claimants" (McAdam, Tarrow, and Tilly 2001, 5). The TMT group—shorthand for Tilly, McAdam, and Tarrow and the project they lead—make a further important specification of their interest. They are talking about "constitutive contention." Constituted contention means the kinds of political conflict that take place among already established political actors making use of already established political means. *Constitutive* contention refers to political conflicts where previously excluded or new actors are making claims and, typically, are making use of new, and often unauthorized, forms of action. Social movements are primary examples of constitutive contention (along with revolution, "democratization," strike waves, and nationalisms).

I think there is agreement in the field on the following definition of social movements: they are collective efforts, of some duration and organization, using noninstitutionalized methods to bring about social change. TMT's approach emphasizes movements whose change-oriented goals ("claims") have a definite political dimension (involve government in some way). Later on, I'll want to closely examine the ways in which such an explicitly "political" definition of movements limits understanding.

TMT have been among the most important contributors, over several decades, to the systematic study of social movements. Their current efforts at codification represent a culmination of their prior separate efforts. Beginning in the 1970s, they, along with others, questioned previously dominant interpretations of protest and movement and helped set social movement studies on a new course.

The kind of thinking they challenged tended to see collective protest as a form of deviance or pathology. The classic study of social movements had roots in notions of "mob psychology." Classic interpretations saw mass action as an expression of social breakdown and anomie: its leaders were often understood as acting out unconscious psychological drives; its participants as driven by irrational ideology. In the 1960s, mass media depictions of the movement upsurge often used these classic stereotypes, but social scientists who came of age as participants or sympathizers with 1960s movements could not accept such characterizations.

The new look of post-1960s social movement studies involved emphasis on movements as "politics by other means," seeing movements as collective efforts to pursue interests with intelligible strategies and rational goals. Understanding movements required not a psychoanalysis of participants, but an account of the ways in which the emergence and evolution of a movement related to the opportunities, threats, and resources available for achieving movement goals. Movement participation was better explained by examining the ways in which participants were embedded in communities and networks than by supposing that they were uprooted or socially alienated. Rather than seeing movements as irrational or destructive forces, it was truer to the historical record to acknowledge their constitutive role in shaping modern societies.

Many of those who studied social movements in the 1960s and 1970s were themselves politically active. My impression then was that they believed that their work ought to aid efforts to achieve social equality, democracy, "emancipatory goals." There was a pervasive awareness after the 1960s that sociology had, at least in the postwar years, largely been at the service of social control. The slogan of the "sociology liberation movement"—a radical caucus at the American Sociological Association (ASA) meetings in 1968—was "knowledge for whom?" Across all the disciplines, there was hot debate about the social function and moral purpose of the social sciences. Mills's challenge at the start of the 1960s became the conscious project of the new generation in the decade's aftermath.

Out of that period there emerged a kind of consensus that if your research was focused on the relatively powerless and disadvantaged, you had an ethical obligation to enable them to use the results; that one ought to be sensitive to the possible ways your work could be used to perpetuate established social arrangements and repress opposition; that the study of social movements ought to provide movement activists with intellectual resources they might not readily obtain otherwise. Such study could enable better assessment of what worked in the way of strategies and tactics, could help activists locate their efforts in historical and structural terms, and could help movements improve efforts to communicate with bystanders and potential sympathizers, interpret the actions of their antagonists, identify opportunities for leverage, and so on.

The new paradigm, emphasizing issues of "resource mobilization," "political opportunity," and "framing," focused on movement strategy as a primary topic. Work in that vein indeed proved to be directly useful to activists; some of the research and theorizing of academic sociologists soon found its way into movement training programs and handbooks (e.g., Gamson 1990; Piven and Cloward 1979; Ryan 1991). It was possible to imagine, if you were engaged in social movement studies, that your teaching, consulting, and direct participation, as well as your research efforts, might have some relevance to the practices and understandings of political activists.[1]

The Decline of Relevance

Along the way, however, the issue of relevance receded for many practitioners, and a much more "professional" and "disciplinary" definition of purpose came to the fore. The professionalization of the post-1960s cohort of academics has been a topic of debate for some years now, and the disconnection between the work of "academic radicals" and the needs of social movements has been bemoaned for at least a decade. Much of that discussion has focused on the burgeoning of esoteric theorizing in literature and cultural studies and in the domain of women's studies and feminist scholarship (e.g., Epstein 1995; Jacoby 1987).

There has been, I believe, a parallel process at work in the academic study of social movements. Writings proliferate that are aimed at establishing, critiquing, or refining "paradigms." The quickest way to access and assess this proliferation is to examine the stack of research compilations that have appeared in the last few years. I have sitting on my desk right now at least six large anthologies of articles aimed at supporting, debating, and contrasting the merits of "resource mobilization" (RM), "new social movement" (NSM), and "political opportunity structure" (POS) perspectives. More and more, the work of younger scholars seems driven by their felt need to "relate" to one or another of such "paradigms"—or to try to synthesize them in some way. Journal articles increasingly analyze social movement experience as grist for the testing of hypotheses or the illustration of concepts.

By the mid-1980s a spate of major review articles and some pioneering research compendia and texts were beginning to appear (e.g., Jenkins 1983; McAdam, McCarthy, and Zald 1988; Morris and Mueller 1992; see also Tarrow 1998, for an authoritative presentation of the founding paradigm). These very useful publications helped codify the state of the field, but they reinforced the trend toward formalization. In 1995 Tilly, McAdam, and Tarrow announced a very deliberate and highly ambitious effort to achieve codification and coordination of the domain. The number of conferences grew apace, and a new journal, *Mobilization,* began publication in 1995; its premier issue featured a programmatic statement by TMT.

Dynamics of Contention (2001) fundamentally revises their earlier efforts at codification and takes account of much criticism, but vigorously reasserts their claim to leadership in defining the domain of "contentious politics" (see Flacks 2003 for a critical review).

Despite the flourishing of debate in movement studies and the many revisions of aspects of their schemes, there is a decided mainstream in the field that is defined by the "political contention" framework that TMT have been putting forward. This consensual agenda for the field is seen as a sign of intellectual progress compared with earlier periods when no agreed-on terminology was evident, and when social processes that bore evident similarities were being studied by research networks that had little contact with each other.

The plethora of research compilations, annuals, journals, and advanced textbooks dealing with social movements is another index of intellectual progress. More systematic research and analysis of movements has been occurring in the last decade than ever before, and much of it makes use of sophisticated methods that enable detailed comparative and historical analysis.

The question nags, however: *what is all this analysis for?* In what way does the validation, elaboration, and refinement of concepts provide usable knowledge for those seeking social change? Does the practice of "normal science" conflict with the *moral* dimension of social movement studies?

Such questions may appear to be anti-intellectual or as seeking a political litmus test for scholarly inquiry. But my worries about the prevailing style of work in the field are as much about its *intellectual* as its moral worth. As Mills argued in his day, abstracted empiricism may appear to be science, but such efforts may turn out to be elaborate exercises in establishing the obvious or trivial—and, even more likely, exercises in refinement that befuddle rather than clarify.

The prevailing conceptual framework, as codified by TMT and others, is not a theory, even if some practitioners are wont to speak of it as such. An intellectual framework is justifiably a theory only to the extent that one can derive some sense of future possibilities from it. This, I think, is surprisingly hard to do on the basis of what TMT have so far produced. The dominant paradigm has certainly provided us with concepts that help explain the past and that sensitize us to questions we might ask in our research. Nothing is wrong with that sort of conceptualizing—in fact, it is indispensable if social movement studies are to go beyond a set of discrete narratives about an array of historical happenings.

Academics, Activists, and the Identification of Political Opportunity

The dominant scheme gives us a conceptual means for explaining the "emergence" of various movements, comparing movement dynamics, and deciding what to pay attention to when we enter a particular movement scene, but it seems it cannot enable us to estimate such emergence and development in advance.

The fundamental proposition in the original TMT model concerns political opportunity: movements emerge to the extent that those in authority are not in a position to repress them (for example, because of their own internal divisions or instability). More generally, "political opportunity" refers to opportunities for access and for mobilization that are provided to a movement by the political environment. This is a fruitful idea for explaining movement emergence. It compels analysts to look not only at the behavior and beliefs of movement participants or at the sources of their grievance, but also at the situation of established political structures and elites. The problem is that one can identify the actually relevant opportunities only *after* a movement has emerged that makes use of them. It is much harder, given the lack of specificity in the various versions of the model, to determine in advance what a movement's potential opportunities may turn out to be.

Post facto explanation is key to historical understanding, but, it seems to me, the most pressing questions concern the future. It is possible to try to inventory plausible opportunities for mobilization that may eventually prove to be relevant—but the concept of political opportunity provides little help in deciding what sorts of opportunity may actually be germane to what sort of mobilizing effort.

Movement activists and organizers are by definition engaged in efforts to anticipate the future, to assess opportunities, and to figure out ways to use them. Yet it is surprising how rarely the historical studies that consti-tute the canon of the political opportunity (PO) perspective focus on the ways activists, in the movements being studied, understood and determined their own opportunities. Indeed, how organizers figure out their oppor-tunities and how movements expand on them are largely unstudied and untheorized by PO practitioners. Activists and organizers with any strategic attitude already know that they need to try to understand the potential points of access and possibilities for alliance in the political environment. Their fundamental practice includes efforts to assess the vulnerabilities of elites and themselves. They are likely to start with the assumption that the established opportunity structure is in fact not hospitable to their efforts and so they have to try to figure out how to make opportunities when these seem largely absent. In a crucial sense, organizers embedded in strategic debate and planning are likely to be more knowledgeable about the nature of political opportunity than are academics who are separated from move-ment scenes.

The study of political opportunity provides an example of how move-ment studies could gain intellectual power if academics and activists were partners in theory and research.

Activist Experience

Another fruitful topic for such partnership is the problem of activist biog-raphy. Biographical study was once a popular topic in the study of social movements. As a result, there is a very considerable literature on the per-sonal development of activists, but work on this theme lost favor in social movement studies as the resource mobilization/political process paradigm became dominant.[2] The structural far outweighed the social psychological in explaining the emergence of social movements.

The structural turn was crucial for enabling movement studies to understand movement participation as rational and movement activity as strategic rather than irrational and expressive. But this turn did not require the jettisoning of the personal dimension of agency. Indeed, understanding activists as a social type remains a critical issue for understanding how social movements work. To the extent that organizers, leaders, movement entrepreneurs, and so on make a difference, understanding their social origins, experience, outlook, and motivational makeup can be critical for understanding the trajectories of particular movements. For example, the shared social origins and identity issues of student activists in the 1960s help account for both the rise and the decline of the student movement.

The study of activist biography can help us respond to Mills's questions about the sources of human capacities to seek freedom. One of the defining characteristics of activists is that they are *people whose actions are not interpretable simply in terms of situation;* they are people who act against institutionalized expectations, accepted belief, conventional values, and goals. How and why some people become engaged in risky, nonconventional activity, when success is at best elusive and causes are often lost, is a topic worthy of attention in its own right. How such commitment is sustained over time is a question that bears on our general understanding of human possibility. Why some people come to consider societal change to be a central priority of their lives is an issue that is fundamentally relevant to the problem of democratic potential. Efforts to understand activist biography can provide insight into central issues of human personality and its socialization, of ideological hegemony and its contradictions, and the relationships between culture and experience. Studying activist motivation and persistence provides important counterweight and challenge to overreliance on rational choice models.

One might suspect that the interrogation of activists about their own lives would be taken as voyeuristic, invasive, or discrediting by those who are subjects of such research. Yet the experience of those who have done this work is that activists are often eager to be engaged in this way. Veteran organizers often welcome the opportunity not only to tell their stories, but to make sense of the inevitable mysteries of their lives and to see their lives in historical contexts. Providing opportunity to reflect on one's life can be therapeutic.

Biographical study continued even when such work was apparently marginalized. Books by Klatch (1999), Robnett (1997), Teske (1997), and Lichterman (1996) have helped reshape understandings of movement dynamics and outcomes by focusing on the life experience of activists and organizers. These efforts by younger scholars, working closely with their activist subjects, may be harbingers of a revival of emphasis on this genre of research, thereby deepening activist-academic connections.

The focus of recent work on activist experience is less on sources of activists' commitment than on their experiences in the movements. Studying the origins of commitment has the practical value of shedding light on how people get recruited to commitment, ideological perspectives change, and movement-relevant identities are shaped. Less studied in the past is another practical question: how can commitment be sustained over time? This can be understood as a relatively short-term matter: how can full-time organizers and staff be nurtured, how can burnout be understood and avoided? Full-time frontline organizing seems to require degrees of discipline and self-sacrifice that don't always mesh with the motivations and aspirations of the youthful idealists who sign up for it. Research on this issue is beginning to be done under the aegis of the labor movement, and a growing number of academic social scientists have been orienting their work to assess many aspects of the activist experience in the "new labor movement" (e.g., Bronfenbrenner 1998; Lopez 2004; Milkman 2000). The labor movement, which has been relatively marginal as a focus of study in social movement research, provides a kind of field laboratory for looking at a wide range of issues about organizing strategies and tactics, and there has been an active effort by key figures in the new national labor leadership to cultivate partnerships with academics. In California, the state legislature funded an Institute for Labor and Employment at the University of California that has for several years been providing substantial numbers of grants for faculty and graduate student research on labor movement–related issues. Meanwhile, a new labor studies section of the American Sociological Association was recently established. Both of these interrelated developments are conscious efforts to bridge between academics and activists that may provide models for how such partnership can evolve. At the heart of these enterprises are efforts to use the experiences and the questions of organizers to generate systematic empirical analyses.

One might fear that such close partnership—and virtual sponsorship—might result in research that simply buttresses the perspectives of union leaders. The published work that has so far resulted from these efforts suggests otherwise. These studies seem to implicitly assume that organized labor needs to come to grips with reality, however disconfirming of prior assumptions or prerogatives this may prove to be. The research ranges from efforts to understand the success rates of various kinds of organizing methods and strategies to efforts to examine the resistance of workers to organizing campaigns, to assess organizer training programs, to examine alternatives to the conventional labor union structure, and to report on the variation of investment by unions in organizing endeavors—all this work highlights limits, barriers, shortfalls, and problems rather than providing images of movement progress.

The emerging sociology of the labor movement aims to support the collective empowerment of workers by enabling those who are seriously committed to that goal to have systematic knowledge about how to achieve it. Much of this work can be defined as applied, yet at the same time much of it is more broadly relevant for understanding the experiences, roles, and potentials of organizers in general.

Lifetimes of Commitment

Many activists are, of course, fascinated by more basic questions about their experience. The biographical study of activists can illuminate how commitment can be sustained over a lifetime. This question is particularly challenging in postmodernity. The usual expectations that ideological or religious conviction and/or strong identity or special qualities of courage or fanaticism can explain long-term commitment no longer hold. Yet, today there are numbers of veterans of 1960s movements who continue to be full-time organizers (and they are now reaching sixty!) or are engaged in continuing activist projects even though they don't have the ideological foundations (and blinders) that seemed to sustain commitment in the generations of the old left. The vicissitudes of activist commitment over the life course have been recorded in countless memoirs and biographies and novels. It is a theme that seems ripe for systematic sociological mining—another way to make the activist-academic bridge.

The Search for Democratic Organization

Recently, Doug Bevington and Chris Dixon, sociology graduate students and activists at Santa Cruz, undertook an informal survey of antiglobalization activists to learn about the intellectual resources and theoretical discourses they used. Their conclusions support the critique I am making here: current literature in the sociology of social movements is not high on activist reading lists; historical and contemporary case studies, biographies, and memoirs are. More important, however, is the inventory that Bevington and Dixon sketch of the theoretically relevant discussion that can be found on activist Web sites and movement-oriented publications.

These discussions focus on issues of strategy, tactics, and movement building and are much preoccupied with how to continuously democratize the movement itself. Here are the main dimensions of that concern, according to Bevington and Dixon:

- The problem of inclusion: how to widen the social bases of the movement with respect to race, ethnicity, and class
- The problem of leadership: how to sustain participatory democracy in movement decision making, overcome cleavages between activist and everyday perspectives, and ensure that the diversity of movement voices can be heard
- The problem of organizational structure: how to evaluate alternative models of internal organization—comparative benefits and costs of centralization/decentralization, formal organization versus network

We can recognize immediately how today's activists continue to wrestle with matters that have been central in academic social theory for at least a century.

When Robert Michels articulated his theory of organizational oligarchy, he did so in light of his own engagement with the movement of his day (German Social Democracy). When John Dewey pioneered a definition of participatory democracy, he did so in relation to his active role as a leader in socialist and trade union activity in the 1930s. When Bill Gamson examined the relation between organizational structure and movement success in *The Strategy of Social Protest,* he did so in response to his engagement with these questions as a participant in the anti–Vietnam War movement. When Piven and Cloward critically scrutinized the assumptions and goals of movement organizers, they did so on the basis of their active involvement with the welfare rights movement.

In short, much foundational work in classic social theory about organization was rooted in the experience of activist intellectuals. That work remains an important resource for today's activists. But current movement experience challenges the understandings of earlier eras, and the key issues remain unsettled. Bevington and Dixon (2003) urge that academic sociologists engage seriously with the debates now flourishing among anti-globalization activists. There is no doubt that such engagement can pay off for the causes of both movement and theory.

A Conclusion: Remember Karl Marx

Karl Marx formulated the single most embracing theory of social structure and dynamics that we have. Yet, of course, he didn't do this work within the confines of the academy. His life's goal was to make his capacities as an intellectual a source of empowerment for the working-class movement. His earliest writings stress that the emancipatory visions of young intellectuals had to be fused with emancipatory struggles of the class "in chains." These struggles, he was sure, could not fulfill themselves unless those who waged them were able to understand the social sources of their collective power and thereby to seize opportunities for social transformation.

In other words, Marx's model is the foundation for contemporary resource mobilization and opportunity structure perspectives. Marx understood that deprivation and oppression were not in themselves the basis for movement. The very notion of class as a framework of mobilization implies that *a group must share resources as well as interests* in order to become a social force. Marx's dialectical style made him search for the opportunities as well as the oppressions inherent in social structure. Capitalism exploits workers, but by creating them it creates its own grave diggers *because the capitalist system in its very nature created opportunities for its own overthrow* (for example, the social space provided by the factory).

One of Marx's central analytic strategies is missing from contemporary theories—namely, his effort to embed power relations in an analysis of the political economy as a whole. Opportunity was not fixed. The more that capitalism organized a global economy and society, the more potential the world's proletariat would have for transformative change. Much of Marx's intellectual career involved the effort to analyze capitalism as a developing and contradictory system, and the ways in which such development would necessitate and make possible collective action from below.

Contemporary work in social movement studies makes only weak and relatively unsystematic connection between macroeconomic conditions and political opportunity. For instance, if one wanted (as quite a few activists want) to analyze the opportunities for a revitalization of the labor movement, one would need to begin with a detailed economic analysis, one that enabled connection between the new economy, evolving macro- and microproduction relations, and how these might necessitate, facilitate, and limit collective action. Marx provided an analysis of this sort in his detailed review of the struggle for the shorter work week in *Capital.* Surprisingly, the structuralism of the political opportunity paradigm stops short of the sort of macrostructural analysis that Marxian theorizing routinely undertakes. (In response to this intellectual gap, Buechler [2000] has attempted a systematic effort to undertake such an analysis.)

But there is an even more basic weakness embedded in opportunity theorists' structuralism. They don't systematically deal with the possibility that *certain kinds of resource and opportunity are considerably more fateful than others.* For Marx, the fundamental source of social power has to do with control over means of production. Because such control is a matter of degree, we can imagine a *gradient of power* available to groups seeking to make social change. Marx makes a theoretical bet that groups, over time, will tend to move along that gradient, striving to maximize the power they can bring to bear. Thus, for example, tactics like mass assemblies, marches, bread riots, and machine breaking—all of which have some effect—will become less important for workers than strategies focused on the withholding of labor (strikes or the threat thereof). Strike-oriented strategies require forms of organization (aimed at expanding webs of solidarity) that will predictably follow from the assumption that workers will over time focus their collective action where it can matter most. This kind of systematic analysis of the logic of power relations is not done in the "political opportunity" project, even by those who claim to be studying "power in movements," or who are documenting "tactical repertoires."

Marx's emphasis on production relations as the primary locus of social power was far too limited for understanding social reality. Class struggles have not followed the paths he predicted; meanwhile, tumultuous social conflict has reshaped society and culture along lines of cleavage other than class.

A post-Marxist theory of power that incorporates class struggle but can account for other frameworks of mobilization and conflict seems both necessary and possible. An excellent illustration of a more general theory of power can be found in a work that has been neglected by political opportunity analysts even though its theoretical perspective seems close to theirs. It is a book by Michael Schwartz, *Radical Protest and Social Structure* (1976), a study of the nineteenth-century Southern Farmers Alliance. Schwartz uses the case study as a springboard for a theoretical discussion on the determinants of organized protest. He summarizes an extended discussion of the powers available to subordinated groups as follows:

> Every functioning system is a set of routinized power relations in effect on a day-to-day basis. This is structural power since the structure could not function without the existence and use of this power. Those . . . subject to this structural power possess a latent power deriving from the possibility of refusing to abide by the power exercised over them. . . . This latent power can be exercised only if the subordinate group organizes itself. . . . The organization of the subordinate group must be carried out independently of the structure itself. . . . Power exercised by a group depends on its place in the structure and its ability to withhold obedience. (177)

Michael Schwartz's effort to define structural power helps us see how we might construct a theory about the powers of the weak by building on Marx's analysis of class power: *the power of the powerless is rooted in their capacity to stop the smooth flow of social life.*

Class-based power, because of its double effect on both the elites and the community, is the most effective way to do this: any structure that depends on the cooperation of subordinates for its functioning provides potential power to those subordinates because of their capacity to refuse cooperation or fulfill expected roles. Social movements, accordingly, can be understood as social formations that seek, over time, to maximize the power available to their constituencies. The "powerless" may engage in or threaten to engage in collective forms of refusal, noncooperation, or noncompliance with the plans, rules, demands, and commands of elites. But as Piven and Cloward (1979) demonstrated in their analysis of poor peoples' movements, institutionally embedded power may not be available to poor communities and groups. Instead, urban movements of the poor, the unemployed, and the disenfranchised exercise power by engaging in forms of collective *disruption* of the ongoing functioning of institutional or community life.

The effective exercise of power derived from defiance, disruption, and noncompliance is rarely easy, because the risks of such exercise are usually profound. Just as workers' strikes are costly to workers themselves (if for no other reason than that they are stopping their actual livelihoods), so other forms of institutional noncooperation disrupt the very activities that members themselves need to sustain their accustomed lives. In addition, acts of noncompliance and disruption can be expected to receive repressive responses. Social movement dynamics are very much shaped by efforts to figure out how to maximize the benefits and minimize the costs to members engaging in power struggle.

In this light, current emphasis on analyzing the conditions for mobilization seems abstract, diffuse, weakly specified. If, instead, we see the underlying strategic aim of social movements as a striving to find the means for structural power, we can develop coherent ways to order our inquiries about opportunity and resources. Our questions will have to do with the conditions and circumstances, the strategies and tactics, the perceptions and motivations that would *increase the readiness of a community or collectivity of people to make use of their potential structural powers,* usually against considerable odds. Helping movements understand their structural power potentials would enable our work to connect with the deepest dilemmas that movement organizers have to deal with.

Marx said that the point was not simply to understand the world but to change it. In saying this, he was not marginalizing intellectual work. On the contrary, the construction of theory is essential to the making of history, provided that such construction is practiced as a dialogue among activists and academics.

Notes

1. Post-1960s efforts to link academic and activist roles were actually part of a long tradition. John Dewey, G. H. Mead, and others at the University of Chicago in the early twentieth century spent much time helping nurture the labor movement (and Dewey throughout his life took leadership roles in union organizing among teachers and in social democratic politics). Paul Lazarsfeld's effort to develop survey research began out of an interest in aiding the Austrian Social Democratic Party assess its political appeals. And the interrelations of scholarship and activism in the lives of such figures as W. E. B. Du Bois and Jesse Bernard are obvious.

2. Here are a few examples: Erikson 1969; Wolfenstein 1967; Keniston 1968. Hundreds of studies on the social psychology of 1960s activism are summarized by Keniston in a book-length bibliography (1973). A sampling of more recent work: Lipsitz 1995; Andrews 1991; Whalen and Flacks 1989; Fendrich 1993. A powerful critique of the dominant perspective is Jasper 1997. Jasper strongly urges the return of biography as a key topic in movement studies, but even he seems largely unaware of the earlier literature.

References

Andrews, Molly. 1991. *Lifetimes of Commitment*. Cambridge: Cambridge University Press.

Bevington, Douglas, and Chris Dixon. 2003. "An Emerging Direction in Social Movement Scholarship: Movement-Relevant Theory." Paper presented at Conference on Social Movements and Social Transformation, Cornell University.

Bronfenbrenner, Kate, ed. 1998. *Organizing to Win: New Research on Union Strategies*. Ithaca, NY: ILR Press.

Buechler, Steven M. 2000. *Social Movements in Advanced Capitalism*. New York: Oxford University Press.

Diani, Mario. 2000. "The Relational Deficit of Ideologically Structured Action." *Mobilization* 5 no. 1: 17–24.

Epstein, Barbara. 1995. "'Political Correctness' and Collective Powerlessness." In *Cultural Politics and Social Movement*, ed. M. Darnofsky, B. Epstein, and R. Flacks, 3–19. Philadelphia: Temple University Press.

Erikson, Erik. 1969. *Gandhi's Truth*. New York: Norton.

Fendrich, James. 1993. *Ideal Citizens*. Albany: SUNY Press.

Flacks, Richard. 2003. "Review of *Dynamics of Contention*." *Social Movement Studies* 2, no. 1: 103–9.

Gamson, William A. 1990. *The Strategy of Social Protest*. Belmont, CA: Wadsworth.

Jacoby, Russell. 1987. *The Last Intellectuals*. New York: Basic Books.

Jasper, James. 1997. *The Art of Moral Protest*. Chicago: University of Chicago Press.

Jenkins, J. Craig. 1983. "Resource Mobilization Theory and the Study of Social Movements." *Annual Review of Sociology* 9: 527–53.

Keniston, Kenneth. 1968. *Young Radicals*. New York: Harcourt, Brace, Jovanovich.

———. 1973. *Radicals and Militants: An Annotated Bibliography of Empirical Research on Campus Unrest*. Lexington, MA: Lexington Books.

Klatch, Rebecca. 1999. *A Generation Divided*. Berkeley: University of California Press.

Lichterman, Paul. 1996. *The Search for Political Community*. Cambridge: Cambridge University Press.

Lipsitz, George. 1995. *A Life in the Struggle*. Philadelphia: Temple University Press.

Lopez, Steven. 2004. *Re-organizing the Rust Belt: From Business Unionism to Social Movement Unionism.* Berkeley: University of California Press.

McAdam, Douglas. 1999. *Political Process and the Development of Black Insurgency, 1930–1970.* Chicago: University of Chicago Press.

McAdam, Douglas, John D. McCarthy, and Mayer Zald. 1988. "Social Movements." In *Handbook of Sociology,* ed. Neil Smelser, 695–737. Newbury Park, CA: Sage.

———, eds. 1996. *Comparative Perspectives on Social Movements: Political Opportunities, Mobilizing Structures, and Cultural Framings.* New York: Cambridge University Press.

McAdam, Douglas, Sidney Tarrow, and Charles Tilly. 1996. "To Map Contentious Politics." *Mobilization* 1, no. 1: 17–34.

———. 2001. *The Dynamics of Contention.* Cambridge: Cambridge University Press.

Milkman, Ruth. 2000. *Organizing Immigrants: The Challenge for Unions in Contemporary California.* Ithaca, NY: Cornell University Press.

Mills, C. Wright. [1959] 2000. *The Sociological Imagination.* New York: Oxford University Press.

Morris, Aldon D., and Carol Mueller. 1992. *Frontiers in Social Movement Theory.* New Haven, CT: Yale University Press.

Piven, Frances Fox, and Richard A. Cloward. 1979. *Poor People's Movements.* New York: Vintage.

Robnett, Belinda. 1997. *How Long? How Long? African-American Women in the Struggle for Civil Rights.* New York: Oxford University Press.

Ryan, Charlotte. 1991. *Prime Time Activism: Media Strategies for Grassroots Organizing.* Boston: South End Press.

Schwartz, Michael. 1976. *Radical Protest and Social Structure.* New York: Academic Press.

Tarrow, Sidney. 1998. *Power in Movement.* Cambridge: Cambridge University Press.

Teske, Nathan. 1997. *Political Activists in America: The Identity Construction Model of Political Participation.* Cambridge: Cambridge University Press.

Whalen, Jack, and Richard Flacks. 1989. *Beyond the Barricades.* Philadelphia: Temple University Press.

Wolfenstein, Eugene V. 1967. *The Revolutionary Personality: Lenin, Trotsky, Gandhi.* Princeton, NJ: Princeton University Press.

Zald, Mayer. 2000. "Ideologically Structured Action: An Enlarged Agenda for Social Movement Research" *Mobilization* 5, no. 1: 1–16.

2

Which Side Are You On? The Tension between Movement Scholarship and Activism

David Croteau

The philosophers have only interpreted the world, in various ways; the point, however, is to change it.
— Karl Marx, "Theses on Feurbach"

Our profession manages to punish us for all of our virtues.
— Robert J. S. Ross, "At the Center and the Edge"

Becoming an academic to support social movements is akin to launching a space program to develop a pen that writes upside down. At best, it is a circuitous route that is surely not the most efficient way of realizing this goal. Still, academics try to do it all the time, probably because of the undeniable allure of the academy. A stable, comfortable, good-paying job in an environment of unparalleled freedom and autonomy is indeed appealing. But in some ways, academia can become a velvet cage that makes it extremely difficult for individuals to make meaningful contributions to social movement efforts. The basic dilemma is that work that is well rewarded within the academy may be largely irrelevant to the real-world concerns of movement activists, while work that is grounded so as to contribute to the strategic advancement of movement efforts is not recognized as significant within the academy. Caught in the middle are the scholars who want to do work that both sustains their academic careers *and* supports social movement efforts. Such individuals often face the hard decision of deciding which side they are on. Are they first and foremost scholars, or are they activists? Many see the choice as a false one; they want to be both. However, the tension between the two roles is considerable.

In this chapter, I argue that the tension between scholarship and activism reflects a longstanding division within American sociology that dates back over a century. I briefly sketch out some episodes in this history and discuss some of the contemporary structural characteristics of U.S. higher education in general, and of the discipline of sociology in particular, that make it difficult to successfully maintain an integrated identity as both scholar and activist. I conclude by considering some of the possible options available to those of us caught in this predicament.

Scholarship and Change: Some Historical Context

"The word 'academic' is synonymous for 'irrelevant,'" Saul Alinsky ([1946] 1969, ix) once wrote. As a college student in the 1930s, the man who later became known for his innovations in community organizing took courses in sociology but was appalled by their lack of connection to the issues of his day. Alinsky later said of this period that he

> was astounded by all the horse manure [sociologists] were handing out about poverty and slums, playing down the suffering and deprivation, glossing over the misery and despair. I mean, Christ, I'd lived in a slum, I could see through all their complacent academic jargon to the realities. It was at that time that I developed a deep suspicion of academicians in general and sociologists in particular, with a few notable exceptions. (1972)

Alinsky was neither the first nor the last student to be troubled by the tension between academic sociology and the need for real-world social change. The issue predated Alinsky and has proven to be persistent to this day.

From Engaged Scholarship to Instrumental Positivism

The early years of American sociology, as embodied in the nation's first graduate department of sociology at Chicago, involved a combination of study and practice (Deegan 1986). In addition to the men who dominated the sociology department proper, a strong contingent of women sociologists were affiliated with it, most famously Jane Addams. Beginning in the early 1890s and lasting a quarter century, many of these women worked with Hull House, the well-known settlement house that also served as an intellectual center of the day. These sociologists pioneered urban social demography techniques while simultaneously pursuing an alliance with local communities as a mechanism for social change. From this position, they took committed stands on aiding the poor, immigrants, and women in a rapidly changing city facing significant social problems.

Most of the men in the sociology department, however, came to view the city as a "laboratory" in which to conduct their work. Its residents were seen as specimens for study rather more than as partners for change. They believed a narrow "objective" orientation was necessary if sociology was to mature into a "real" science within academe. Thus the Chicago School eventually moved away from using social scientific knowledge in partnership with the community to affect change. In 1920, all the women affiliated with Chicago's sociology department were transferred en masse to the social work department, poignantly symbolizing the split between study (sociology) and ameliorative practice (social work). The subsequent community research in the department, increasingly dependent on funding from various Rockefeller foundations, remained sympathetic to the plight of the "less fortunate," but no longer had a change-oriented focus.

In the ensuing decades, the shift initiated at Chicago was carried much further elsewhere. Moving dramatically away from the often qualitative methods and community-based concerns of the Chicago School, departments at Harvard and Columbia were among the leaders in promoting statistically oriented instrumental positivism that relied heavily on survey methodologies. Funding for this work came from large foundations, including Russell Sage and the Rockefeller Foundation, sometimes channeled through other organizations such as the Social Science Research Council (SSRC). Feagin and Vera note that at the SSRC, "the goal was not to create a social science relevant to public policy—but one that accented quantitative and business-oriented research" (2001, 93).

Later, as this approach came to fully dominate mainstream sociology, government funding became extremely important. In 1960, the National Science Foundation established a Division of Social Sciences. Between 1956 and 1980, private research money to the social sciences nearly doubled, from $21 to $41 million, but government funding increased fourteenfold, from $30 to $424 million. Feagin and Vera observe that with an instrumental-positivist orientation, "It seems that a majority of the sociologists who sought funding from government agencies or private foundations made a conscious attempt not to do research on controversial social issues" (2001, 89).

These developments marked the creation of an artificial division that became increasingly entrenched within sociology. The two dominant mainstream research roles that became available to sociologists involved "basic" research—the advancement of disciplinary knowledge for knowledge's sake—and "applied" work—using social science methods to address narrowly defined issues in areas demarcated by funders. To this day, this division is an influential one in the discipline.

The Scholar-Activist Tradition

The tradition of linking sociological research with social change did not come to an end with the banishment of the Chicago School's women to the social work department. Indeed, it wasn't long before some sociologists began to challenge the emerging orientations in sociology. The fundamental issue was not limiting research to "practical" applications but what knowledge would be produced and for whom.

In 1939, Robert Lynd was already famously asking, "Knowledge for what?" In roughly the same period that Alinsky had become disillusioned with the irrelevancy of sociology, Lynd took the social sciences to task for, among other things, virtually ignoring the impact of the Great Depression on American society. Such massive blind spots existed, he believed, because the social sciences had split into two dominant blocks, neither of which was adequate. On the one hand, there was the "scholar" who was "becoming remote from and even disregarding immediate relevancies" and, on the other hand, there was the "technician" who was "too often accepting the definition of his problems too narrowly in terms of the emphases of the institutional environment of the moment" (Lynd 1939, 1).

Instead of engaging with the pressing issues of the day, Lynd argued that social scientists were "hiding behind their precocious beards of 'dispassionate research' and 'scientific objectivity'" (1939, 181). Rather than emphasizing work that had some social utility, social science was content to fill in "the infinite odd bits of the jigsaw puzzle of the unknown." In contrast, Lynd advocated that "it is precisely the role of the social sciences to be troublesome, to disconcert the habitual arrangement by which we manage to live along, and to demonstrate the possibility of change in more adequate directions" (ibid.).

Lynd was not alone in his critique, and such thinking eventually led in 1951 to the establishment of the Society for the Study of Social Problems (SSSP) as a progressive alternative to the American Sociological Association (ASA), which tried to legitimize the work of critical sociologists and other professionals. In the midst of the social movement upheavals of the 1960s, the effort to link scholarship and activism reached a new prominence and presented a considerable challenge to mainstream sociology.

"Radical Sociology" in the Sixties and Beyond

The 1960s and 1970s saw a number of efforts that, in varying ways, emphasized the importance of making sociological research relevant to addressing real-world concerns. These included the Sociology Liberation Movement, the Women's Caucus (later Sociologists for Women in Society), and the Black Caucus (later the Association of Black Sociologists), all of which challenged the mainstream, dominant sociology of the day. Sociologists played key roles in other efforts of the period, such as the New University Conference, that sought to unite faculty and student support for student protest movements (Oppenheimer, Murray, and Levine 1991).

Collectively, these efforts were seen by some as the development of a new "radical sociology." One 1971 volume on the subject opened this way:

> Mainstream, contemporary sociology is largely the creation of cold-war liberals who, for the most part, have been content to observe and ratio-nalize the operations of the American colossus from a position of privi-lege in the name of science. The emerging radical sociology rejects and condemns this posture and sees its responsibility as that of opposing such forces. (Colfax and Roach 1971, 3)

In various ways, radical sociology—fueled by the impertinent questions of graduate students—challenged the myth of "value-free" social science and exposed the complicity of some academics in perpetuating systems that enabled injustice. Liberal sociologists were condemned for their willingness to "advise the military on ways of mobilizing support for its programs and develop, in the name of economic growth and democracy, rationalizations for the exploitation and pacification of the domestic poor and the Third World" (ibid., 6).

Also targeted for criticism was disengaged "bourgeois radical scholar-ship" that

> often provides the scholar with a degree of institutionalized protection from the obligation to become directly involved in the social issues of the day. In much the same way as empiricism has served to keep most sociologists from having to examine the values implicit in and underlying their work, preoccupation with the formalism of scholarship can often make it possible for the radically inclined scholar to avoid the demands, dilemmas, and ambiguities of radical activism. (Colfax 1971, 85)

In its own way, the "radical sociology" of the period advocated a new praxis integrating scholarship and social change and once again raised the basic question of "knowledge for what?"

Not coincidentally, this same period was one of dramatic advancement for the field of social movement studies. Younger scholars—some with di-rect movement experience—challenged and refuted many of the earlier as-sumptions about the nature of social movements and protest actions. Their pioneering work on resource mobilization reflected the pragmatic issues facing activists. Thus, the closer link between activism and scholarship in this era was a catalyst for fundamental change in social movement studies.

Despite these and other ensuing changes that introduced more diversity into the sociological landscape, such as the resurgence in qualitative methodology sparked in part by feminist scholars, the tension inherent in the scholar-activist role continued.

The Continuing Tension between Scholarship and Activism

As the cursory history above indicates, the efforts to integrate scholarly work with social change have been considerable. But despite the best attempts of committed scholars, there has not been a lasting change in the basic tension between academia and activism.

In 2001, Feagin and Vera added yet another chapter in the quest for a sociology that "is concerned with alleviating or eliminating various social oppressions and with creating societies that are more just and egalitarian." Following in the tradition sketched out above, the point of what they term "liberation sociology" is "not just to research the social world but to change it in the direction of democracy and social justice" (1).

While we should applaud the important contributions and advances made by such scholars, the reality remains that academic sociology continues to be relatively unreceptive to the calls for integrated scholarship and activism. After a century of struggle, and despite some recent calls for more "public sociologies," such approaches are still uncommon. To varying degrees, the tension between scholarship and activism is felt broadly throughout the university in programs like women's studies and African-American studies. The situation is especially ironic and dire for those of us specifically interested in social movements and social change. The sociological study of social movements is still vexed by an echo of Lynd's seventy-year-old question: knowledge for what?

A century of struggle and an honor roll of committed scholars have failed to fundamentally change the barriers facing scholar-activists in the academy. To understand why, we need to examine some of the key factors that have contributed to the tensions faced by such scholars. I now turn to five of these contributing factors.

Politics

Imagine an employee who proposes to her boss that a portion of her work time should be devoted to organizing her coworkers into a labor union to advocate for better wages and working conditions. We'd surely think her incredibly naive to the ways of power in the workplace. Yet in some respects, scholars who want to use their academic positions to advance social movement causes are proposing something quite similar. More than ever, the vast bulk of higher education—especially its major research universities—is fully integrated into the dominant political economy. Universities are octopuses whose tentacles are intertwined with their business and government counterparts. Schools train workers for future employers. The private sector funds research. Government funds a part of public universities, provides tax breaks for private ones, and supplies a sizable chunk of the basic research funding for all universities. In more provincial settings, universities are often major players in local politics, affecting land use decisions, contributing significantly to local economies, and so on.

Critical sociologists have been aware of this for decades. In 1968, one wrote that "the universities no longer serve only the somewhat luxurious function of socializing elites and invigorating the going value system; they are now far more closely integrated into the political economy. They are as indispensable to its functioning as the factory, the bank, and the government agency" (Flacks 1970, 73).

In more recent years, higher education hasn't *served* big business, it has *become* big business. Like their corporate counterparts, universities now rely on contingent labor both inside and outside the classroom, develop branding campaigns, refer to their presidents as CEOs, and present employees with "customer service" awards. Students are captive consumers who are bombarded with advertising from credit card companies, whose campuses sign exclusive contracts with soft-drink companies, and whose cafeterias are increasingly campus-based fast-food franchises. Perhaps most important, much of the research work done on campuses is increasingly connected directly or indirectly to corporate interests, especially in the lucrative areas of medical and technological research. In 2001, *Academe* devoted an entire issue to the theme of "Selling Out? Corporations on Campus" (American Association of University Professors 2001), and the corrosive influence of these changes on university life are widely discussed in both academic and popular press outlets (e.g., Johnson, Mattson, and Kavanagh 2003; Nelson 1997; Press and Washburn 2000). The ideal of universities as the neutral incubators of objective knowledge to be freely shared to benefit humanity is especially incongruous with the era of privatized for-profit universities, university ownership of intellectual property, politicized government funding, and corporate-funded research with publication restrictions.

It would be peculiar indeed for an institution so fully enmeshed in the status quo to provide a cozy environment for those whose mission was to assist in challenging that state of affairs. Given the dominant trend of corporatization in higher education, why would we look to academe as an easy resource for social change? It's a different story if we are talking about how to manage social problems (as in much of contemporary social work), achieve efficient social control (witness the tremendous growth in funding for criminal justice in recent years), administer economic growth programs (urban planning), and so on. These tasks are quite consistent with the maintenance of social order and the status quo and are therefore comfortably pursued within academia. The bottom line is that other areas of "applied" work or professional training don't face the difficulties that social movement scholars do because their subject matter does not present a significant challenge to the status quo, but instead holds the promise of a more smoothly functioning society.

The critical study of social movements does not offer such a comforting agenda. "Activist research," as Francesca Cancian defines it and of which engaged social movement scholarship might qualify, "aims at challenging inequality by empowering the powerless, exposing inequities in the status quo, and promoting social changes that equalize the distribution of resources" (1993, 92). Such research is fundamentally about how those without power organize themselves to most effectively challenge those with power. This inevitably involves conflict. Unlike social service, charity, or volunteerism, the promise of social movement organization is the creation of an autonomous power base from which people can pursue their own self-defined interests. Such efforts can be a threat to powerful institutions, including universities.

Publication Conventions

Informal disciplinary conventions mark the boundaries of what type of research and writing will be rewarded within research universities. Crudely put, there are two major yardsticks by which academic productivity tends to be measured (and rewarded): prestigious publications and external funding. These features dramatically influence the hiring/tenure/promotion process, especially at more esteemed research universities.

Publication in the discipline's more prestigious outlets, especially its elite journals, signals acceptance by one's most influential peers. Theoretical development is usually paramount in such journals, so even work that may have practical implications is usually framed so as to highlight theoretical contributions to the discipline in order to maximize the chances of publication. Consequently, the most prestigious social movement scholarship, published in the field's "best" journals, tends to focus on theory development that contributes incrementally to paradigm development rather than having any utility for movement practitioners. The strategic implications of more pragmatic efforts that result from scholar-movement collaborations rarely make it into such journals. Movement activists looking for strategic guidance to inform their efforts would be hard-pressed to find much of use in the discipline's top journals.

These journals have been oriented to the quantitative analysis of large survey data sets, sometimes to the near exclusion of other methodologies (Feagin and Vera 2001, 114–24). (This narrow orientation has periodically led to debate and controversy regarding the editorial makeup of these journals.) Such surveys, however, have not been an especially prominent approach in the study of social movements, presenting another hurdle for scholars seeking access to these elite outlets.

The issue of publication is not a trivial one for the career of an academic scholar. Hall notes that knowledge in the university

> is the very means of exchange for the academic political economy. Tenure, promotion, peer recognition, research grants and countless smaller codes of privilege are accorded through the adding up of articles, books, papers in "refereed" journals and conferences. . . . Academics are under economic, job survival or advancement pressures to produce in appropriate ways. (2001, 176–77)

He suggests that the research process is distorted by such structural pressures "in spite of one's personal history, in spite of ideological commitment, in spite of deep personal links with social movements or transformative processes" (177).

Any successful junior faculty also learns that form is as necessary as substance to succeed in these rarefied climates. The requisite skills include mastering the field's jargon, tempering language so as to evoke a detached scholarly stance, and proper genuflection to the leaders in the field. As Ryan notes, such tactics often result in academic language that is "impenetrable to non-specialists" and that "devolves into a secret language of social movement scholars" (2004, 111–12). This, in turn, undermines the ability of scholars to relate with activists. She continues:

> Collective actors who do not speak the secret language of social movement theory are seen as atheoretical, or as sources of raw material in the colonial tradition. This hurts relation building. Activists rarely see social movement theorists honor their ideas much less recognize that activists theorize constantly. Perceiving theorists as being more interested in each other than in front line experience, activists withdraw as well.

Thus the valuing of publications with highly abstracted theoretical context coupled with difficult language contributes to the perpetual gap between academic and activist.

Funding

The other criterion—in addition to publication—by which academic success tends to be measured is the ability to generate external funding from government and, to a lesser degree, private foundation sources. Many university employment ads routinely include some variation of the line, "Candidates should have evidence of success in obtaining external funding." Research grants not only cover the cost of conducting research but also provide considerable benefits for the university. Some of the grant money usually goes toward supporting graduate students, thereby reducing the cost of operating a graduate program while giving students direct research experience. Faculty, too, are often supported on these grants, again reducing costs for the university. Best of all, the most desirable research grant—available from just a couple of government agencies—compensates the university significantly for overhead expenses. Schools can take a large percentage off the top of such grants and use the funds to meet general operating expenses. It is no wonder that in an age of cash-strapped universities the pressure to generate more externally funded research has been increasing.

But external money comes with a catch. The most obvious is that the range of fundable research is controlled by the funding agencies. To obtain significant funding—and to do so repeatedly—one must present proposals that conform to the program specifications laid out by the agencies. The practical reality is that major funding agencies are nearly always interested in work that stays safely within acceptable parameters of conventional thinking. Research likely to confirm or suggest only incremental adjustments to the status quo is more acceptable. Proposed work that begins with critical assumptions or that suggests support for fundamental change stands little chance of being funded. Making external funding an employment criterion can—intentionally or not—work as an informal ideological screen.

Funding as a route to academic success, therefore, presents another unique challenge for scholars interested in doing social movement research. Remarkably little of the work in the field of social movements is externally funded by major—or *any*—grants. Compared to many other social science topics, the study of social movements appears to be drastically underfunded. Researchers who even try to obtain major grants must often reframe their research agenda into safe avenues that might be more palatable for funders. Proposals that explicitly suggest collaboration with social movements in order to promote fundamental social change are unlikely to be serious contenders for government money. Why would we expect otherwise?

As a result, researchers must often turn to smaller foundations to piece together modest amounts of money to cover expenses or must pursue work that can be done without a budget. Either way social movement researchers are at a distinct disadvantage in pursuing mainstream academic careers. The absence of significant funding marginalizes social movement scholarship in the eyes of educational institutions increasingly fixated on externally funded research. Mainstream research addressing mild policy reforms, rather than work that engages with concrete and strategic issues connected to specific contemporary struggles, is better able to compete for major funding and, therefore, is more likely to be a route to academic success.

Constituency

This rather sad state of affairs facing the university-based movement scholar has developed, in part, because of the absence of a significant constituency in the broader community that advocates for more movement scholarship. Historically, the openings for more progressive efforts within the university, such as the introduction of African-American studies and women's studies, have been the consequence of significant social movement activism taking place outside of the university. That is, activism off campus has helped to create space on campus for progressive academics to do their work. In recent years, the influence of progressive social movements has been displaced by the ascendancy of corporate power that, in turn, has transformed much of higher education to reflect the needs and interests of the business sector. Social movement scholars—along with progressive scholars from other disciplines—have been left largely isolated in their efforts.

One problem is that the field of social movement study has no real applied component. Applied sociological work—even broadly conceived—is less valued in many sociology departments than theory development and basic research. However, many types of applied work and "engaged scholarship" have flourished in the academy, and in recent years interest within sociology in blending research with practice appears to have grown. Since the late 1970s the American Sociological Association has had a section on sociological practice. During the 2000 ASA annual conference, this section held special joint meetings with the Society for Applied Sociology—a separate professional association—dubbed "Unity 2000." But this trend has not spilled over into the study of social movements.

Most applied work involves professional training in fields such as social work, urban planning, and even labor studies. Each of these fields, to varying degrees, focuses on preparing students for specific employment. Scholarship on the field and related issues is an integral part of the missions of these programs. Such programs have a ready-made constituency among graduates who go on to practice in the field and among employers who hire these students. With the exception of labor studies, such efforts are likely to be uncontroversial and potentially lucrative for the university.

If such a model applied to social movement research, much would be different. If a key purpose of social movement courses was to train future activists, the content of such courses would have to focus on pragmatic dilemmas of organizing, various strategic models of social change, a situated analysis of power and its strategic consequences, and so on. (Various organizer training manuals, such as Bobo, Kendall, and Max 2001, are suggestive of the range of issues that might be highlighted.) Research would probably follow suit, incorporating a much more strategic orientation. Social movement scholars would have a more readily identifiable constituency relying on their work and likely supporting their efforts.

In the real world, this is not the case. The social movement sector, excluding more mainstream advocacy groups, is probably not large enough to support the employment of a significant number of graduates. As a result, courses and scholarship are usually not grounded in the issues with which activists actually grapple. Even in cases where scholars do manage to forge connections with social movement groups, such groups are unlikely to have the money to significantly support research efforts. From the perspective of university administrators, such alliances are troubling politically and generate no monetary benefits for the university. More attractive collaborations would be safe and lucrative efforts with public schools, social service agencies, or law enforcement. Without the affirmation of an external constituency for their work—via funding or political support—movement scholars are left in a vulnerable position within academia.

The Higher-Ed Hierarchy

We need to remember that in the status-conscious system of higher education there exists a distinctive institutional and departmental hierarchy. In a nutshell, the pressure to publish in the field's "best" journals and/or generate significant external funding tends to be closely associated with the most desirable jobs. Those jobs usually come with lighter teaching loads, PhD students with whom to collaborate, and more supporting resources (travel and start-up monies, technology, sabbaticals, and so on), thus enabling more scholarship. Consequently, in order to have the institutional support to pursue a significant research agenda, one must usually produce a certain type of work, work that is often irrelevant to movement activists and is written up in language that is relatively inaccessible to outsiders. Pursuit of such a career can amount to a deal with the devil. While a few scholars manage to maintain a scholar-activist orientation in such positions, the hurdles and temptations along such a route are formidable.

Conversely, refusal or inability to conform to the dominant disciplinary conventions means greatly diminished job prospects. While an existence at less-prestigious institutions, such as liberal arts colleges or lower-level research universities, may provide some freedom from narrow disciplinary norms, this comes at a price. Employment at such institutions usually means heavier teaching loads, limited or no access to graduate assistants, and a lack of institutional resources, all of which make research—especially time-intensive collaborative research—difficult, if not impossible.

Those wishing to pursue a career that integrates the scholar-activist role face a conundrum. Obtaining a more prestigious appointment where research is most feasible may require conforming to disciplinary conventions that makes the resulting research useless for the advancement of social change. Obtaining an appointment where the pressure to conform to disciplinary conventions is less acute may mean not having the time or resources to actually carry out relevant research.

The Elusive Goal of Scholar-Activist: Three Potential Paths

Despite the obstacles, some scholars aim to use the security, stability, and freedom of a tenured academic position to conduct research and do writing that provides useful assistance to progressive social movement efforts. This elusive goal is based on integrating two very different roles: academic scholar and movement activist. Some strict positivists would see the two roles as simply antithetical, since the first requires detached objectivity and the latter suggests partisan engagement. But the roles are difficult to integrate precisely because the university as currently constructed is *not* a neutral entity but instead is usually allied with parties that reinforce the status quo rather than promote progressive social change. Academics choosing to support movement-based social change efforts face institutional barriers that make such work difficult. Because of these hurdles, aspiring scholar-activists seem to evolve in one of several common ways.

The SCHOLAR-Activist

Some scholars come to prioritize their academic careers. A quarter century after an attempted "sociology liberation movement," Flacks commented on the adjustment of scholar-activists to the confining realities of academia:

"[W]e have become members of the university, involved more than we ever expected with problems of personal survival, career advancement, and institutional niche making; we have accepted, more than we would have thought possible, the terms, canons, and criteria of conventional academia as unchangeable" (1991, 26). Staughton Lynd put it more starkly: "We ought to take very seriously the fact that the university corrupts radicals more often than it destroys them" (1970, 62).

Thus, some scholars become successful in academia but end up doing work that is largely irrelevant for social movement efforts—even though the work may be *about* social movements. There are many reasons why this work is not useful for movements. Some work may simply not address issues with which activists are concerned. Some may involve broad social criticism or may focus narrowly on social problems without considering how social change might occur. (Sociology, especially, has a long history of work that points out problems without suggesting realistic avenues for change.)

Regardless of the reasons, many scholars do not recognize, or are unconcerned with, the irrelevancy of their work to movement efforts. They may have at one time viewed themselves as activists, but eventually their role as professor begins to overshadow their activist sympathies. In some cases, they may simply not realize that what *they* see as politically interesting work is simply not helpful to potential movement allies. Some scholars blame movement activists, whom they criticize for being atheoretical and overly fixated on short-term pragmatic concerns. Still other academics recognize the disconnect between their scholarship and activism and take comfort in their *teaching* as their political work. In a variation on the old saying, "those who can, do; those who can't, teach," they recognize their inability to effect social change but hope they can inspire others to do so.

Another important way to maintain a successful academic career while continuing the pursuit of change is to moderate one's goals and work to improve social services or promote limited reform rather than advocate for fundamental change. There are avenues available for liberal scholars who are willing to operate under such conditions. Participatory action research (PAR), a form of collaborative research, offers some promise in challenging the traditional barriers. Researchers try to couple their training with the expertise of community partners and produce work that can be used by the community partners to advance their efforts.

A number of academic publications have explored the theoretical justifications, methodological issues, and practical implications of this sort of research (e.g., Greenwood 1998; Maguire 1987; Nyden et. al. 1997; Reason and Bradbury 2001; Stringer 1996). However, the origins and impetus for PAR have often been rooted *outside* of the academy. Hall observes:

> participatory research was very largely theorized and disseminated from a social movement or civil society base. Among the original premises were the importance of breaking what we referred to as the monopoly over knowledge production by universities. This was not in the least a form of anti-intellectualism, but was a recognition that the academic mode of production was, and remains, in some fundamental ways linked to different sets of interests and power relations from those of women and men in various social movement settings or located in more autonomous community-based, non-governmental structures. Much of the energy and impulse for deepening the understanding of participatory research came from the social movement contexts in Latin America, Africa, Asia, the Caribbean and elsewhere. (2001, 176)

Because it emerged from active civil society and social movement bases, PAR has always included an activist orientation. For example, in 1978 the International Participatory Research Network, based outside of universities, defined "participatory research" as involving "a whole range of powerless groups of people—the exploited, the poor, the oppressed, the marginal," as originating "in the community itself," as having as its goal "the radical transformation of social reality and the improvement of the lives of the people themselves," and envisioning the researcher as "a committed participant and learner in the process of research, i.e., a militant rather than a detached observer" (cited in Hall 2001, 173).

However, as PAR is adopted and brought into traditional academic institutions, it tends to lose much of its militant edge. Because of the confining factors described above, much of PAR work seems limited to improving the efficiency of service delivery or developing mild reform strategies. Such efforts diverge significantly from more direct challenges to power posed by social movement efforts.

In addition, attempting to utilize an approach to research that was developed largely outside of academia—while still positioned within academia—is no easy task. In one analysis of participatory research scholars, Cancian concluded that researchers "with the strongest ties to community groups tend to be the least successful in academia and to have the most conflict with their departments. The major requirement for academic success in research universities—publishing regularly in academic journals—is incompatible with doing research that is controlled by community members and that includes radical social change" (1993, 105). So even scholars who pursue some form of PAR, an approach that explicitly seeks to bridge the gap between researchers and others, find themselves struggling with the tensions inherent in their identity as scholar-activists.

The Scholar-ACTIVIST

A second evolutionary path for aspiring scholar-activists is to prioritize activism at the expense of scholarship. This is most feasible after tenure is obtained. In such situations some scholars may decide to write primarily for a broader audience, abandoning journal publications aimed at peers. Such a shift is likely to be uncomfortable since it will probably bring negative sanctions from administrators and colleagues who expect conformity to the disciplinary conventions. It is also by no means certain that such a shift in orientation will necessarily result in work that is of real assistance to movement efforts. As a result, some academics eventually leave (or are dismissed from) academic life, turning instead to more directly aiding social justice efforts. Such an abandonment of an academic career usually comes at a significant financial cost and almost always precludes the sort of autonomous research and writing that made academia attractive in the first place. But for some, the costs are worth the benefits of more fully realizing their activist values.

The SCHOLAR-ACTIVIST

Finally, there are those who continue their effort to maintain an integrated scholar-activist identity. As noted above, some academics do manage to produce work of relevance to social movement efforts—but often with the consequence of having to cling to the margins of academia.

A scholar intent on succeeding in mainstream academia while simultaneously addressing an activist audience must learn to produce two versions of their scholarship—one for consumption by colleagues and a translation for a more activist audience. This extra burden presents a unique hurdle for movement scholars that most colleagues do not face. As a result, it can be especially stressful. Cancian concludes from her discussion with those who adopted it that the two-career strategy—one in academia, one oriented to social change—is "very demanding on the researchers' time and energy. One childless woman observed that if she had children, she would not have the time to be an activist as well as a successful professor" (1993, 103). Since the activist version of such publications is not particularly rewarded—and may be seen by some as mere popularizing—the implicit professional pressure is to focus on prestigious journals and leave the translation to others.

Other Paths, Other Problems

Imagine a sociology program in social movements that aimed to "meet the needs of activists as members and leaders in their social movement organizations, as active citizens in their communities, and as responsible individuals in a democratic society." Such an approach would likely be praised as refreshingly direct by some scholars and condemned as too applied and unscholarly by others. But such an approach would not be new. It already exists in some labor studies programs—one of whose self-descriptions is the basis for the quote above (Indiana University Division of Labor Studies 2003).

It is interesting that labor studies, based in one of the nation's oldest and largest social movements, has long taken a different approach to research and education than the bulk of social movement studies. As a result, it exists as an exception to some of the dynamics described above. While the history of labor studies is a diverse one with varying degrees of success that should not be romanticized, some elements of the better labor studies programs do suggest some alternatives regarding the relationship between academics and activists.

Labor studies scholars generally tend to be much more closely aligned with the labor movement than social movement scholars. There are a number of reasons for this. First, some labor studies programs have the explicit goal of educating workers and training current or future union leaders. Therefore, the need to understand union wishes and ongoing placement of graduates in union jobs encourages closer ties. Second, some labor studies programs exist on the margins of academia with one foot in traditional universities and the other in more populist adult education efforts. Sometimes the programs even have a unique structural position in the university distinguishing them from traditional academic departments. This has led to significant tensions within the labor studies community, with some striving for more mainstream academic respectability by becoming more fully integrated in the university while others focus on retaining the more direct applied links to labor that occur outside of the university. Existing at the margins can be very trying and can make labor studies programs more vulnerable to budget cuts and political attacks, but it also offers some freedom from the confining professional conventions of more mainstream academia. Third, organized labor has often served as an external constituency supporting labor studies programs both politically and monetarily—precisely what most traditional social movement scholars lack. This can make it difficult to criticize the union establishment. But at its best, such support can lead to enormous benefits.

It bears repeating that labor studies have had ongoing difficulties existing at the margins of academia and have had to withstand attacks from both inside and outside of the academy. (Perhaps such attacks indicate a level of threat posed by labor studies to those in power that does not exist in more traditional social movement studies.) Still, it is a different tradition that has resulted in academic work that is often much more strategically oriented than traditional social movement efforts (e.g., Bronfenbrenner et. al. 1998).

Interestingly, the tradition of closer connections between labor studies scholars and activists has had an impact in sociology. In recent years, a Labor and Labor Movements section of the American Sociological Association has been formed, separate from the older Collective Behavior and Social Movements (CBSM) section. The newer section has stood in critical support of the labor movement and has worked collaborative events into the ASA meetings, such as meetings between AFL-CIO officials and sociologists to discuss research agendas of mutual interest.

Such efforts may prove to be a fruitful meeting ground, but they will not change the structural realities in which academics operate. Changing the university would involve long-term collective response by those within it, in ongoing collaboration with allies outside the academy—something that appears nowhere on the horizon.

It may be, as in the 1960s, that activism will find academics on campus, this time in the form of unionization and living wage campaigns among university staff, grad student union drives, affirmative action battles, and other campus-based activism. Perhaps these efforts will be a spur to more change-focused research.

It may also be that the most successful fusion of activism and scholarship will not come from academics' deepened appreciation for collaboration with social movements but from social movements' deepened appreciation for the value of research. The labor movement, again, provides an interesting example. As the assault on unions has contributed to the declining number of union members in the United States, some labor unions have explored new strategies for leveraging power over employers and reducing the hostile environment in which they must operate. More sophisticated corporate campaigns, along with strategies of community collaboration, have increased the demand for skilled researchers who can generate necessary campaign information and help develop organizing strategy. Thus, there are a small but growing number of PhDs among the rank of labor researchers. These researchers—embedded within a social movement—may be the ones who make the most valuable long-term contributions to our understanding of movement dynamics.

Conclusion

To be a writer may require a room of one's own, but to be an activist requires an organized collective effort. Universities, unfortunately, are far from ideally suited to serve as common ground between the two. Instead, they are structured to accommodate the individual scholar. Those satisfied with contemplating the world from afar or in the abstract—even radical social critics—can find a comfortable home there. Those engaged in practical efforts that reaffirm the status quo or promote mild reform can also pursue lucrative academic careers. But those who are intent on trying to develop—in collaboration with social movements—scholarship that promotes fundamental social change face a formidable challenge that may only be growing. Universities, in ways both subtle and overt, are hostile to the efforts of such scholar-activists. Survival in this environment is more likely with collective organization of like-minded scholars, as has been done at various times in sociology's history. Brave souls will continue to make the effort to integrate their scholar-activist identity, and no doubt some will succeed. But for many others, being in a university eventually means being forced to decide which side they are on—and being prepared to live with the consequences of that choice.

Note

Thanks to Charlotte Ryan and Bill Hoynes for comments on this chapter. Special thanks to Steve Lyng for commenting on the chapter and, especially, for a decade of conversations related to these topics.

References

Alinsky, Saul. [1946] 1969. *Reveille for Radicals.* New York: Vintage Books.
———. 1972. "A Candid Conversation with the Feisty Radical Organizer."
    Playboy 19 (March): 59+.
American Association of University Professors. 2001. "Selling Out? Corporations
    on Campus." *Academe* 87, no. 5. At http://www.aaup.org/publications/
    Academe/01SO/So01toc.htm.
Bobo, Kim, Jackie Kendall, and Steve Max. 2001. *Organizing for Social Change.*
    Santa Ana, CA: Seven Locks Press.
Bronfenbrenner, Kate, et al. 1998. *Organizing to Win: New Research in Union
    Strategies.* Ithaca, NY: Cornell University/ILR Press.
Cancian, Francesca M. 1993. "Conflicts between Activist Research and Academic
    Success: Participatory Research and Alternative Strategies." *American
    Sociologist* (Spring): 92–106.

Colfax J., David. 1971. "Varieties and Prospects of 'Radical Scholarship' in Sociology." In *Radical Sociology,* ed. J. David Colfax and Jack L. Roach, 81–92. New York: Basic Books.

Colfax, J. David, and Jack L. Roach. 1971. "Introduction—The Roots of Radical Sociology." In *Radical Sociology,* ed. J. David Colfax and Jack L. Roach, 3–21. New York: Basic Books.

Deegan, Mary Jo. 1986. *Jane Addams and the Men of the Chicago School, 1892–1918.* New Brunswick, NJ: Transaction Books.

Feagin, Joe R., and Hernan Vera. 2001. *Liberation Sociology.* Boulder, CO: Westview.

Flacks, Dick. 1991. "The Sociology Liberation Movement: Some Legacies and Lessons." In Oppenheimer, Murray, and Levine, *Radical Sociologists and the Movement,* 17–27. Philadephia: Temple University Press.

Flacks, Richard. 1970. "Radicals in the Universities." In *Where It's At: Radical Perspectives in Sociology,* ed. Steven Deutsch and John Howard, 71–77. New York: Harper and Row.

———. 2004. "Knowledge for What? Thoughts on the State of Social Movement Studies." In *Rethinking Social Movements,* ed. Jeff Goodwin and James M. Jasper, 135–53. Lanham, MD: Rowman & Littlefield.

Greenwood, Davydd J. 1998. *Introduction to Action Research.* Thousand Oaks, CA: Sage.

Hall, Budd L. 2001. "I Wish This Were a Poem of Practices of Participatory Research." In *Handbook of Action Research,* ed. Peter Reason and Hilary Bradbury, 171–78. London: Sage.

Indiana University Division of Labor Studies. 2003. "50 Years of Labor Education." At http://labor.iu.edu/lshistory.htm.

Institute for Labor and Employment. 2003. "About the Institute." At http://www.ucop.edu/ile.

Johnson, Benjamin, Kevin Mattson, and Patrick Kavanagh, eds. 2003. *Steal This University: The Rise of the Corporate University and the Academic Labor Movement.* New York: Routledge.

Lynd, Robert. 1939. *Knowledge for What?* Princeton, NJ: Princeton University Press.

Lynd, Staughton. 1970. "The Responsibility of Radical Intellectuals." In *Where It's At: Radical Perspectives in Sociology,* ed. Steven Deutsch and John Howard, 61–70. New York: Harper and Row.

Maguire, Patricia. 1987. *Doing Participatory Research: A Feminist Approach.* Amherst: University of Massachusetts.

Marx, Karl. [1845] 1978. "Theses on Feurbach." In *The Marx-Engels Reader,* ed. Robert C. Tucker. New York: W. W. Norton.

Nelson, Cary, ed. 1997. *Will Teach for Food: Academic Labor in Crisis*. Minneapolis: University of Minnesota Press.

Nyden, Philip, Anne Figert, Mark Shibley, and Darryl Burrows. 1997. *Building Community*. Thousand Oaks, CA: Pine Forge Press.

Oppenheimer, Martin, Martin J. Murray, and Rhonda F. Levine, eds. 1991. *Radical Sociologists and the Movement*. Philadelphia: Temple University Press.

Press, Eyal, and Jennifer Washburn. 2000. "The Kept University." *Atlantic Monthly* (March): 39–54.

Reason, Peter, and Hilary Bradbury, eds. 2001. *Handbook of Action Research*. London: Sage.

Ross, Robert J. S. 1991. "At the Center and the Edge: Notes on a Life in and out of Sociology and the New Left." In Oppenheimer, Murray, and Levine, *Radical Sociologists and the Movement*, 197–215.

Ryan, Charlotte. 2004. "Can We Be Compañeros?" *Social Problems* 51, no. 1: 110–13.

Stringer, Ernest T. 1996. *Action Research: A Handbook for Practitioners*. Thousand Oaks, CA: Sage.

3

Knowing What's Wrong Is Not Enough: Creating Strategy and Vision

Cynthia Peters

From what our people received in benefit in this war, I saved an example of "humanitarian aid" for the chiapaneco indigenous, which arrived a few weeks ago: a pink stiletto heel, imported, size 6½ . . . without its mate. I always carry it in my backpack in order to remind myself, in the midst of interviews, photo reports and attractive sexual propositions, what we are to the country after the first of January: a Cinderella. [. . .] These good people who, sincerely, send us a pink stiletto heel, size 6½, imported, without its mate . . . thinking that, poor as we are, we'll accept anything, charity and alms.

—Subcomandante Marcos

Politicians lie. Corporations steal. These are almost truisms in U.S. culture today.

In my experience as an activist, tabling on the streets and talking to people at educational forums, and in the union-based ESL and high school diploma classes I teach through SEIU Local 2020, I regularly hear insightful critiques of how U.S. institutions work. "Wars kill poor people and make rich people richer," says one immigrant worker. "The boss is nothing but a thief in a suit and tie," says an African-American union steward. "Why lobby the government for change when corporations control everything?" asks a Vietnam vet I talked to in front of the post office soon after 9/11. "U.S. wars are about imperialism," says a white Irish American marine whom I recently met in a bar, and who served in Beirut in 1983, Panama in 1989, and the first Gulf War. "And then I've got to come home to Nazi-chusetts," he adds, referring to the antidemocratic (former) Massachusetts Speaker of the House, Tom Finneran, who shelved a popular referendum on clean elections. "The system is rigged to favor men," says a victim of domestic violence and a single mother. "They get better pay, they think they can control us, we have the babies, and there's no way to break out of the cycle. Welfare acts like another guy in your life."

Gramsci argued that systems of domination require both the "force of the dominant and consent of the dominated" (Kaufman 2003, 20). Intellectuals play a critical role in producing ideology that legitimates and rationalizes domination, and universities are where they hone their knowledge-in-service-of-empire skills. In *Disciplined Minds,* Jeff Schmidt calls graduate and professional schools "intellectual boot camp," where the mission is to produce "obedient thinkers" (2000, 2). People with advanced degrees—the coordinators, managers, and professionals who make the decisions that others must follow—take on careers where it is their job to "follow assigned ideologies." Their nonprofessional counterparts are only required to "follow assigned procedures" (279). Is it any wonder that they are better positioned to more accurately perceive how systems work and how they hurt?

For decades, progressives have oriented themselves toward reaching out to people with alternative information and analysis. *If people only knew* what the "war on terrorism" was really about, how the tax system favors the wealthy, how corporations rip off workers, how people of color are systematically disadvantaged, and so on, they would surely rise up to defeat injustice. Indeed, as we saw during the 2003 war in Iraq, populations in countries where the mainstream media are less constrained by U.S.-oriented propaganda were more likely to protest. In the United States, there is so much disinformation pumped through our collective consciousness, surely the mission of providing accurate information is an utmost priority for any social change movement. Even if our megaphone is minuscule compared to media behemoths, progressives should continue uncovering and circulating the underreported toll of U.S. empire.

Progressive academics have played an invaluable role in the effort to counter mainstream propaganda. Historians, economists, sociologists, political scientists, anthropologists, and professors in women's studies and African-American studies have used their tenured positions and access to university resources to publish books and articles that illuminate how oppression works and how it hurts people. Academics' contributions to social change organizing are too numerous to mention, but I offer a glimpse, which I hope will at least remind us of the great wealth of material that has been produced in the last few decades: Historians Howard Zinn, Philip Foner, and Linda Gordon used their academic positions to tell the histories of grassroots communities, labor struggles, and women and families. Frances Fox Piven and Richard Cloward did groundbreaking work on how domestic policy is used to "regulate the poor." Ward Churchill, bell hooks, and Manning Marable all have tenured university positions but are closely connected with movements that have informed and inspired their activism and their writing. Their books have provided direct momentum to antiracist struggles. Media research by people like Noam Chomsky, David Croteau, Edward S. Herman, Bill Hoynes, and Charlotte Ryan has given activists an understanding of the role of the corporate media and has supplied activists with concrete social change tools. In addition to providing much needed research and documentation, radical academics also have supported independent media by publishing their work with alternative presses such as South End Press, Common Courage Press, Monthly Review, and many others.[1]

Thus far, producing and disseminating information has been the most productive result of collaboration between activists and academics. But what if we have done our job almost too well? What if—due to progressive efforts or not—there are millions of Americans who do see the writing on the wall? They are fed up with corporate greed and political expediency. They acknowledge that corporations care only about their profits, that politicians lie, and that voting is barely worth the trouble. They understand that many of the systems that govern us are corrupt. They don't need activists or academics to expose the lies or uncover the machinations that lead to increased concentration of wealth and decreased democratic participation.

What if what is missing is not information and understanding of all that is wrong, but rather a sense that it is worth trying to do something about it?

In numerous workshops and role plays that I have helped conduct about how to talk about the war, we ask people to write down the question they most dread having to answer. Over and over again, activists say they are less worried about being cornered on historical details, the specifics of UN resolutions, or the nuances of U.S. foreign policy. What they worry about having to deal with is the person who agrees with them about what is wrong but believes there is no point in trying to change it. In his excellent study of working-class people's relationship to white, middle-class social change movements, David Croteau quotes one worker as saying the things that are wrong in the world are akin to bad weather. "A lot of times I don't like the weather," she says, "but I don't wrack my brain trying to think up a way to change it. . . . If it's raining . . . I go inside. I don't try to stop it from raining" (1995, 72).

Activists need a way to address widespread fatalism. To do this, we need to educate ourselves about our victories and how we have grown even when we have lost certain battles. We need to respond to crises in ways that lead toward institutional change, or at least ways that signal how institutional change would lead to better lives. In other words, we need a strategy to win real change, not just temporary Band-Aids. And we need to be convincing that another world is possible—which we can only do if we've put some creative thinking into what this other world might look like. Academics could help reshape and advance social change work by joining forces with activists to address these more or less missing elements (call them *victories, strategies,* and *visions*) of our activism. If widespread dissent and disaffection could be combined with a sense that organizing works, that long-term strategy can be embedded in short-term struggles, and that a better world is possible, then we would have the potential to be a massive and truly danger-ous social change movement.

For progressive academics, moving from information dissemination to strategy and vision may be a difficult step because the process may call into question their own rationalizations for the career they have chosen. Conceptualizing how to dismantle repressive institutions would endanger the academic's elite role in just such an institution. Compelling visions of a better world presumably will not include the same caste system that gives rise to current distinctions between professionals and nonprofessionals, a distinction that many academics are not just wedded to, but spend signifi-cant time replicating and justifying. Isn't the expertise that can be honed in cloistered ivory towers important to maintain? Aren't some theories too difficult for most people to understand and so the discussion about them rightfully belongs in obscure and inaccessible journals? Isn't it right and proper for some people to make decisions for others, get social accolades for holding such positions, and contribute to ongoing hierarchies—the point of which is to stifle democratic participation?

Noam Chomsky says that it is the responsibility of intellectuals to "speak the truth and to expose lies" (1987, 60). Although institutional pressures (funding sources, internal hierarchies, the pressure to publish in certain elite journals, and so on) make such a mandate challenging, some radical academics have taken it seriously and have dedicated their lives to documenting the painful toll of repressive institutions such as capitalism, imperialism, racism, sexism, and homophobia. Their contribution has been invaluable and much of it has been disseminated through a sophisticated network of alternative media that has succeeded in saving some radical academics' work from oblivion.

But what of the social movement theorists—those who have taken on the project of trying to understand how social movements occur, why people participate in them, and how they can be catalysts for change? This is important work. Understanding our movements, their histories, and the theoretical frameworks that guide them should help activists avoid costly organizing mistakes. The study of movements should, if we were doing it correctly, help us have better movements. But it is rare to find social movement theory being published through progressive outlets that see themselves as servicing the movement. It is rarer still to hear activists responding to or in any way reflecting on social movement theory coming out of the academy.

The fault lies partly with activists, who are frequently (and understandably) consumed with coping with current crises. By focusing primarily on today's battles, activists don't sufficiently orient themselves toward winning the war in the long term. Perhaps this is because our movements share some of the fatalism we see in the mainstream. We don't *really* think we can win, but we think it is worth attempting to put out some of the fires and maybe win reforms here and there (Albert 2002). If activists were more visionary, more seriously oriented toward winning profound change, perhaps we would look to social movement theory for guidance in critiquing and analyzing what we need to win. Clearly, we need to look beyond what we have taken so far from academia—the documentation of how bad things are. We need to look for the evidence of what works and why—not as an exercise in understanding, but because we want it to inform our work, improve our skills, make us better at what we do so that we can win.

What could academics do (particularly social movement theorists) to push forward the work of social change? Academics should become activists themselves. They should create meaningful channels for interacting with and building bridges to other activists and their work. And they should find ways to share resources. In this way academics will gain a clearer sense of what is missing (and much needed) in social change discourse.

When I asked Syracuse-based activist Brian Dominick how he thought academics and activists might more usefully interact, he replied, perhaps not even half jokingly, that it would be better for academics to keep to their lofty debates. At least that way, he reasoned, they would be less inclined to dominate and attempt to control activist projects, which would degenerate as a result. "Shutting up in public would be the thing I'd have to say that academics can best offer activists," suggested Dominick.[2] Indeed, academics must be highly disciplined about not using class privilege and "expertise" to unfairly dominate activist agendas. They must be careful about bringing the equivalent of the "pink stiletto heel, size 6½, imported, without its mate" to other people's work. But these warnings are not meant to close doors. Rather, they should inspire us to open channels between activists and academics based on mutual respect, a desire to learn from each other, and honest appreciation of each other's strengths and weaknesses.

Be an Activist Where You Are

University professors who want to help move social movements forward could start by following the Zapatista mandate to be an activist where you are. Only individuals talking and planning in groups can decide how best to direct their efforts, but surely academics, like all the rest of us, have dozens of choices. Academics work in institutions that replicate race, class, and gender oppression. They operate according to norms that reinforce the idea that it is sensible, desirable, and even humane for some people to do the thinking, conceptualizing, and coordinating while others clean the toilets. They reward the already wealthy with educations that prepare them for lives as members of the ruling class, and they prepare working-class people for low-wage, rote jobs.

These aren't necessarily reasons to leave the university. "Stay and fight," Jesse Lemisch exhorts in a talk he gave at a Columbia University conference on the history of activism (2003). "The university is a critical site of struggle for many reasons," adds Eric Mann, the director of the Los Angeles Labor/Community Strategy Center:

> First, from the United States to the Third World, the university is home to the student movement. The student movement is essential as a radical, and at times, revolutionary force in society. Second, the university has growing corporate ties that allow for direct struggle with many of society's most powerful and visible forces. Finally, the university is a central cultivator and disseminator of the ideology of dominance. (1999, 770)

Being an activist does not mean studying—or being a participant observer in or a visitor to—someone else's struggle. Nor does teaching count as activism. As a professor, you may equip your students with important radical theory and perspective. You may do other things that professors do that are important politically, like serve as the academic advisor for a radical student group or speak at campus rallies, and so on. But real activism means actually taking on an organizing challenge yourself, working collectively with others, and doing the slow, plodding, tedious work of bringing people together to make change.

In his book about the way professionalism undermines democracy, Jeff Schmidt (2000) offers three general guidelines for radicals who are professionals. Academics who wish to broaden their contribution to social change work might start here.

First, identify primarily as a radical, not as a professional, so that you do not bring to your work the "same elitism, the same inequality of authority and ultimately the same hierarchy of 'somebodies' and 'nobodies' that turns people off to the status quo in the first place and sparks their interest in the opposition" (Schmidt 2000, 265). During the fall 2002 janitors' strike in Boston, a few professors at Simmons College strategized about ways they could actively support the cleaners in their building. They talked about canceling classes, offering classes off campus, and joining picket lines. But most professors wanted to show their support only by donating money. A labor struggle over health benefits and slight wage increases for the "help" did not rank as something that should impinge on class time. In the scheme of things, janitors' work does not count for much. It is meant to be invisible. Professors' anxiety around the strike centered on how their offices would get clean—not on how a class-based struggle would play out. In other words, their identity as professionals who do thinking work all day and enjoy clean and tidy environments due to no exertion of their own determined their response to the janitors more than their identity as radicals.

Second, Schmidt says, "You must hold a very critical view of the social role of your profession and of the institution that employs you" (2000, 265). If you understand clearly the role that the academy plays in the social structure, you will more effectively identify short-term reforms that will help bring about the long-term change that you are aiming for. For example, in May 2003, USAID offered $3 to $5 million in grants to U.S. universities for embarking on "partnerships" with Iraqi institutes of higher education. The goal was to provide "a critical avenue to strengthen intellectual diversity in Iraq and prepare Iraqi youth for leadership and employment opportunities in a competitive global economy," says Dana Peterson with USAID's Asia and Near East Bureau (USAID 2003). Representing the invader, victor, and occupier of nearly defenseless Iraq, U.S. bureaucrats apparently have no need to gloss over their unilateral plans for this freshly subordinate country. U.S. guns brought Iraqis to their knees, and now U.S. universities will help get an elite few on their feet again in preparation for "leadership and employment" in the U.S.-dominated global economy. USAID officials do not even show any sign of concern that U.S. universities might balk at the opportunity to play handmaiden to such a frank and antidemocratic assertion of global power. Has anyone asked the Iraqis what help they want, if any, from U.S. universities? Has anyone contemplated whether it is even possible for the country with the biggest guns and the most single-minded pursuit of global profit to contribute anything to "intellectual diversity" in Iraq? It's the age-old pattern—after the troops come the missionaries—but too many academics do not see how they are pressed into service of the empire. U.S. academics could protest and suggest alternatives to USAID's plans in Iraq that could result in a better short-term outcome (no-strings-attached donations to Iraq, for example) and, in the process, illuminate and undermine U.S. hegemony in the world.

Third, "Your politics must make a difference in the world. You must make your radical outlook count for something somewhere; it must guide you in some activity, on or off the job" (Schmidt 2000, 266). One example of radical academics making a difference in the world is the Media Research and Action Project (MRAP) at Boston College, also discussed elsewhere in this book. Directed by William Gamson and Charlotte Ryan, MRAP's mission was to take what academics have learned about how the media work into marginalized communities. Their weekly seminars brought together scholars, activists, and journalists in an effort to help social change movements identify barriers to media access and develop strategies to overcome those barriers.

Use Schmidt's guidelines as a standard against which you can measure your activist work. On sometimes cloistered college campuses, internal debates around dormitory rules, grading norms, curriculum changes, and so on can seem like the height of struggle when in fact they have few repercussions for building a social change movement. Part of the work of being an activist where you are is to ask yourself where and how it is most important to use your energy, whether your efforts are contributing to something broader, and whether you are building relationships with other activists inside and outside the campus community.

If being an activist in the academy doesn't suit for whatever reason, then be one in the neighborhood where the university is located or in the neighborhood where you live. The reason for this, at least in part, is simple: we will not win, we won't even come close to winning, unless every single one of us is an activist. No matter who you are or what line of work you are in, you should be doing something to nurture the relationships and build the organizations that contribute to a loose network that someday will amount to a powerful pressure on corrupt social institutions.

There is no particular prescription for how to do this. There are many variables, including one's own inclinations and abilities. The university is a good place to organize a petition drive around the USA Patriot Act. Professors might organize other professors to support graduate student teaching assistants (TAs) in their struggle for fair pay. They might find ways to disrupt divisions of labor on campus by, for example, declining to give TAs all the papers to grade. Speaking of grades, maybe professors could work with students and faculty to abolish grades altogether. Or maybe university teachers will go home from work in the evening and join their neighborhood peace and justice group in their effort to institute rent control, raise consciousness about U.S. war plans, or stop the spraying of pesticides in the park where the kids play. Maybe there are professors who loathe the thought of extra meetings and so would become paralyzed by the challenge to be an activist where you are. But there is plenty of work for these folks, too. They can maintain the database for some worthy organization, write the grants, edit the bulletins, or design the leaflets. No matter which of these activities a person chooses, he or she will be exposing him- or herself to the challenges of making change—of creating and sustaining momentum toward a better world.

Develop Relationships with Activists

Perhaps most important, academics will develop relationships with activists, which will help keep them honest and grounded in what the real point of it all is, lest they succumb to pressures that lead them to believe it is just about publishing that next paper or one-upping some colleague in an intellectual feud that only a few other colleagues even understand. "Intellectuals, the educated classes, are the most indoctrinated, most ignorant, most stupid part of the population," Chomsky (in Ross 1990, 101) reminds us. There are two reasons. "First of all, as the literate part of the population, they are subjected to the mass of propaganda. There is a second, more important and more subtle reason. Namely, they are the ideological managers. Therefore, they must internalize the propaganda and believe it. And part of the propaganda they have developed is that they are the natural leaders of the masses" (ibid.). Not developing relationships with activists leaves you with little support to withstand the pressure to carry out what Schmidt calls "assigned ideologies."

Besides some structured-in humility for those who have been crowned the "natural leaders," there are other reasons why academics and activists must bridge the gulf between each of their efforts. By collaborating on projects, activists and academics will generate more useful work. The bimonthly progressive economics magazine *Dollars and Sense* has an interesting model for integrating academics into a progressive project: academics as well as non-university-based intellectuals work on the collective that publishes it. Everyone does everything, from editing to fund-raising to schlepping boxes around the office. The noneconomists get editing and writing help from their better-trained (at least in that field) colleagues, and the economists learn firsthand about current organizing challenges, as well as how to keep a movement operation going. *Dollars and Sense* also produces half a dozen or so books a year, such as *Real World Micro* and *Real World Macro,* that mirror beginning-level college texts but feature progressive- and activist-oriented economic analyses. These books, which are edited by a mixed group of activists and academics, bring social change activism as well as analysis into the classroom and form a critical bridge between activists and academics.

Dollars and Sense provides just one model of developing materials that activists and academics can both benefit from. But surely there are many more. We just need to think of them. Key to any model, however, is that it functions as a two-way street.

Klare Allen, organizer with the environmental justice group Alternatives for Community and the Environment (ACE), reflected on the challenges of building relationships with people in academia and stressed the importance of maintaining grassroots leadership:

> Here in Roxbury, we are surrounded by academic institutions that are nationally known, and that seem to know everything in the world that there is to be known, and yet there's no clear way for us to benefit from all this knowledge that's housed right next door. We know we can't work with Harvard as an institution. Instead, we're trying to build a relationship with the people within Harvard. We're asking them to organize themselves. We're inviting them to come out to our community meetings and just listen. Then they can go back and report on what they saw and understood. After a while, they can figure out what they have in their pool of resources to offer. After they've been to the ninth meeting, then maybe they'll be in tune enough to know how to enter in, to know what makes sense to offer. This is what institutional folks can do [to support activist struggles]. And if the home-base organizers have made sure that people are at the center of the strategy, then they will have been very clear about what their needs are. There will be a strong enough core to evaluate what is being offered. Does it make sense? Will it help? These are baby steps, but this is how we have to do this work. (2004)

Another example of activist/academic collaboration has been unfolding in Boston recently. Academics in social work and psychotherapy are learning from a tenants' rights group (City Life/Vida Urbana) that has been organizing study groups following a Freirian model of problem posing (Freire

2000). Participants identify what *they* see as wrong in their communities. They discuss why these problems exist and finally propose what action they might take to ameliorate the situation. Starting with the basic widespread problem of unaffordable rents, for example, the discussion often leads to a critique of private property, the concentration of wealth, racism, the role of the welfare state, and links between local and global privatization. Actions include immediate reform, such as rent control, and more long-term goals, such as undermining capitalism. According to facilitator Elena Blanco, participants speak from a personal place—bringing humor, pain, and a great deal of hard-won experience to the study group. In the process of sharing their stories and their challenges, participants discover themselves as co-analyzers of what is happening. They begin to feel better because they realize that they are not alone, that their problems generate from a system, and that there are ways they can join together to fight for change.[3]

The study groups help participants see themselves as the experts of their own situations. For many, this is a radical and empowering moment, and one that Bill Madsen, writer, therapist, and postgraduate professor of social work, hopes to learn more about. Author of *Collaborative Therapy for Multistressed Families* (2001), Madsen believes the study group model helps participants achieve something he has strived for in his work, i.e., the problematizing of the constraints and obstacles that people face rather than the people themselves. Madsen thinks the study group facilitators are asking questions that lead people to think of themselves as actors. In what could be a successful example of activist/academic collaboration, he has asked the facilitators to present their study group model at an upcoming academic conference of people in the mental health field. In return, he hopes, activists might leave the exchange with more insight into how to support people who are making radical shifts in how they think about themselves and their role in the world.[4]

Share Resources

If activists and academics had more organic connections, ideas about how to share resources would naturally emerge. But academics could be more proactive about it. They could, for example, set up focus groups with radical activists to exchange ideas and learn from each other. Through this process, activists could identify materials that they might benefit from or that would be useful in their organizing. Academics could use their institutional base to develop the materials, and activists could be the editors and the field testers.

Taking research cues from social change movements is not exactly a great career move for academics, but it may be a necessary and worthwhile sacrifice. It redistributes access to knowledge and information. Indeed, it means that activists get to help determine what the knowledge base is. Participatory action research (PAR) takes this model a step further. Not only do activists help determine the subject, they participate in the research, and the research has an advocacy component. Academics analyze and "help solve the real-world problems of the people they once might have called their research subjects," according to Laura Hershey (2001). In one PAR example, researchers took their cue from people in the disability rights community and examined the effects of changes in the Canadian Pension Plan on disabled women. The result was a revealing study that could be used by activists and policy makers alike in their efforts to press for better benefits for disabled people.

What if there were some channel of communication that allowed activists to say to PhD students, "Here are the things we wish we knew more about." As Justin Podur, an antipoverty and antiwar activist from Toronto, explains, activists need more opposition research. Left academics spend too much time studying social movements and "other" cultures or subgroups and not enough time trying to understand "corporations and systems of authority and control, with a view to dismantling them, or even finding weaknesses that could be exploited—even on very microscale." For example, in Toronto, Podur continues, "It would be helpful for academics to produce maps of all the buildings that are abandoned and have questionable ownership, and hand that over to squatting movements."[5] Boston-based tenant organizer Mark Pedulla echoes the need for community-directed research. "We need research on organizing models both nationally and internationally. We need research on strategies and tactics that are being used in different social locations. And we need research on what public policy alternatives are available."[6]

Sharing resources, besides being a fair and equitable thing to do, is strategic on a number of levels. Perhaps the most important of these resources is time and privilege. Many university professors have more flexible schedules than most workers do. Many have summers off and occasionally get sabbaticals. Tenured professors don't have to worry so much about publishing and should be able to devote themselves more energetically to social change work. They don't spend the whole day doing rote, boring work and should be more capable of pitching in at this level when it comes to movement work. Too many privileged people join movements expecting to replicate the class perks they enjoy elsewhere in life. They want to do the conceptual work, speak at the events, and write the articles while someone else stands at the copier machine, does door-to-door canvassing, and keeps the phone tree running smoothly. Participating in the movement-building ("shit") work helps privileged people get acquainted with what may have previously been invisible labor. Freeing up others to do the speaking, writing, and debating gives those with less access to such empowering roles a chance to grow in those skills.

By balancing rote and conceptual labor (Albert and Hahnel 1991), activists and academics contribute to breaking down class divisions, a moral as well as strategic goal. They address classist behaviors on a microscale, and in the process reveal new ways of organizing work. More people of more varied backgrounds gain a public voice and shape the movement's direction and the public's perception of the movement. Academics carry lessons back with them and perhaps encourage research into alternative modes of organizing work, thus contributing to the vision work that we so desperately need to help address the fatalism people feel regarding social change.

In addition to time and privilege, academics have access to material resources. We often see activists teaming up with university groups in order to be able to host conferences or talks in campus lecture halls for free or low cost. But they could do more. Why not lobby universities to make library cards available to activists? As an activist and writer on a limited budget, one of my biggest challenges is not having institutional support for research. It would be helpful to have the support of a good librarian, a well-stocked library, and Lexis-Nexis. Why not develop a special program for activists to be able to take classes for free? Why not invite activists to coteach seminars? Why not ask activists what night classes would benefit them and then rally some professors together to teach them?

"Ideas are also weapons."

Probably the single most important thing a radical academic can do is to blur the line between thinking about social change and acting on it. Not that there is no distinction between thinking and acting. There is and should be. Activists who are not in universities take time for planning, thinking, and reflecting on their actions. We theorize about what we do (though we may not call it that). We can't do effective social change work without the benefit of ideas or without an understanding of history and current context. "We can't build movements without history," says queer theorist and cultural critic Michael Bronski.[7] Our thinking is constantly informed by our actions, but it is probably not adequately informed by history and by others' actions. In this activists could directly benefit from academics. Historians and social movement theorists know stuff about movements that we don't because they have the time and the space and the access to libraries necessary for study.

Yet academics are sharing with *each other* the insights that come from study. They are holding conferences, publishing journal articles, and debating various social movement theories that activists don't know the first thing about. If social movement theorists are doing anything useful, *then we need to know about it.* Is there any other academic field where the theorists are so divorced from the practitioners? Scientists read, understand, contribute to, and are influenced by the journals in their field. Activists, on the other hand, have very little to do with social movement literature in any capacity. We are missing out on the opportunity to learn about and reflect on anything other than what is unfolding in the narrow parameters of our own organizing work. Living in the United States at a time of unprecedented rollbacks of rights and protections at home and unilateral aggression abroad, this is an inefficiency we can hardly afford. Activists could benefit greatly from having access to more debate, more theoretical exchange, more ideas and knowledge about what works, what doesn't, and why.

Meanwhile, the theorizing that academics do should not—*must not*—happen in a vacuum. It must be informed by something more than what they read in books. It should be informed by activism. This could happen by reading what activists write, by having more connections to activist communities, and by participating in activist struggles. All of these ways of being informed by activism are important. Academics can't be expected to have lived experiences in every kind of political struggle that they study or comment on. Jesse Lemisch's assertion that "a good dose of tear gas makes us think more clearly as historians" (2003) may be true for some, but it should not be a mandate to all. Good analysis or commentary does not depend on direct experience. It is valid to keep in touch with activists less directly through meetings and newsletters, and so on. But it is still essential for an academic—especially a social movement theorist—to take on the challenge of making change.

"There are habits of the mind that I think are important for a healthy engagement with the political world," writes activist and academic Cynthia Kaufman (2003, 3). I have argued that *being an activist, building relationships* with activists, and *sharing resources* with activists will stretch scholarship—pushing and prodding academics to play a more productive role in social change movements. Meanwhile, activists need the opportunity to theorize about our work—to develop the "habits of the mind" that will help us be most effective. "Theorizing," it seems, is just a word that describes thinking, analyzing, and organizing knowledge and understanding. We need the opportunities to learn about how others think and about what theoretical tools they bring to their work. We need to explore ways that academics can help activists move beyond the educational model of organizing: if we teach them, they will follow. It is true that facts, data, knowledge can be weapons. Whole movements have grown up around newly exposed injustice. But as Marcos says, "Ideas are also weapons" (2000). Most important, they can help us break the habits of the mind that keep us in the current activist holding pattern—one that encourages us to not even see our victories, much less learn from them; that keeps us focused on daily emergencies rather than long-term strategy; and that tells us it is not worth envisioning a better world because minor reforms on the current set of horrors is the best we can do.

Notes

Thanks to all the activists and scholars who took time out of their busy schedules to share their ideas with me. Thanks to Michael Albert, Klare Allen, Dawn Belkin Martinez, Paul Kiefer, Sharon Kurtz, Justin Podur, Charlotte Ryan, and Paul Saba—for their conversation, advice, research, and example. Thanks to editors David Croteau, Bill Hoynes, and Charlotte Ryan for taking on this project and providing helpful guidance.

1. It is clearly unwise to try to capture the extent of progressive academic scholarship in one paragraph. The result is clearly inadequate. Still, I offer this glimpse as exactly that. There are many thousands of contributions.

2. Brian Dominick, e-mail correspondence to author, July 10, 2003.

3. Elena Blanco, unpublished interview by author, August 8, 2003.

4. Bill Madsen, unpublished interview by author, August 25, 2003.

5. Justin Podur, e-mail correspondence to author, July 8, 2003.

6. Mark Pedulla, e-mail correspondence to author, August 28, 2003.

7. Michael Bronski, unpublished telephone interview by author, June 25, 2003.

References

Albert, Michael. 2002. *Trajectory of Change.* Cambridge, MA: South End Press.

———. 2003. *Parecon: Life after Capitalism.* London and New York: Verso Press and www.parecon.org.

Albert, Michael, and Robin Hahnel. 1991. *Looking Forward: Participatory Economics for the Twenty-First Century.* Boston, MA: South End Press.

Allen, Klare. 2004. Interview by Cynthia Peters. *Z Magazine,* 17, no. 7–8 (July–August): 31–34.

Chomsky, Noam, 1987. "The Responsibility of Intellectuals." In *The Chomsky Reader,* ed. James Peck, 59–82. New York: Pantheon Books.

Croteau, David. 1995. *Politics and the Class Divide: Working People and the Middle-Class Left.* Philadelphia: Temple University Press.

Freire, Paulo. 2000. *Pedagogy of the Oppressed*. New York: Continuum Press.

Hershey, Laura. 2001. "Academics in the Service of Activism: Scholar/Advocates Engage in Participatory Action Research." *Disability World*. At http://www.disabilityworld.org/07-08_01/il/par.shtml.

Kaufman, Cynthia. 2003. *Ideas for Action: Relevant Theory for Radical Change*. Cambridge, MA: South End Press.

Lemisch, Jesse. 2003. "2.5 Cheers for Bridging the Gap between Activism and the Academy; or, Stay and Fight." *Radical History Review* 85 (Winter): 239–48.

Madsen, William. 2001. *Collaborative Therapy with Multi-stressed Families: From Old Problems to New Futures*. New York: Guilford Press.

Mann, Eric. 1999. "Radical Social Movements and the Responsibility of Progressive Intellectuals." *Loyola of Los Angeles Law Review* 32 (April): 761–90.

Marcos. 2000. "Ideas Are Also Weapons." *Toward Freedom Magazine* 49, no. 6 (November): 7–9.

———. 2003. "Chiapas, the Thirteenth Stele: Part Two, A Death." *ZNet*, July 25. At http://www.zmag.org/content/showarticle.cfm?SectionID=8&ItemID=3957 (accessed July 7, 2004).

Ross, Andrew. 1990. "Defenders of the Faith and the New Class." In *Intellectuals: Aesthetics, Politics, Academics,* ed. Bruce Robbins, 101–33. Minneapolis: University of Minnesota Press.

Schmidt, Jeff. 2000. *Disciplined Minds: A Critical Look at Salaried Professionals and the Soul-Battering System That Shapes Their Lives*. New York: Rowman and Littlefield.

USAID. 2003. "USAID Sectoral Consultations—Transcript: Higher Education and Development Conference." At http://www.usaid.gov/iraq/vid_live060503_t.html (accessed July 7, 2004).

4

Movement Strategy for Organizers

Richard Healey and Sandra Hinson

As nonacademic activists/scholars, we have been asked to reflect on the gap between social movement scholars and the movements they study. Over the last eight years, we have engaged in discussions with movement-oriented scholars around many questions: What would make scholarship more compelling for activists and organizers? What problems and challenges can movement-oriented scholars help activists address? What kinds of relationships can scholars and activists have, and how might those relationships enrich scholarship and address activists' needs? We consider these and other questions as we survey the needs of the social movement organizations we work with—statewide coalitions, labor-community alliances, community-based social change groups, and progressive regional networks. Based on our own efforts to bring theory to bear on social movement organizing, we would argue that there are many places where activists and organizers would benefit from more reciprocal relationships with scholars around questions of theory, strategy, leadership, and forms of organization.

Others in this volume are offering critiques of the current state of social movement scholarship as a way of illuminating the factors that inhibit activist-scholar collaboration. We focus more on barriers to collaboration that are connected to the current state of social movements. For a long time movement organizations have been caught up in efforts that are short-term, fragmented, and reactive. Similarly, academics have tended to be specialized in their research and reactive to research trends rather than movement trends. We offer suggestions on how this came to be, as well as ideas for helping movement groups move beyond these limitations. We also point toward promising trends—greater attention to political education, leadership development, coalition building, and infrastructure—that we see manifest in renewed efforts to become more strategic. These trends carry with them opportunities for more collaboration.

We start with an assertion: despite the anti-intellectual leanings of many activists and organizers, as noted by Darnovsky, Epstein, and Flacks (1995) and others, many movement activists and organizers are receptive to theoretical insights if they see a way to apply them to their own work. Some activists relish opportunities to engage in critical analysis and reflection and to be challenged to move beyond their usual approaches. At the same time, there are many barriers—structural, institutional, social, and cultural—that keep activists from seeking out and taking advantage of the strategic and analytical resources that are available. Too often, theoretical and analytical resources and spaces feel more like a luxury than a necessity.

The Grassroots Policy Project: Strategy for Movement Building

The assertions, analysis, and descriptions in this chapter are based on the organizations we work with and other groups with whom we are familiar. These organizations are struggling for social, economic, and racial justice. Their long-term missions include major changes in our society that would expand democracy; promote social, economic, and racial justice, good stewardship of the land, human rights and dignity; and pose challenges to concentrated power and wealth, though not necessarily all of these issues are paramount in any one group.

Our organization, the Grassroots Policy Project (GPP), works with social change groups representing a wide range of constituencies located around the country. Some, like the Tenants' and Workers' Support Committee in Alexandria, Virginia, are community-based, with predominantly low-income Latino and African-American constituencies, while others, like Wisconsin Citizen Action, are statewide coalitions that bring together urban and rural, labor and environmental, white working-class, African-American, immigrant, and gay and lesbian constituencies. Another kind of social change group we work with can be called labor-community alliances, like the Connecticut Center for a New Economy (CCNE) in New Haven. Groups like CCNE address the needs of low-income workers as *workers*— for living wages, collective bargaining, and dignity on the job—while also supporting economic and quality of life issues that affect the *communities* in which the workers live—affordable housing, social services, community reinvestment, and a voice in political decision making.

Kurt Lewin once said, "There's nothing so practical as a good theory."

At GPP, we encourage groups to explore the practical and, we would argue, necessary benefits of good theory. Like good popular education, a good theory doesn't tell people what to do or think, but it does help them figure out what they know as well as what they would like to understand better. It gives people tools and frameworks for discovering, synthesizing, evaluating, and rediscovering things about the social and political contexts in which they are working and for engaging in collective analysis, planning, and action for democratic social change. GPP brings particular elements of social movement research and theory into trainings and materials for organizers and activists.

Our engagement with social change groups takes many forms, from political education workshops on power analysis and issue framing to in-depth series on planning and strategy development. We develop sessions that provide a political context for all the activities that groups are engaged in. At a practical level, we might work with a group on areas such as organizing, coalition building, communications, and electoral engagement. Our work is informed by a theory about social change in America, using three interrelated concepts: *power, worldview,* and *strategy.* When we work with groups on strategic development, we use this theory of social change as a guide for the organization to adopt and implement *strategic shifts*—to expand the strategic potential of their campaigns and organizing efforts. We will say more about these concepts in the following sections.

The members of the organizations with whom we interact are asking how and why the corporate-conservative movement has shifted the political terrain so successfully over the last thirty years. To answer this question, groups must closely examine the ways in which power and social change operate in America. For this kind of analysis, groups need good theory. Movement leaders' desire for this kind of analysis provides an opening for dialogue about theory and practice, ideas and action.

The State of the Movement

For the past twenty years or more, most social change organizations have been on the defensive: shoring up past victories and warding off further attacks on progressive gains from past social movements. Since the 1980s, the right has been successful in eroding New Deal reforms as well as gains made in the 1960s and early 1970s on civil rights, environmental protection, women's rights and reproductive health, and so much more. These well-organized attacks have brought into painful relief the limits of prevailing models of organizing and movement building on the progressive left. For a host of reasons, groups are becoming more aware of and concerned about the huge gap between their mission and their daily work. Most of their energies go into fighting immediate political battles, struggling to stay afloat financially, doing turnout for events, dealing with staffing issues, servicing members, and so on.

The staff and leaders of these groups recognize that their day-to-day work is often reactive, fragmented, and tactical. They are self-critical and interested in "moving to the next level," as they would say, though they are not always sure what that next level might be. Groups are willing to examine tools and practices that might help them narrow the gap between their mission and their daily work. At GPP, our goal is to help organizations continue to be effective in their immediate struggles while at the same time begin to develop the power and capacity to address their long-term and strategic goals.

The phenomenon that we are calling the *mission gap* has a long history. It can be traced back to the German Social Democratic Party in the nineteenth century, in their discussions about linking work on immediate reforms to their long-term goal of revolution. The tendency of social change organizations in the United States to focus on immediate reforms at the expense of social transformation also has a distinguished history. Many of the explanations for U.S. reformist tendencies have been condensed in phrases such as American exceptionalism, the legacy of anticommunism, bread-and-butter trade unionism, and Alinsky-style organizing, among others.

The social movements of the 1960s were a departure from narrowly focused approaches to social change—a time when diverse constituencies made broad demands for authentic democracy, economic and social justice, and a more enlightened foreign policy. These demands were located in a wide range of issues and causes. Yet, at the close of this tumultuous period in U.S. history, many social justice activists, trade unionists, environmentalists, and community organizers became wary of big challenges to the status quo and about the dangers of *ideology* as a factor in isolating and marginalizing groups from the American mainstream. During the 1970s, organizing became more focused on mobilizing large numbers of people to support narrowly cut issue campaigns and public interest advocacy. Nonideological approaches to issue-focused organizing and mobilizing began to replace more transformational, intensive engagements around theories, ideas, and analysis.

There are parallels between the rise and fall of transformational, movement-oriented organizing and the decline of activist-academic engagement. Prior to the mid-1960s, most sociologists and political scientists who studied organized activism and dissent would not have bothered themselves with the question of how they should relate to the organizations they studied. In the 1960s, academics became activists in the civil rights and antiwar movements, and scholarship followed along, seeking to understand and advance social movements as "politics by other means." Activist caucuses and individual academics saw a role for themselves in helping to advance social movement goals. In the 1960s activists in the New Left embraced new theories of social change each year, inspired by Marx, Weber, Gramsci, Marcuse, Sartre, Mills, Mallet, and other theorists. The activists were interested in scholarship and intellectual and historical analysis.

The New Left's successors of the 1970s—public interest groups, ACORN, Citizen Action, the Industrial Areas Foundation, and others—were more concerned about connecting with what they thought of as the *real* America. They focused on *organizing*, not the false promises of *theory*, and became more interested in Alinsky than Aronowitz. These trends in social movements have contributed to the recent decline in activist-academic engagement. The short-term orientation of movement organizations over the last thirty years has had the effect of eroding meaningful activist-academic relationships. The time and money crunch that activists and organizers face and the incentives for visible short-term work drive the wedge in deeper. Declining movement infrastructure means there are fewer institutional and relational linkages and even fewer models of or spaces for collaboration as part of movement building.

Organizing trends emerging from the 1970s have produced some impressive victories in terms of environmental laws, women's rights, GLBT issues, and advancing community efforts for local investments, to name a few. Indeed, their approaches seem very pragmatic and realistic. And yet, these kinds of single-issue advocacy approaches may no longer be adequate to the challenges of the moment.

Theoretical Resources for Social Change

We are suggesting that renewed interest in analysis and political education on the part of activists carries with it the potential for renewed engagement between scholars and activists. Many activists and organizers are interested in theory that corresponds with their sense of urgency about the need to roll back the gains of the corporate conservatives and the cultural right. There is growing recognition among many leaders in labor, community organizing, environmental groups, antipoverty advocacy, and cultural activists that fragmented, issue-by-issue approaches have failed to build progressive power. As leaders shift more of their focus toward building movement infrastructures that could include research, policy, and academic institutions, roles for scholars become more evident. Within the context of infrastructure, we can imagine roles, relationships, and many possibilities for joining together scholarship and action.

We will use the remainder of this chapter to illustrate how GPP uses research and theory from sociology and political science. Our starting point is a favorite from both fields, theories of *power.*

Power Analysis

While there are many unexamined assumptions about power among activists, the leaders we work with say they want to build power, not just have access to it and influence with decision makers. In fact, most of the organizations we know about, not just the ones we work with directly, think and talk about power and have some ideas about building power. Probably the most common approach to power derives from "commonsense" (in the Gramscian sense of the term) observations of local politics and decision making. Common sense suggests that power is the ability to get people to do things they don't want to do, and organizers say that there are two sources of power—organized people and organized money. Common sense and good organizers have built impressive organizations that have achieved important victories for millions of people over the past thirty years.

This approach to power is familiar to social scientists; we might think of it as pluralism seen through the eyes of a pragmatic community organizer. It has all the strengths and weaknesses of pluralist models of decision making in America. It is better than a belief that power is something other people do and that an organization will win because it is "doing the right thing." The modified pluralist model makes sense. It offers measurable results in a way that is easy to understand. This is important in terms of the "incentives structure" to which most movement organizations are subservient: foundations and large donors give money to things that they can understand and measure. GPP works with organizations that have operated with this model and under these incentives. Using these approaches, groups have achieved significant victories. Nevertheless, the leaders of these groups are dissatisfied and self-critical. They want to do something more than all-out mobilization for a legislative victory (or defeat), or one more electoral cycle that seems just like the last one. They want to be less reactive. These feelings have opened the door to a broader discussion about power and strategy.

The Three Faces of Power

Most groups engage in some form of power analysis, whether it is mapping current players or imagining what our society would look like if progressives had power on a larger scale. Since we are also deeply interested in questions of power, we can engage groups about something we are mutually interested in.

The tools that groups use for power analysis tend to provide one-dimensional snapshots—force-field analysis, mapping the alignment of groups and resources, and so on. Power maps are particularly useful tools for developing issue campaigns and tracking their progress. A good power map also can illuminate the need for longer-term strategies to shift power relations in a region. However, these one-dimensional tools do not lend themselves to an analysis that pushes the theoretical boundaries beyond groups' pluralist assumptions.

As we struggled to find and develop better tools for power analysis, we needed a theory that could explain the shift in the political agenda over the past thirty years. Better yet, we wanted a theory that could help groups move to a more proactive level of contesting for power. For the past four years, we have used an analysis of power derived from Stephen Lukes's book, *Power: A Radical View* (1974). We started with Lukes's three dimensions of power, which we summarize as (1) observable decision making based on observable differences of interests; (2) non–decision making based on observable differences of interest (i.e., agenda setting) via the "mobilization of bias"; (3) decision making and non–decision making based on preventing people from understanding and articulating their real interests.

As we did workshops and trainings using these concepts, we found that in going from the academic sphere to the activist organization, we needed to

- translate ideas and terms,
- shift from analysis to strategy,
- and adapt the strategy to concrete circumstances.

The first task is translation. Lukes's book was intended as an intervention in a long-running academic debate, not as a manual on strategy. His framework needs some translation for the situations activists face in their organizing, networking, coalition building, media and communications strategies, and so on. The first face of power—observable decision making—is familiar to the activists we work with and needs little or no translation. The second face of power needs a complicated kind of translation. The idea of getting something onto the political agenda, or keeping something off the agenda, makes a kind of immediate sense. Translating *mobilization of bias* into *organizational power* makes sense, but it leaves out too much of the large-scale, networked organizational structure we are interested in. All the organizations we know think about capacity building, but rarely about the relation of organizational power to long-term goals and to the architecture and the ideological and political glue that holds disparate organizations together. It is the networked and goal-oriented structure that we want to get at in translating the phrase *mobilization of bias* for activists.

We define the second face of power in terms of *developing infrastructure*. That is, organizations create formal and informal networks to wield power for achieving larger goals. Coalitions, trade associations, overlapping boards, and country club memberships are ways of building ties between organizations to pursue common goals. We use the term *political infrastructure* to indicate the most developed and coherent networks of organizations that have implicit or explicit goals that go beyond the immediate interests of the member organizations.

This last point is the most interesting one: how and why do organizations work together in ways that go beyond their self-defined or manifest goals? For example, the Christian Coalition, the NRA, and the Business Roundtable are part of the corporate-conservative infrastructure. To better understand the relationships between them, we ask, how do members of the NRA, whose members endorse stated goals regarding guns, understand their organization's relationship to corporate interests? There is a tension between the NRA's manifest goals and its activities as part of the corporate-conservative network. Managing this kind of tension is a key aspect of conservative strategy. For progressive and left social change activists and organizers whose focus has been single-issue politics, the absence of an infrastructure has made it extremely difficult to navigate the inevitable tensions between social, economic, and environmental justice goals, not to mention identities.

The third face of power is about the commonsense notion that people derive much of their conceptual framework from society at large. We define the third face as using cultural beliefs, norms, traditions, histories, and practices to shape political meaning, the ways that people understand the world around them, their roles in the world, and what they see as possible. This definition of the third face provides a fairly clear translation of Lukes. It was his inclusion of the third face that led to the word *radical* in the subtitle of his book. Our translation is intentionally naive in that it avoids what we might call the ideology problem. Flacks and others have noted that social movement scholars tend to avoid dealing directly with questions of ideology. As Flacks puts it, "Once upon a time, the study of ideology in relation to action was a topic of major interest, but it is one of those questions that now are out of fashion" (2002).

This also parallels trends in social movement organizing. In order to work with groups on bringing worldview into their work, we have to confront at least thirty years of resistance to talking about ideology as part of organizing. The 1970s saw a rise in public interest and community organizing that was decidedly nonideological, as exemplified by the common saying, "organizers check their ideology at the door." One aspect of the legacy of Alinsky and the professionalization of organizing was the tendency to avoid ideological struggle. One assumption that took hold in both community organizing and public interest advocacy is that organizers should avoid talking explicitly about ideologies. The prevailing wisdom in organizing was that, when people come together around a common interest or to solve a particular problem, the experience of collective action to achieve a goal will precipitate a shift in their consciousness. This reinforced the notion that organizers did not need to directly engage members in ideological discussions and analysis. This evolving orthodoxy about nonideological organizing was bolstered intellectually by Boyte's writings about "free spaces" (Fisher and Kling 1990). Alternatively, congregation-based organizing generally saw Judeo-Christian beliefs as the ideological basis for their work.

We use the term *worldview* to describe the terrain of struggle around the third face of power, in part to avoid the connotations associated with the word "ideology." We talk about how people are influenced by multiple, often contradictory, belief systems. We stress that though there is a dominant worldview, people live with contradictory beliefs and behaviors. Further, their instincts and beliefs can move in either democratic or authoritarian directions. We also stress the centrality of race in shaping political consciousness. Without a larger framework that moves people from specific interests toward a critical analysis of social and power relations, most who get involved in a single-issue campaign will lose interest after the specific campaign is done. They are less likely to see and feel the connections between their own issues and the struggles of others in their communities and in the larger world.

We have noted that translation is the first task in moving from the academic to the activist sphere. The second task is to shift from analysis to strategy. The three-faces framework is a nuanced and layered *analysis* of how power operates in our society. Activists need more than analysis. They need a way to *operationalize* a theory of power. They need a theory that suggests ways to build power adequate to their goals and purposes. And they need to do so in terms of their own circumstances, so a theory of power and social change has to be contextualized to different circumstances.

From the Three Faces of Power to a Strategy for Power

Shaping a strategy for long-term social change begins with an assessment of where the progressive social change movement as a whole has been and where it is now, in terms of its long-term goals. We use the three-faces framework to suggest that, as a whole, progressive organizations

- allocate too much of their resources to the first face of power;
- build their own group's power but don't think in terms of building infrastructure;
- ignore or misunderstand the third face of power. While they are getting better at framing messages, they are not contesting for power by challenging the dominant worldview and promoting an alternative to it.

We will illustrate these assertions by describing our work with Wisconsin Citizen Action (WCA).

Wisconsin Citizen Action is a statewide membership organization as well as a coalition of labor, women's, environmental, and other organizations. It is just over twenty years old. Its two codirectors have been highly respected organizers and leaders for about as long, and they have been with WCA for eight years. It is generally considered the leading progressive coalition in Wisconsin. When we started working with WCA three years ago, they were running more than six issue campaigns, including work on campaign finance reform, health care, and education. They played a major role every two years in state elections. In spite of their victories and the victories of other groups, Wisconsin, like the United States, was moving in a more conservative direction. Building on their existing strengths and victories, the codirectors were looking for a larger strategy that could address the difference between winning so many specific battles and yet seemingly losing the larger war.

At that point, in the summer of 2001, the Grassroots Policy Project began what would become an ongoing relationship with WCA. We started with a series of trainings with the board and then the staff on power, worldview, and strategy, using the three faces of power as our framework. The stated goal of the trainings was to help WCA develop an understanding and strategy for building sustainable power by linking current work to long-term goals. Our trainings with WCA began by looking at how the right has used the second and third faces of power. Most of the people involved were already aware of the interlocking nature of think tanks, media, advocacy, the Republican party, and the religious right, so talking about how conservatives used the second face of power made sense to them. Worldview was a bigger challenge.

WCA and Worldview

Here is how we defined *worldview* for WCA:

> Worldview is the variety of beliefs, both formal and informal, that individuals and groups draw upon and inherit from the larger social world in

which they live. While many different ideas and belief systems in our society compete for attention, some are more dominant than others. With
most of our issues, we see elements of a "dominant worldview" at work,
one that draws upon themes, assumptions, and ideologies that are part of
the mainstream American cultural heritage. Political and social issues or
problems are defined and interpreted for people within the larger world
of meanings—the images, assumptions, stereotypes and beliefs that
make up the dominant worldview.

We went on to define *themes* as critical, basic elements of worldview
that are used over and over again to tie down the meanings of higher-level
terms or, in discourse theory, how they act as floating signifiers. We argued
that the corporate-conservative infrastructure has a limited number of
basic themes that ground most of their worldview, and we focused on three
themes that are critical to the politics of the past three decades:

- *Rugged individualism.* The brand of individualism we are referring to
  is the heroic, rugged, go-it-alone individualism of popular myth. This
  is the "lift yourself up by your own bootstraps" individualism that
  inhabits the myths associated with the American Dream.
- *Role of government/antigovernment.* Antigovernment themes are used
  to call into question all government efforts at addressing social, economic, or environmental needs. This theme is particularly effective
  when linked with race, which serves to further stigmatize activist government. Public sector programs are deemed inefficient and
  wasteful—if not harmful—unless they are programs that maintain
  order or advance U.S. "interests" through the military or police.
- *Competition and the market.* As an aspect of social relations, competition is seen as a natural force that separates the winners from the
  losers. If we have freedom of choice, then we can pick what is best for
  ourselves, which is the genius of the market. At its worst, this theme
  is used to define democracy as being synonymous with consumer
  choice. If someone is a loser in our economy, they only have themselves to blame.

These themes have deep roots in American history. As with any ideological element, they have been used within different political traditions,
their meaning shifting depending on the context and linkages with other
themes and worldview elements. Conservatives have linked them tightly together in a fashion that gives them a much more sharply inflected meaning
(see Hall 1983 and 1995 for more on chaining themes together). Starting in
the 1960s, conservatives linked them to race and gender as well. We do not

claim that these themes, along with race and gender, exhaust the conservative repertoire. We asked the participants to analyze conservative articles and ads on every issue they were concerned with—education, health, taxes, and so on. During our sessions with WCA, the board and staff members saw that these themes were used in every instance. They noted that conservatives do not talk about issues or policies in an ad hoc manner and that these themes, which resonate on many issues and across broad sectors of the population, undergird most conservative discourse. Furthermore, having these fundamental ideological themes provides one kind of glue to hold the corporate-conservative infrastructure together.

At this point we did a lot of exercises on framing. *Framing* refers to the ways that groups use elements of worldview to give meaning to an issue or social problem. We used frame analysis materials developed by Charlotte Ryan (1990) and the Media Research and Action Project to help the participants deconstruct issue frames they encountered in the news, in popular culture, and in everyday life. Their own analysis of conservative themes on their issues was strong evidence about what we called the dominant worldview.

The clincher for WCA was an exercise in which we first asked them to role-play a conservative group developing a speech on an issue. Every group realized that they were extremely good at generating conservative discourse using these themes. Then we asked several small groups to work on a progressive discourse or rap on three or four issues that countered the conservative frame. This turned out to be much harder work. The participants quickly recognized that they had no progressive analogue to the conservative themes and the role they play in conservative ideology. They realized that there was no necessary connection or overlap between the frames that WCA used for the issues it worked on.

This insight about the power of the dominant worldview was the crucial step in the board and staff's understanding about the need for a strategy in order to build in all three faces of power. It helped them make sense of many aspects of their work, for example, why so many rank-and-file members of unions and other organizations vote Republican or oppose issues that WCA supports. It helped explain why using a "values" term, such as *fairness,* does not shift how people think about health care funding—its meaning is not easily redefined because it is already defined for most people by its strong links to the three key conservative themes noted above. Given how much of WCA's resources were focused on legislative and electoral struggles, these insights meant that a long-term strategy would entail a reallocation of resources, from first-face work to more work in building infrastructure and a progressive worldview.

WCA made changing worldview and, as they said in a board planning document, "inspiring new thinking about the role of politics and government" part of its key strategies for building power. As one of the planning team members put it, WCA's work in this area "means opening up people's sense of what's politically possible, countering dominant themes in political discourse with more progressive themes, and taking steps to actualize and point to our vision of what our world should be like." WCA recognized that this vision provided a framework for deeper affiliate and member connection to its work. People and organizations might come and go if their main connection to WCA was on a specific issue, but if they saw WCA as the place to act on their progressive values and make a difference, they would see it as a source of hope, power, and change.

Some board members have found the discussions and training so valuable that they have in turn invited WCA to lead workshops on worldview with members of their own organizations. This is a new and exciting opportunity to reach various grassroots membership bases with a progressive message and invitation to action. As WCA launches its new campaign to impact tax and budget policy in Wisconsin, a core component of the first phase is a series of such workshops on the issues.

WCA and Infrastructure

For WCA, building power in the second face has meant making some shifts in both their organizing models and coalition relationships. As a result, they are starting

- to build more sustained membership involvement by supporting community-based projects and engaging members in more events about issues and elections;
- to identify and develop progressive candidates for public office, especially with women's groups and in communities of color;
- to strengthen partnerships among leaders of their member groups;
- to engage in leadership development with board members;
- and to build commitment among their board and member groups to support a proactive progressive agenda instead of working issue by issue.

Groups like WCA are striving to move beyond a loose coalition of disparate interests toward fostering a more coordinated progressive infrastructure. The critical element that WCA is grappling with is why and how its member organizations should orient to WCA's long-term goals, in addition to their own organization's mandate and goals. For example, an environmental organization can sit on WCA's board; their own goals typically relate only to environmental issues. What happens when an issue of workers' rights or corporate subsidies comes up at the board? Does the environmental leader see herself as a WCA leader who is looking at the issue in terms of WCA's mission and work or only through the lens of her own organization? Will that leader take an issue like workers' rights back to her organization and find ways to involve the rank-and-file members?

Generalizing those questions, we argue that a powerful, progressive infrastructure should be more than a collection of organizations; it can be an integrated, coordinated, and strategically oriented network of different kinds of social change groups, representing diverse constituencies and issues that can impact state, regional, and national politics. Think tanks, policy and research groups, training and education institutes, and other "intermediaries," including social movement scholars, should be integrated into this infrastructure.

WCA and Strategy Development

Until recently, the identity of WCA has been as an organization that works on discrete and immediate goals, as one of the leading organizations in Wisconsin on progressive legislation and state elections. Put another way, WCA has been very successful in the first face of power struggles. WCA's directors asked us to work with them because they wanted to do more. We are learning together what that might mean. Through the training sessions, the planning process, and implementation phases, WCA has identified and is working toward bringing about the following strategic shifts in their work, to attempt to continue to be successful in legislative and electoral work and also to link that work to long-term social change goals:

- *Strategic electoral engagement.* WCA has generally followed the usual electoral cycle of supporting candidates in the last few months of each two-year cycle. Messaging has been based on polling, focus groups, and intuitions about what works. They want to move toward doing electoral work all year long, understanding the electoral arena as one where lots of work can be done on infrastructure building and worldview. For example, they are working with their member organizations to find and train candidates for office who can articulate a progressive worldview. They want to support candidates who can work with their member organizations to reach the rank and file in various ways so that during an election there is a larger, more unified base among the rank-and-file members who are ready to support a candidate with a progressive worldview and agenda.

- *From issue campaigns to a progressive agenda.* A legislative issue campaign focuses on moving swing legislators over to our side, usually on a specific aspect, such as education or health care or another area of concern. WCA wants to link such legislative campaigns to a progressive agenda that represents a broader and deeper articulation of what kind of education, health care, housing, workers' rights, jobs, and racial and gender justice WCA stands for. The progressive agenda, sometimes termed a new social contract, should act as a framework for the specific legislative issues that give them a deeper meaning for various constituencies, which as isolated campaigns they would not have.

- *From messages to progressive worldview.* Good organizers and legislative advocates are taught to "stay on message." For example, they don't want to confuse someone they are organizing on health care with some discussion about campaign financing. The message is tightly focused, which makes a lot of sense for the first face of power struggle. WCA is moving toward being able to frame all of their issue work based on a progressive worldview, so that the frames reference and reinforce each other.

- *Leadership and member development.* WCA is struggling to shift from a top-down coalition model toward working with board members, the rank and file from their organizations, and other affiliates in processes that create more of a common identity and a growing ownership of WCA's longer-term goals. This strategic shift will require further resources to be implemented on a larger scale.

- *Reshaping the organizational culture.* Board and staff both are working to reshape the culture from one that is staff driven and compartmentalized to one that is relational, collaborative, and interconnected. The staff believes, and we agree, that this is not an add-on. Suffice it to say, figuring out what these shifts mean for their day-to-day work and how to carry them out while continuing intensive work on existing program areas requires enormous creativity and energy from the entire staff.

Much of GPP's work with WCA in the last year has focused on the challenge of implementing these shifts. The nature of this role has often meant deliberately working with a creative tension between the immediate demands of first-face strategies (legislative, direct action demands, and electoral) and the different commitment required to build in the second and third faces. Clearly this tension will never entirely resolve itself. However, as WCA continues to work on implementing these strategic shifts, they can navigate the tensions by making all aspects of their work as interconnected and reinforcing as possible.

Developing a Progressive Worldview

Our work with Wisconsin Citizen Action and other groups would be much easier if we could hand them a progressive worldview. In our workshops, people ask us "what are our three points, or themes," that are comparable to the three themes that undergird a corporate-conservative worldview. Our answer is not very satisfactory. While we can suggest some elements of what might become a progressive worldview, we cannot create it on our own. There is no unitary, condensed set of themes or words that represent the definitive *progressive worldview* any more than there is such a thing on the right.

We engage the groups in exploring elements of progressive worldview from social movement history, liberatory ideas and themes from U.S. history, popular culture, and the ideas and experiences of subcultures and marginalized communities. This past year, a number of core values and beliefs have emerged from our workshops with statewide coalitions and labor/community groups. Here is a summary of the elements we hear most often:

Democracy

- Active participation in all aspects of the political process. It is part of personal development and about freedom as an individual to be part of our collective life.
- Individual and human rights are fundamental to democracy; corporations and the market should serve society, not dominate it.
- Democratic rights in the workplace, including the right to organize.

Personal Autonomy and Development

- Respect for all individuals.
- Social/public guarantees of equal access to the prerequisites for autonomy and development.
- Public intervention to safeguard personal rights and autonomy.

Mutual Responsibility

- Personal autonomy and mutual responsibility have to be linked together to create the kind of human beings and society that is our goal.

Social Justice

- Respect for difference.
- Social/public guarantees and intervention for individuals, families (all

domestic groupings), and communities for their dignity, health, and development.

Family, Community, Society

- Everyone needs to be part of loving, supportive relationships. This extends from childhood to old age and means respecting and nurturing the relationships of all people—those who live alone, those in traditional and new forms of domestic partnerships, communities—and supporting all of these, society itself.
- Public guarantees that all of us can grow up and live in a healthy and sustainable environment.

Equality

- All human beings are inherently and equally worthy of respect and dignity.
- All forms of domination are infringements on equality and should be ended.

Participants often respond to a list like this with some caution, if not outright suspicion. Is this a laundry list of slogans, or values to use in a speech, or something to help them frame an issue that they are working on? We suggest these as a point of departure, as a way to engage the groups in a discussion of what each participant actually believes in, what their activism and commitment is rooted in. For the organizations we work with, this is not an easy discussion (see Lichterman 1996 and Hart 2001 for more on this challenge). We challenge the participants to explore how the meanings of individual themes change when linked with the other themes. Through framing, we illustrate how it becomes more difficult for themes to be assimilated into the dominant worldview when they are linked together in frames that tell a story about every issue the organizations work on.

We will continue to explore the theory and practice of developing a progressive worldview. Fairly quickly, with any group, the discussion of such a goal has to turn to more practical concerns, and so we work with organizations on framing, using these and other progressive worldview themes. When we do workshops on framing and message development, we emphasize that a good message must be embedded in a larger strategy and must be practical enough to reach a specific audience about the issue or set of issues that we are working on. These two sides of messaging are constantly in tension with each other. One way to navigate the tension is to check each message by asking the following question: are we saying anything today, in this message, that will undermine our efforts tomorrow to promote a broader social justice agenda?

Roles for Scholars: Developing Collaborative Relationships

From our vantage point, as activists and nonacademic scholars who are constantly nudging leaders to analyze their work in more critical ways, we find that activist groups need scholars to challenge them, to cast critical light on the things they are struggling with, and to encourage them to be more reflective, analytical, and strategic.

Despite the problems we have described here—the fragmentation of groups and issues, the short-term and nonstrategic approaches that have prevailed since the mid-1970s, the decline of movement infrastructure, and so on—we do see some very promising trends. In particular, we see a renewed interest in strategic analysis around power and the role of ideas. We see efforts to build lasting networks and coalitions that are more democratic and bottom-up, less top-down, than the coalitions of the past. Organizers and leaders in the labor movement, in statewide and regional coalitions, in national advocacy groups, and at the local and community levels are seeking new ideas and opportunities to work more proactively and to connect their work to something larger—something that could become a more coherent movement for social change.

Some grassroots-based leaders and activists want scholars to provide technical support and resources and nothing else, certainly not leadership of any kind. This desire can lead them to put academics into a box—as with so many other resources, activists and leaders would like to be able to take movement-oriented academics out of the box only when they need them. Scholars who are active in movements, and who have stakes in those movements, may object to being assigned such narrow and compartmentalized roles. Robert Bullard, professor of sociology at Clark Atlanta University and environmental justice activist, suggests an alternative approach: activist-academics could be part of a network that contains multi-class and organizational membership, bridging the gap between grassroots and scholarly sectors and creating more mutual relationships and accountability through the network (Sen 2003).

For scholars, being self-conscious about their position and social locations, and the power dynamics that can come into play, is very important and essential for establishing trust. Navigating the differences in social locations, education levels, class, and race is especially challenging with grassroots leaders who have had little exposure to the world of academia. At the same time, scholars should not let this keep them from engaging fully with activists and grassroots leaders. Furthermore, scholars need some critical distance and autonomy, even as they form closer relationships with activists. Scholars need spaces where they can pursue ideas and engage in research that is not necessarily popular or practical or immediately applicable.

We want to encourage engagement between academics and activists, and we want that engagement to be more than technical support. We envision a movement infrastructure in which the ties between activists and academics can be negotiated as part of shared movement-building strategies. The tensions that are inherent in the different social locations of activists and scholars and in the different ways that the results of collaboration are used will always be there. However, as Bullard suggests, these tensions can be put to positive use through networks in which more organic connections can take root. In such a network, scholars would get feedback that helps them make their work more available and useful for activists.

References

Darnovsky, Marcy, Barbara Epstein, and Richard Flacks, eds. 1995. *Cultural Politics and Social Movements*. Philadelphia: Temple University Press.

Fisher, Robert, and Joseph M. Kling. 1990. "Ideology and Activism: Two Approaches to 'Leading the People.'" In *Dilemmas of Activism: Class, Community, and the Politics of Local Mobilization*, ed. Joseph M. Kling and Prudence S. Posner, 31–45. Philadelphia: Temple University Press.

Flacks, Richard. 2002. Remarks at the "Hope and History" conference, Boston College.

Hall, Stuart. 1983. "The Great Moving Right Show." In *The Politics of Thatcherism*, ed. Stuart Hall and Martin Jaques, 19–39. London: Lawrence and Wishart.

———. 1995. "The Whites of Their Eyes." In *Gender, Race, and Class in Media*, ed. Gail Dines and Jean M. Humez, 18–22. Thousand Oaks, CA: Sage.

Hart, Stephen. 2001. *Cultural Dilemmas of Progressive Politics*. Chicago: University of Chicago Press.

Lichterman, Paul. 1996. *The Search for Political Community*. Cambridge: Cambridge University Press.

Lukes, Steven. 1974. *Power: A Radical View*. London: MacMillan.

Ryan, Charlotte. 1990. *Prime Time Activism*. Boston: South End Press.

Sen, Rinku. 2003. "Who's Got the Power?" *Race, Poverty, and the Environment* 10, no. 1: 26–28.

II
Bridging the Divide:
Lessons from the Field

5

Housing Crisis: Gaining Standing in a Community Coalition

Kevin M. Carragee

Boston, like many cities in the United States, has experienced an expanding housing crisis in the last decade. Rapidly escalating rents and home prices have forced many poor and middle-class residents to relocate in search of more affordable housing. In Boston, the housing crisis is exacerbated by the failure of many colleges and universities to house their undergraduate students on their campuses. For example, by the late 1990s, 25 percent of undergraduates at Boston College—approximately 2,225 students—lived in off-campus apartments and homes in the Allston-Brighton neighborhood of Boston. This increases the pressure on an already overburdened housing market, with students displacing many working- and middle-class families because of their ability to pay higher rents.

This paper examines an intervention from 1998 to 2000 designed to highlight the severity of Boston's housing crisis and to stress the complicity of universities and colleges in contributing to this crisis. Working with community groups and with the Media Research and Action Project (MRAP), I sought to make the policies of city government and a local college more responsive to the needs of working- and middle-class residents of Boston. In this chapter, I consider the opportunities and challenges confronting interventions designed to secure social and political reform, devoting close attention to how coalition building and media strategies enhance mobilization.

These interventions stand in sharp contrast to traditional forms of academic consulting. Applied social science research in general and communication consulting in particular have failed to address significant issues and problems in American society. They also have served to advance the interests of powerful groups and organizations while neglecting the challenges confronting marginalized communities and groups (for more detailed discussions of this issue, see Deetz and Mumby 1990; Frey et al. 1996).

I begin by outlining the severity of the housing crisis in Boston, devoting particular attention to the Allston-Brighton neighborhood where the crisis is significantly influenced by the abdication of local colleges and universities to house their students. I then trace the Boston College Community Task Force's efforts to press for more on-campus housing for students of Boston College, one of the three universities in Allston-Brighton. I locate the intervention as part of a broader effort of the Media Research and Action Project to assist marginalized groups in their efforts to secure social justice. I conclude by discussing the nature of the intervention. This discussion highlights issues relating to my relationship with a specific community group (what I will call "standing"), the creation of coalitions to secure political and social change, and the framing of housing issues.

The intervention had some success, which illustrates how concepts derived from social movement theory, particularly insights derived from framing research, can inform collective struggles for social and political reform. Working with a variety of community groups, I helped direct city and news media attention to the contribution of universities and colleges to Boston's housing crisis. This led to the city's rejection of Boston College's initial master plan for the years 2000 to 2005 because of its inadequate expansion of on-campus housing. Facing community and city pressures, the college increased its commitment to house additional students in dormitories from 450 to 800 over a five-year period. This fell short of community demands for 1,200 additional dormitory beds by 2005, but it represented one of the few instances where community pressures forced significant revisions to Boston College's proposed master plans.

The Housing Crisis in Boston

While a full discussion of the character and causes of Boston's housing crisis exceeds the scope of this chapter, it is necessary to provide a brief sketch of the severity of the crisis and its consequences in order to place the intervention in its proper social and political context.

In recent years, rents and home prices in Boston have increased significantly, reflecting one of the lowest housing vacancy rates in the country. Boston home prices and rents are among the highest in the United States. Factors contributing to this rapid escalation in prices include an expanding demand for housing due to economic growth in greater Boston, the limited increase in new housing construction in the city given the scarcity of land available and appropriate for new housing, the gentrification of particular city neighborhoods, real estate speculation, the decline in federal support for the creation of affordable housing, and the failure of Boston-area colleges and universities to house their students.

The character and consequences of this housing crisis can be illustrated by examining trends in housing in the Allston-Brighton neighborhood of Boston. Allston-Brighton has 70,000 residents; most residents are middle or lower income. The neighborhood's median household income in 1998 was $44,583, but one-third of its residents earned below $25,000 (Allston-Brighton Community Development Corporation 1999). Paradoxically, despite skyrocketing rents and home prices in the 1990s, Allston-Brighton's poverty rate actually increased from 20.1 percent in 1990 to 23 percent in 2000 (Boston Foundation 2002).

The rapid escalation of rents and home prices in the 1990s led to the relocation of many long-term residents. Average rents for family-sized units, for example, increased 71 percent between 1992 and 1998, from $927 to $1,588. The average rent for a one-bedroom apartment in 1999 exceeded the entire gross pay of a full-time minimum wage worker. A report by the Allston-Brighton Community Development Corporation, a nonprofit organization focusing on housing issues, indicated that "public and private participants in the housing industry generally agree that rents that consume more than 30% of household income constitute a burden on a family's financial health. In 1998, a four-person household earning the median income would have had to pay 43% of its income to rent a three-bedroom apartment in Allston Brighton" (Allston-Brighton Community Development Corporation 1999, 6).

Focus group research conducted by the Allston-Brighton Healthy Boston Coalition revealed widespread concerns that escalating rents and home prices had forced many residents to relocate. The coalition's report concluded that the "impact of the high cost of housing is pervasive. Middle class participants reported that they could not afford market rate houses. Housing is also affecting young professionals. Many interviewed reported that they do not believe they can afford to buy a home and raise families in this neighborhood" (Allston-Brighton Healthy Boston Coalition 2002).

The failure of local universities and colleges to house their students contributes to the housing crisis in Allston-Brighton. The neighborhood is home to three major universities: Harvard University, Boston College, and Boston University. While Harvard houses almost all of its undergraduate students, Boston College and Boston University have for decades failed to do so, forcing thousands of students to find apartments in the community.

As a consequence, by 1999 students in private housing accounted for approximately 22 percent of Allston-Brighton's total population (Allston-Brighton Community Development Corporation 1999).

The presence of so many students in the private housing stock not only significantly influences rental prices, but also has profound consequences on prices for homes. Increasingly, two- and three-family homes in Allston-Brighton—formerly a means by which working- and middle-class people gained home ownership—are purchased by absentee investors eager to reap large profits by charging exorbitant rents to college students. Absentee landlords frequently charge six undergraduate students $500 each for a three-bedroom apartment, producing $36,000 a year in rental income. This trend has made it increasingly difficult for working- and middle-class families to remain in Allston-Brighton either as renters or as homebuyers. As a result, the percentage of family households in Allston-Brighton declined from 36.2 percent to 32.7 percent from 1990 to 2000 (Boston Foundation 2002). Allston-Brighton's owner occupancy rate of 20 percent compares unfavorably with the citywide average of 36 percent. A 1999 report revealed that "all types of home purchase are beyond the means of the average Allston Brighton household" (Allston-Brighton Community Development Corporation 1999, 38).

The negotiations between community groups and Boston College concerning the college's institutional 2000–2005 master plan, therefore, took place within the context of a steadily worsening housing crisis for the city of Boston in general and for Allston-Brighton in particular. This context much informed the negotiations and conflicts.

The Media Research and Action Project

My lengthy involvement with the Media Research and Action Project considerably shaped my intervention focusing on the housing crisis in Boston's Allston-Brighton neighborhood. Integrating the concerns of sociologists and communication researchers, MRAP assists social movement organizations and community groups in securing political and social change. This often has involved enhancing the ability of these groups to advance their demands in the public arena, including the news media (for more detailed discussions of MRAP's work, see Ryan, Carragee, and Meinhofer 2001; Ryan, Carragee, and Schwerner 1998).

MRAP's focus on social movements and community groups rests on the assumption that meaningful social change is rooted in collective action. This focus highlights the importance of agency and the role that meaning making plays in the mobilization process. Within this context, the news media represent critical symbolic arenas in which collective actors attempt to advance their definitions of political inequality and injustice.

The experiences of MRAP, gained by working with more than two hundred social movement organizations, community groups, and nonprofit organizations since 1986, have underscored the utility of framing research and its insights to the practical challenges confronting collective efforts to secure political or social reform. In its applied work, MRAP has examined the complex interaction between the frames advanced by the social movement and community groups we assist, the frames advanced by opposing groups and organizations, and the frames employed by journalists in their news stories. Within this interaction, social movement organizations and community groups frequently work at a considerable disadvantage because of their relative lack of economic and cultural resources. Nonetheless, MRAP has had success in assisting these groups in advancing frames that have attracted sympathetic news coverage.

Frames organize discourse, including news stories, by their patterns of selection, emphasis, and exclusion. By framing issues, social actors define what is and what is not relevant to an issue. In a review of research exploring the use of frames in journalistic discourse, Robert Entman writes that frames "select some aspects of a perceived reality and make them more salient in a communicating text" (1993, 52). Considerable research has examined the character of frames in news discourse and the influence of these frames on public perceptions of issues and events (Carragee 1991; Croteau, Hoynes, and Carragee 1996; Gamson 1992; Gamson and Modigliani 1989).

Multiple social actors, including politicians, organizations, advocates, and movements, sponsor frames and influence journalistic framing of issues. News stories, then, become a forum for framing contests in which political actors compete in sponsoring their preferred definitions of political issues. The ability of a frame to dominate news discourse depends on a variety of complex factors, including the sponsor's economic and cultural resources, the sponsor's knowledge of journalistic routines, and the frame's resonance with broader political and social tendencies in American culture. Given the practices of American journalism and the significance of resources in the successful sponsoring of frames, framing contests routinely favor elites (Gamson 1992; Ryan 1991).

Beyond its attention to framing processes, MRAP has stressed the significance of developing coalitions in its applied work with social movement organizations and community groups. Marginalized groups by their very nature lack resources and power, making it vital that they seek allies in their efforts to secure political and social change. Building coalitions depends on effective communication between organizations and groups. This is no small task given the lack of resources of these groups and the demands placed on these limited resources by challenging political and social circumstances. The emphasis on coalition building and on the significance of effective communication reflects the major features of resource mobilization theory and research within sociology (see, for example, Gamson 1990; McAdam 1988; Morris 1984).

The Intervention

When I joined the Boston College Community Task Force, a coalition of community groups representing Allston-Brighton in its interaction with Boston College, in 1998, I became directly involved in a number of contentious social and political issues: the concept of standing, the forging of new coalitions in an effort to bring political pressure on Boston College to construct additional dormitories on its campus, and the reframing of the long dispute between the Allston-Brighton community and Boston College concerning the presence of college students in the neighborhood's residential housing.

The Concept of Standing

Standing involves the granting of voice to groups, organizations, and individuals, allowing them to speak in public forums on controversial social and political issues. Groups, organizations, and individuals with standing have the ability to advance their claims concerning social and political issues within particular public arenas; those without standing do not. Ferree, Gamson, Gerhards, and Rucht remind us that "not every actor has an equal chance to have a voice in public discourse" (2002, 86). Elites by virtue of their power and resources routinely have standing; marginalized groups struggle to attain it.

I use the concept of standing in a dual sense. First, it relates to the social and political position of the Boston College Community Task Force in terms of its relationship with Boston's broader political environment. Second, it refers to my own relationship with the task force; that is, my own standing as a member of this group. In this sense, I seek to expand Ferree, Gamson, Gerhards, and Rucht's use of this concept (2002) because they essentially limit its application to the news media, neglecting that social actors struggle for standing in multiple public forums and that individual actors work to acquire standing within groups.

The task force has standing in a very specific sense: ideally, it represents the community's interests in its discussions and negotiations with Boston

College. Its standing is formally acknowledged by city government because the task force plays an important role, albeit one limited by structural inequalities, in representing the community's views in the development of five-year master plans by Boston College. The Boston Redevelopment Authority (BRA), the city's major planning agency, must formally approve these plans. The granting of standing to community groups like the task force in negotiations concerning the institutional master planning process represents the culmination of a long struggle to open urban planning to citizen voices.

Historically, the task force and Boston College have been at odds on a range of issues, including college purchases of additional land in Allston-Brighton, the expansion of the college's football stadium, the scope of community benefits provided by the college to Allston-Brighton, the size of the college's PILOT payments to the city (payments in lieu of taxes for city-provided services), and the college's failure to provide on-campus housing for large numbers of its students. In short, tension and conflict characterize the relationship between the task force and Boston College.

Long-serving task force members regularly criticize the BRA in particular and city government in general for not better protecting the interests of Allston-Brighton residents in their negotiations with the college. Certainly, the task force has few of the resources available to the college in its effort to influence city policy. Boston College is a powerful institution in the city, with active community affairs and public relations departments. It regularly uses consultants on a wide range of issues involving its relationship with the city. It benefits from the large number of its alumni who work in city agencies (often characterized by critics as the Boston Irish Mafia). Its chancellor, J. Donald Monan, S.J., has extensive contacts with the city's corporate and political elites, many of whom are Boston College graduates. In contrast, the task force is composed of working-class and middle-class residents who are active in their community. Most members work full-time, and the task force represents only one of many civic engagements or responsibilities for many of its members. Simply put, the group is resource poor, lacking money and time to pursue its interests.

Partly because of its scant resources, the task force has only limited standing in Boston's broader political environment. While city government formally recognizes the task force's role in the master planning process, it routinely has ignored the group's objections to particular features of past Boston College master plans. Prior to 1998, the task force had not established relationships with groups or organizations focusing on housing issues in Boston. Similarly, the task force had only limited experience in dealing with the news media.

The task force's limited standing in Boston's broader political environment also was a product of how its long-serving members perceived their role. Most preferred what I call private politics rather than public politics; that is, the task force routinely and almost exclusively relied on direct negotiations with the college and with the BRA to advance its interests. This approach relied on appeals to the college and to the BRA to safeguard community interests. These appeals, including demands for more on-campus housing and opposition to the expansion of the college's football stadium, often failed, producing increased conflict between college representatives and task force members and charges that the BRA better represented the college's interests than the community's. The task force neglected the processes of public politics—the mobilization of broader public support, the effort to attract news coverage to particular controversies, the forging of broader coalitions with like-minded groups and organizations—in its effort to shape the decision making of the college and the city. In fairness, the processes of public politics demand considerable time and resources; task force members lacked both.

My own standing on the task force was a product of my lengthy involvement in civic issues in the Allston-Brighton community where I had lived since 1990. Because of this involvement, I was invited to join the task force in 1998. Much of my local political involvement was tied to my work in forming the Hobart Park Neighborhood Association (HPNA), a community group, in 1992. This group has sought to build and sustain a sense of community in one of Brighton's neighborhoods while also focusing on improving basic city services. The group has been involved in anticrime efforts, the revitalization of a public park, and improving the neighborhood's access to the Charles River. By 1999, I was serving as copresident of the HPNA.

My lengthy involvement in the neighborhood's civic and political life provided me with a particular standing on the task force, a standing distinct from my identity as an academic who had a particular set of skills that could benefit this group. This standing, I believe, shaped the intervention in decisive ways, contributing to my own effectiveness and to the broader effectiveness of the task force. Because of this standing, I was not seen as an academic consultant divorced from the experiential world of Allston-Brighton residents.

My status as a renter who had become deeply involved in the life of the community also may have shaped perceptions of my civic engagement. Most long-term task force members were homeowners. They respected my engagement in community issues, and for some I became an example of how the escalating housing crisis made it increasingly difficult for even middle-class residents to purchase a home in Allston-Brighton.

My academic training and my experiences with MRAP, of course, shaped my work on the task force in multiple ways, informing the strategies I recommended and providing me with skills in public speaking and media relations that helped the task force in its effort to influence Boston College and city government. Most members of the group recognized these skills as useful, but they were not seen as the skills of an outsider, a professor or academic consultant. Instead, they perceived me primarily as a resident or activist who happened to be a professor. This distinction, I believe, made a crucial difference in how my recommendations concerning strategies and tactics were taken by task force members. Most significant, my particular standing in the group made some members, although certainly not all, more receptive to my ideas.

My conversations and interactions with task force members over time support the interpretation that my standing in the group was linked to my civic engagement, not my status as a professor. For example, task force members seldom asked about my teaching, research, or academic training. In contrast, conversations frequently focused on the problems confronting the community, including the Hobart Park area, or my family's difficulty in finding an affordable home in Allston-Brighton. Within this context, I believe that task force members perceived my recommendations concerning strategies or tactics as rooted in an experiential world they shared, the life of an active resident of Allston-Brighton.

I do not believe, therefore, that my academic credentials and the skills associated with them were decisive to my standing on the task force. Task force members, after all, had become increasingly distrustful of the academic world because of long-standing tensions with Boston College. They felt, with justification, that Boston College, while gaining an international and national reputation, had harmed their community. College officials, according to task force members, played "word games," developing impressive statements and documents that underscored their commitment to the local community but engaging in actions that harmed it.

A compelling example of what task force members perceived to be the college's word games relates to negotiations concerning community benefits. These benefits are designed to mitigate the negative impacts Boston College has on the Allston-Brighton neighborhood. Past benefits have included small grants to community groups, assistance to local schools, and employment opportunities for local residents. In negotiations for the 1995–2000 Boston College master plan, members of the task force believed that they had obtained fifty four-year scholarships for Boston residents as a community benefit. The college, however, interpreted the complexly worded agreement, drafted by college officials, by counting each year of a scholarship as a single scholarship. As a result, only twelve Boston residents received scholarships for all four years of their education at Boston College.

Deeply angered by the college's interpretation of the agreement, task force members made it a priority to gain four-year scholarships for fifty Boston residents in the 2000–2005 master plan. This produced tense negotiations with college officials, with task force members repeatedly accusing Boston College of betraying and undermining the earlier agreement. I recall one task force member pounding her fist on a table as she shouted: "Fifty means fifty. Fifty kids on four-year scholarships."

Because of the task force's persistence, the college, after much conflict, included fifty four-year scholarships in its 2000–2005 master plan as a community benefit, a deeply satisfying victory for the task force. At the time of this writing, forty Boston residents have received these scholarships, ten students each year from 2001 to 2004. The task force continues to monitor Boston College's commitment to this agreement.[1]

I do not want to provide a romanticized definition of my interaction with other members of the task force. Conflicts did occur. Some objected to my repeated recommendations for actions more consistent with what I have called public politics; they remained more comfortable with the private politics traditionally practiced by the task force. Some of the conflicts no doubt were tied to experiential differences between particular task force members and me. The vast majority of task force members were born and raised in Allston-Brighton (they would not say Boston); I was not. Most are homeowners; I rented. Most have high school or college degrees; I was one of the few who had an advanced degree. Most describe themselves as moderate or conservative Democrats; I am a progressive, increasingly frustrated by the rightward drift of the Democratic party. These differences matter, and they no doubt informed at least some of the conflicts between particular task force members and me; however, these differences would have mattered much more if my standing on the task force was tied to academic consulting or to the efforts of a researcher-activist who sought to help a marginalized group struggle against a powerful institution.

Forging Coalitions

Social movement research and theory has highlighted the need for community groups and social movement organizations to forge coalitions with other advocacy groups in order to increase their ability to shape public policy (see, for example, Gamson 1990). The forging of coalitions becomes even more significant for organizations and groups, like the task force, lacking resources. The task force, however, had neglected the importance of coalition building given its past reliance on private politics. This was a contradiction in that the task force itself represents a coalition of multiple community groups in Allston-Brighton.

Based on my experience in community activism with the Hobart Park Neighborhood Association and my knowledge of the efficacy of coalition building given my experiences with MRAP, I was well positioned to link the task force to other advocacy groups, especially groups that focused on Boston's evolving housing crisis. As a consequence, the task force received support from a number of groups in its successful effort to influence the BRA to reject Boston College's preliminary master plan. The Allston-Brighton Community Development Corporation; the Alliance of Boston Neighborhoods, a city-wide coalition of community groups; and the Greater Boston Interfaith Organization (GBIO), an activist group focusing on housing issues, supported the task force's position and urged the BRA to press Boston College to house additional students on-campus. The support of GBIO was particularly significant because of this group's ability to mobilize support for its position and its increasing influence on public officials.

My past contacts with these groups allowed me to serve as a link between them and the task force. I had worked with the Allston-Brighton Community Development Corporation on housing-related issues and through it had met with activists in GBIO. I also had interacted over time with the head of the Alliance of Boston Neighborhoods because of our common interest in and opposition to plans to privatize public spaces in Boston. These past interactions made it easy for me to call and write these organizations to gain their support for the task force's positions.

My previous activism and civic engagement, then, provided me with a network of relationships that I could rely on as a means to gain additional support for the task force in its conflict with Boston College. I had established affiliations with individuals and groups linked to the traditional Allston-Brighton community through my involvement with the Hobart Park Neighborhood Association, the Allston-Brighton Little League, and the Roman Catholic grammar school my daughter attended. This was the social world of many of the task force members, a world of neighborhood groups, youth sports, and the local church and parochial school (and this corresponded to the social world of my childhood in New York City). But I also had links to progressive individuals and groups, particularly housing activists. I felt a degree of comfort in both worlds, although there were certainly tensions between them. Some task force members, for example, distrusted the Allston-Brighton Community Development Corporation, complaining of its "leftist" political orientation.

The support of multiple organizations and groups increased the political and social power of the task force, connecting it to a network of groups advocating for public policies that would relieve Boston's significant housing crisis. The broader nature of the coalition now opposed to the college's preliminary master plan increased the political pressure on Mayor Thomas M. Menino, the BRA, and city councilors to seek modifications in the plan. The support of these groups came as an unwelcome surprise for Boston College, which had previously been able to interact with an isolated task force.

The interactions between these groups had mutual benefits. The task force obtained support from citywide groups with broader constituencies, GBIO, and the Alliance of Boston Neighborhoods. This support highlighted the housing crisis as a problem influencing the city as a whole, not just Allston-Brighton. The task force also benefited from statistical data on the housing crisis produced by GBIO and by the Allston-Brighton Community Development Corporation. The CDC's report *Rising Rents, Closing Doors* was particularly significant because it provided statistical evidence concerning the severity of the housing crisis in Allston-Brighton. In turn, GBIO and the Alliance of Boston Neighborhoods gained insight on the degree to which Boston's housing crisis was exacerbated by the failure of colleges and universities to house their students. Finally, unlike the other groups, the task force had formal standing in the city's institutional master planning process and, therefore, had the ability to influence the BRA in its evaluation of Boston College's master plan.

The ability of the task force to secure major modifications in the college's master plan provides a striking example of the effectiveness of coalition building for community groups and social movement organizations. Coalitions allow underfinanced and underresourced groups to increase their ability to influence public policy.

Reframing the Issue

My most significant influence on the task force concerned a shift in its framing regarding the presence of so many Boston College students in residential housing. Traditionally, the task force had framed the failure of Boston College to house its students on campus in terms of quality of life: the presence of students in residential neighborhoods produced late-night parties, public drunkenness, poorly maintained homes and apartments, and parking difficulties. This framing of the problem highlighted tensions between young, transient students and older residents of Allston-Brighton. Boston

College and the city of Boston responded with a lengthy litany of practices and strategies designed to control and punish troublesome students.

The quality of life frame had severe limitations from the perspective of the task force's efforts to influence Boston College to construct more on-campus housing. Its emphasis on unruly student behavior displaced responsibility from Boston College to individual students who behaved improperly. This frame easily allowed the college to cite its efforts to curb offensive student behavior as proof that it was responsive to community needs. The task force historically made little effort to attract news media coverage of the problem. For journalists, the problems highlighted by the quality of life frame appeared to be an inevitable consequence of living in a Boston neighborhood dominated by three major universities. In short, the news media viewed this frame as old and tired, with limited news value beyond Allston-Brighton. I recall, for example, a veteran *Boston Globe* reporter initially asking me "what was new?" about community conflicts with Boston College regarding the presence of its undergraduate students in apartments and homes in Allston-Brighton.

Most significant, the quality of life frame neglected the major *structural* consequences of the presence of large numbers of undergraduates in residential housing: escalating rents and home prices, the displacement of working and middle-class families from Allston-Brighton, and declining owner-occupancy rates given the increasing number of absentee landlords who viewed the neighborhood as a particularly attractive investment opportunity. The broader housing crisis within the city of Boston exacerbated these trends in the late 1990s, producing an unprecedented housing crisis for Allston-Brighton.

In reframing the issue we focused on these structural consequences, defining Boston College's failure and the failure of other Boston-area universities to house their students on their campuses as a major influence on Boston's housing crisis. Activist groups focusing on housing issues, like GBIO, advanced the same frame, thus increasing the frame's presence. Unlike the quality of life frame, the housing crisis frame assigned responsibility for the problem to Boston College, not its students. The solution to the problem from this perspective was not additional oversight by the college and city on students living in Allston-Brighton, but the construction of on-campus housing. This frame resonated with many Allston-Brighton residents who faced rapidly escalating rents and home prices; it also resonated with some homeowners who had witnessed or who feared the consequences of the increasing number of two- and three-family homes purchased by absentee landlords. Finally, this frame resonated with a news media focus on

Boston's escalating housing crisis. The increasing news coverage of housing issues represented a victory for housing activists who had become savvy in both their organizing efforts and their courting of news attention.

These resonances produced extensive news media coverage on the conflicts between Boston College and the task force. Not surprisingly, the local newspaper, the *Allston-Brighton Tab,* devoted considerable coverage to these conflicts; indeed, the *Tab* frequently placed stories on the evolving dispute between the task force and Boston College on its front page. The newspaper also repeatedly endorsed the task force's recommendations in its editorials. While coverage by the *Boston Globe* and the *Boston Herald* was considerably less extensive, both newspapers devoted far more attention to the master planning process than in past years. The housing crisis frame much influenced news stories in all three papers. News media attention to the dispute represented another pressure on both the college and the city to respond to community concerns. The very public nature of the controversy played an important role in influencing the BRA to demand additional on-campus housing from the college.

I served as the chief link between the task force and the news media, writing news releases, preparing op-ed columns, calling reporters, representing the group at public meetings where reporters were likely to be present. In all of these efforts, the task force stressed the housing crisis frame, avoiding or minimizing the quality of life frame. Through my own teaching and research and through my work with MRAP, I had developed an understanding of news media practices and routines. This knowledge benefited the task force in its efforts to attract coverage. Although these efforts sometimes succeeded, failures occurred as well. News releases attracted little or no coverage; an open letter to the president of Boston College generated a story in the *Tab,* but failed to do so in the *Globe* or *Herald.* These failures serve as a warning not to romanticize this intervention.

While most members of the task force welcomed the additional news coverage, others viewed the effort to attract news media attention with skepticism, given their belief in and reliance on private politics. Certainly, the task force could better control its framing of the issues in direct negotiations with the college and with the BRA when compared with its interactions with the news media. A news media strategy entails real risks because reporters and editors are free to reject frames proposed to them and advance their own definitions of issues and problems. In addition, news media demands for information placed additional burdens on a community group lacking resources. Some members of the group expressed unease and dissatisfaction with my role as a public advocate for the task force. These complaints produced what I saw as a cumbersome and unwieldy review process of potential material designed for the news media. The time-consuming nature of this process sometimes diminished the ability of the group to attract news coverage given the deadline demands of journalists. In fairness, however, this is a difficult issue. Advocates for groups remain responsible to the group as a whole, and I recognize the need for democratic decision making. My experience with the task force illustrates the very real tensions between the desire to attract news coverage and the need to safeguard collective decision making in a collective effort.

Conclusion

My work with the Boston College Community Task Force illustrates an alternative to traditional forms of academic consulting. By working with marginalized groups, researcher-activists can make contributions to the struggle for needed political and social reform. Too often traditional academic consulting has served the interests of the powerful at the expense of communities and groups lacking power. The intervention described in this chapter and similar projects conducted by others demonstrate that expertise gained in our teaching and in our research can be applied to efforts to secure progressive change.

This intervention also underscores how concepts derived from social movement theory and research can help to shape struggles for social and political reform. My actions were informed by my past activism, by my long participation in the Media Research and Action Project, and by theorizing and research on social movements.

This experience illustrates the particular benefits of interventions linked to issues and causes in our immediate communities. I benefited from a particular type of standing with members of the task force, a standing based on my lengthy involvement with pressing community issues in Allston-Brighton. This standing did not eliminate conflicts within the task force concerning my recommendations, but I believe it reduced the scope and depth of these conflicts. My relationship with this community group would have been fundamentally altered if my interaction had been based on the traditional model of academic consulting. Acting locally, then, can enhance the effectiveness of our interventions because it allows us to be part of a collective effort to secure reforms, rather than outside experts removed from the experiential world of those we seek to assist.

In a recent symposium on the need to reinvigorate links between sociology and broader publics confronting significant problems in American society, Burawoy writes that "professional sociology [a sociology of theory and empirical research] provides the ammunition, the expertise, the knowledge, the insight, and the legitimacy for sociologists to present themselves to publics or to powers" (Burawoy et al. 2004, 105). I think there is considerable truth in Burawoy's claim. My standing with the Boston College Task Force, however, reveals that ammunition, expertise, knowledge, and insight also can be gained by engagement with the collective efforts of community groups and social movement organizations; this is the legitimacy of "compañerismo," a legitimacy established and sustained by relationships and engagement, that Ryan describes in her contribution to the same symposium (ibid., 113). For members of the task force, my involvement with the issues and problems confronting the Allston-Brighton community provided me with the expertise, knowledge, and insight that really mattered.

Finally, this intervention demonstrates the very real constraints confronting efforts to secure meaningful social change. More than one thousand Boston College students remain in residential housing in Allston-Brighton; they represent a very small fraction of undergraduates who live in the community and in other Boston neighborhoods. The failure of universities and colleges to house their students remains a *systemic* problem in Boston. This problem cannot be resolved by isolated and underresourced task forces; it requires policies enacted and enforced by city government. Similarly, the broader structural problems contributing to Boston's housing crisis demand action by government agencies on the local, state, and national levels. Boston's housing crisis worsened between 2000 and 2002, with housing prices increasing by 37 percent (Boston Foundation 2002). The task force's actions did not and could not resolve Allston-Brighton's housing crisis. That crisis remains and its consequences for working- and middle-class families continue to be felt.

Note

1. From my perspective, the complex and vague language used by Boston College officials in their oral and written communication with community residents represented purposive ambiguity. Through "word games," the college maintained multiple options for future actions. At other times, college representatives used language to obfuscate, rather than to inform. Regarding organizational uses of strategic ambiguity, see Sellnow and Ulmer 2004.

References

Allston-Brighton Community Development Corporation. 1999. *Rising Rents, Closing Doors.* Boston: Allston-Brighton Community Development Corporation.

Allston-Brighton Healthy Boston Coalition. 2002. *The Allston-Brighton Community Needs and Assets Assessment Report.* Boston: Allston-Brighton Healthy Boston Coalition.

Boston Foundation. 2002. *Creativity and Innovation: A Bridge to the Future.* Boston: Boston Foundation.

Burawoy, Michael, William Gamson, Charlotte Ryan, Stephen Pfohl, Diane Vaughan, Charles Derber, and Juliet Schor. 2004. "Public Sociologies: A Symposium from Boston College." *Social Problems* 51: 103–30.

Carragee, Kevin M. 1991. "News and Ideology: An Analysis of Coverage of the West German Green Party by the *New York Times.*" *Journalism Monographs* 130: 1–30.

Croteau, David, William Hoynes, and Kevin M. Carragee. 1996. "The Political Diversity of Public Television: Polysemy, the Public Sphere, and the Conservative Critique of Public Television." *Journalism and Mass Communication Monographs* 157: 1–55.

Deetz, Stanley, and Dennis Mumby. 1990. "Power, Discourse, and the Workplace: Reclaiming the Critical Tradition." In *Communication Yearbook 13,* ed. James A. Anderson, 18–47. Newbury Park, CA: Sage.

Entman, Robert. 1993. "Framing: Toward a Clarification of a Fractured Paradigm." *Journal of Communication* 43, no. 4: 51–58.

Ferree, Myra Marx, William Gamson, Jurgen Gerhards, and Deiter Rucht. 2002. *Shaping Abortion Discourse: Democracy and the Public Sphere in Germany and the United States.* New York: Cambridge University Press.

Frey, Larry, W. Barnett Pearce, Mark Pollack, Lee Artz, and Bren Murphy. 1996. "Looking for Justice in All the Wrong Places: On a Communication Approach to Social Justice." *Communication Studies* 47: 110–27.

Gamson, William. 1990. *The Strategy of Social Protest.* Belmont, CA: Wadsworth.

———. 1992. *Talking Politics.* New York: Cambridge University Press.

Gamson, William, and Andre Modigliani. 1989. "Media Discourse and Public Opinion on Nuclear Power: A Constructionist Approach." *American Journal of Sociology* 95: 1–37.

McAdam, Doug. 1988. *Freedom Summer.* New York: Oxford University Press.

Morris, Aldon. 1984. *The Origins of the Civil Rights Movement.* New York: Free Press.

Ryan, Charlotte. 1991. *Prime Time Activism: Media Strategies for Grassroots Organizing.* Boston: South End Press.

Ryan, Charlotte, Kevin M. Carragee, and William Meinhofer. 2001. "Framing, the News Media, and Collective Action." *Journal of Broadcasting and Electronic Media* 45: 175–82.

Ryan, Charlotte, Kevin M. Carragee, and Cassie Schwerner. 1998. "Media,

Movements, and the Quest for Social Justice." *Journal of Applied Communication Research* 26: 165–81.

Sellnow, Timothy, and Robert Ulmer. 2004. "Ambiguity as an Inherent Factor in Organizational Crisis Communication." In *Responding to Crisis: A Rhetorical Approach to Crisis Communication,* ed. Dan Millar and Robert Heath, 251–62. Mahwah, NJ: Lawrence Erlbaum.

6

Media Research and Media Activism

William Hoynes

Academics and activists have long shared an interest in understanding the forces that shape news coverage. Both social movement researchers and movement activists often pay close attention to media coverage, looking at how political debates are framed and how activist organizations are represented in the news. Although academics and activists often ask similar questions about news media, and often come to similar conclusions about media coverage, the potentially beneficial relationship between them remains underdeveloped. This chapter explores my own experiences doing research in support of media activists as a window on broader questions about academic-activist collaboration.

Since the early 1980s, social movement researchers have paid increasing attention to the relationship between media and social movements. Todd Gitlin's *The Whole World Is Watching* (1980) focused on the relationship between the U.S. news media and the "new left," examining the role of news in the rise and ultimate demise of the student left in the 1960s. Gitlin's analysis of the complex dynamic between media and movement, particularly the powerful ideological role of the major news media and the pitfalls for movements of the media spotlight, helped to define an enduring set of questions for research and theory at the intersection of social movements and media sociology.

More recently, a growing body of research and theory has explored both media coverage of social movements and media strategies of movement organizations. In the second edition of his now classic *The Strategy of Social Protest* (1990), Gamson argues that mass media are a key factor in analyzing post–World War II social movements, and researchers interested in how both media and movements "frame" issues have been particularly attentive to what Gamson and Wolfsfeld (1993) call the "transactional" relationship between news media and social movements.

In exploring this relationship, social movement theorists have defined media as potentially valuable resources for movement organizations, looked at the media as part of political opportunity structures, and identified media as a terrain of political and cultural contestation (see, for example, McAdam, McCarthy, and Zald 1996; Ferree et al. 2002). Media, then, are both cultural forces that shape the field of mobilization and an arena of political activism itself. And neither movement activists nor journalists are passive in this relationship. One of the real contributions of social movement scholarship is this illumination of the push-pull of media-movement relations, which highlights both the strategic agency of activists and the journalistic norms and practices that do so much to shape media coverage of social movements.

At the same time that social movement scholars were turning their attention to media as a site of political activism, media researchers were reconstructing the largely neglected history of what I call *media activism.* McChesney's *Telecommunications, Mass Media, and Democracy* (1993) is perhaps the most significant work of this kind, but it is emblematic of a larger body of research that explores organized efforts to shape the terms of media policy in the United States (see, for example, Engelman 1996; Starr 2000; Streeter 1996). McChesney highlights the period between 1928 and 1935, when education, labor, and religious activists challenged the emerging corporate broadcasting industry, arguing for a policy that would promote the public, noncommercial development of broadcasting. These media activists ultimately lost the battle, but only after their efforts helped to produce a 1935 bill in the U.S. Senate that would have made all broadcast licenses null and void while setting aside 25 percent of all the top AM frequencies for educational institutions. They are part of a long history of activists—from those trying to promote radio as a form of two-way communication in the years before 1920 to those who advocated for a public broadcasting system in the United States in the 1960s—who have focused their political activity around media policy (Douglas 1987; Hoynes 1994). By highlighting the history of political contest surrounding media policy, media researchers have shown with great clarity that the U.S. media industry is not a natural occurrence but is the result of continuing political struggles and policy choices. If social movement scholars have shown that media matter to movements, media researchers have demonstrated that activism is linked to the organization of the media industry.

For many activists, the major media—or more commonly in activist circles, the "mainstream media"—are a fundamental problem: difficult to reach and generally perceived to be unsympathetic, mainstream news media are the subject of much criticism among activist groups. Activists are likely to see mainstream news as an arena that promotes elite interests and presents a very narrow set of perspectives about current events. Since activists generally pay close attention to the issues around which they are organizing, they often have very specific analyses of the shortcomings of mainstream journalism. In this context, activists' substantive critique of mainstream news commonly defines the economic structure of the media industry and the close relationship between reporters and officials as the primary reasons that news is so unfriendly to activists and their alternative perspectives.

In addition, as Ryan (1991) demonstrates with great clarity, there are good reasons why activists believe that mainstream news is dismissive or even hostile to activist groups. Most activist groups lack both the institutional legitimacy and the resources to be part of standard news routines, so they have to work hard to get the attention of journalists. Just as important, reporters are often suspicious of activists, whom they often define as "special interests" with an ax to grind rather than credible sources. In short, many activists understand that they have limited access to news—they rarely see their own views on display in the mainstream media—and see this as a result of the structure and organization of news media. Activists typically reject the notion that news provides a "mirror" of the world, arguing instead that news reflects the interests of political and economic elites.

But activists often have a double-edged relationship with the news media. Despite their criticisms of mainstream media, many activists still believe that media are a potentially valuable resource for social movements. Even though activists understand that the news is not a level playing field, media remain a central concern for many movements. Although they often deeply mistrust mainstream news, many activists implicitly define media coverage as an informal measure of success. Prominent and favorable news coverage of a demonstration or the publication of an op-ed by a local activist—perhaps because these are so rare—is likely to give activists a sense of accomplishment. Many activist groups will circulate mainstream news coverage of their actions and news items that quote their members as widely as possible, targeting both current members and potential supporters. Mainstream news coverage can confer a kind of legitimacy on a social movement organization—giving the organization visibility and, at least temporarily, putting activists' concerns on the agenda. From a strategic standpoint, many activists understand that media coverage can be a key, if volatile, part of efforts to mobilize supporters, since mainstream media can reach a much broader public than internal newsletters or phone trees. It is not uncommon for activists to have a sophisticated critique of the mainstream news media, both subscribe and contribute to independent media, and at the same time seek mainstream media coverage of their political efforts.

While social movement theorists, media researchers, and activists often share a broad set of questions—those that focus on the complex, two-way relationship between media and social movements—the work of scholars and activists remains largely in separate domains. Social movement theorists study media coverage of social movements and the framing strategies of movement groups, but with rare exceptions (see Ryan 1991; Gamson 1992) have done little to explore the implications of their evolving understanding of media-movement relations for movements themselves. Similarly, many activists are aware of social movement and media scholarship that tries to clarify media's role as both resource and constraint for activist organizations, but see it as too abstract to be useful for building media strategies. As a result of this persistent disconnect, both scholarship and activism have been shortchanged. Research and theory has only just scratched the surface of activist experiences with media, and movements are only vaguely familiar with what researchers have learned about media and social movements.

Media Activism

Over the past two decades, a new social movement has emerged that defines media as the target—not just a resource or constraint but the explicit focus—of mobilization efforts. Media activists seek to change both the structure and content of mainstream media, and they use a wide variety of tactics to alternately woo and pressure journalists, call public attention to the failures of mainstream media, build public support for policies aimed at promoting diversity in media ownership and content, and support alternative media across the range of media platforms. This still-emerging form of activism raises important questions about the relationship between activism and media research because research has been a key component of the repertoire of media activism.

For more than fifteen years, my work as a media researcher has been linked to the project of media activism. But this has evolved in a way very different from what I had anticipated. Rather than study media activism as a movement itself or work with activists on strategic challenges, much of my work (often with my colleague David Croteau) has been media research that media activists have found useful. Since shortly after its founding in 1986, I have worked with Fairness and Accuracy In Reporting (FAIR), a leading progressive media activist organization in the United States. FAIR defines its mission as working "to invigorate the First Amendment by advocating for greater diversity in the press and by scrutinizing media practices that marginalize public interest, minority and dissenting viewpoints" (*Extra!* 2003). In the remainder of this chapter, I want to explore my long-standing research relationship with FAIR and, along the way, delve into the terms and goals of such collaborative efforts between media researchers and media activists.

When I first encountered FAIR in 1987, the founders of the organization had an articulate critique of the shortcomings of the major news media in the United States and a clear sense that news could do a far better job of representing the full range of perspectives on current issues and events. FAIR's founders were writers and activists, and they were skilled at producing careful media criticism. I first became acquainted with FAIR when Bill Gamson handed me a special issue of their newsletter (now magazine) *Extra!* that described the absences in U.S. news coverage of conflicts in Central America, emphasizing the success of the Reagan administration at manipulating the news media. At the time, I was working on a study of media strategies of the Central America solidarity movement—activists who opposed U.S. intervention in the region—and exploring the broader symbolic contest about U.S. foreign policy that Central America activists were fighting. With Cold War assumptions shaping both the political debate on Capitol Hill and mainstream news coverage of U.S. involvement in Central America, FAIR's brand of media criticism, which highlighted these taken-for-granted assumptions and suggested alternative ways of framing the situation, was a breath of fresh air. More generally, FAIR suggested to *Extra!* readers, mostly activists at the time, that activists needed to talk back to the news media and develop strategies to pressure journalists to broaden their coverage of the ongoing conflict in the region.

Shortly after reading this special issue of *Extra!* I traveled to New York City to meet with FAIR's director Jeff Cohen about the possibility of doing a collaborative research project. FAIR had recently received a small grant from the Fund for Investigative Journalism to support research for an article on ABC's prestigious late-night news program *Nightline*. They had a core idea that I immediately saw as part of a broader tradition of research on news sources: they wanted to analyze *Nightline*'s guest list, the roster of experts and officials who appear each night to discuss the top story of the day. No one had previously studied *Nightline* in this way, and the program was at the height of its popularity and influence in the late 1980s, with its host Ted Koppel among the most highly respected journalists in the United States.

What FAIR staff lacked were the background and skills to conceptualize and conduct a systematic study of *Nightline*'s guest list. This seemed like a very good fit: FAIR needed the research skills and legitimacy that come with academic research, and I sought resources to support my research and an opportunity for connecting my research and activist concerns.

The Nightline Study

In the spring of 1988, David Croteau and I set out to design a study of *Nightline*'s guest list and to work out the details of our collaboration with FAIR, making decisions that laid the foundation for our decade-long work with each other and with FAIR. The terms of our collaboration with FAIR were relatively straightforward. They would provide resources to support the research (the funds from their small grant would pay us a small sum for our time and effort), help us to acquire either videotapes or printed transcripts of *Nightline* programs, and give us complete autonomy in designing, carrying out, and writing up the research—and we would deliver a completed study in approximately six months. While details of publication were not entirely clear, we agreed that FAIR would publish the study in *Extra!* and that we retained the option of writing a different version for publication in a scholarly journal.

In addition, since FAIR activists had a great deal of knowledge about both the news media and *Nightline* itself, we agreed that it would be mutually beneficial to work together to identify the underlying questions and goals of the study. We sought to design a study that was consistent both with FAIR's interest in a critical evaluation of journalistic decisions about scheduling guests and with our interest in what we saw as potentially valuable research on news sources and the media framing of policy debates. While we were not thinking about a long-term research relationship with FAIR, we were cognizant of some of the dilemmas of collaborative research and sought to balance our scholarly and activist concerns by defining a project with underlying *questions* that we defined as both politically and intellectually valuable.

Identifying these questions was simple enough: who appears on *Nightline* and how does the makeup of the guest list shape the framing of policy debates? But designing a study to answer these questions was far more complex. FAIR wanted research that would provide data, preferably quantitative, on the political orientation of *Nightline*'s guest list, based on a classification of guests along a left-center-right or liberal-moderate-conservative continuum. However, it was clear to us that this was not a viable approach. While we might be able to use voting records to characterize elected officials on a liberal-conservative scale, we knew that judgments of the political orientation of *Nightline*'s guests would be far too subjective and reflect our own political leanings as much as those of the guests. We needed to design a method that would allow us either to infer the political consequences of the guest list constitution or look more carefully at the relationship between guests and the framing of policy debates on particular issues. A direct measure of the political leaning of guests was simply not feasible.

After much discussion with FAIR activists about the inherent problems of a simple political classification scheme and a reaffirmation that both parties—researchers and activists—shared a commitment to a credible research design, David and I developed a methodological framework that highlighted measures of demographics, institutional affiliations, and the degree and form of participation of *Nightline* guests, coupled with qualitative case studies of several key issues that *Nightline* covered regularly. We spent the next several months reading, coding, and analyzing *Nightline* transcripts that covered a forty-month period from 1985 to 1988. In the fall, we presented a draft of our study to our colleagues at Bill Gamson's weekly MRAP seminar in the Sociology Department at Boston College (BC) and to FAIR. Responses and criticism from both activists at FAIR and our colleagues at BC helped us to clarify and sharpen our analysis and to keep in mind the three distinct audiences for the study—media activists, journalists (including staff at *Nightline*), and media researchers.

We delivered a final version of the study, "Are You on the *Nightline* Guest List?" (Hoynes and Croteau 1989) to FAIR in early 1989. In the study, we argued that "*Nightline*'s choice of subjects and guests helps to define a narrow political terrain in a way that reflects the interests of the show's elite participants." The cover indicated that we were the authors of the study, which was prepared *for* (not by) FAIR. Now our work was done, or so we thought. FAIR planned to publish an edited excerpt of the study in *Extra!* and "release" the complete study as part of a media campaign in February 1989.

To our surprise, FAIR was remarkably skilled at publicity work and the study received widespread media attention, with stories about the study appearing in scores of daily newspapers and talk radio stations. Most news stories included comments by FAIR's executive director Jeff Cohen about the significance of the study's findings, and virtually all of the media coverage noted FAIR as the organization that released the study. This was good news for FAIR, providing the organization with visibility, and, for at least a moment, FAIR's critique of the American news media was prominently featured in the mainstream media itself.

The *Nightline* study, as it quickly became known, was successful on several fronts. FAIR made national news, reaching both journalists and a broader public; at the same time, they published a special *Nightline* issue of *Extra!* that served their core constituency of media activists. Our work received a great deal of attention outside of the academic community, was well received by both scholars and activists, and helped to define a useful method for further media research. In addition, *Nightline*'s host and executive producer responded publicly to the study, something that would never have happened with an academic study published solely in a scholarly journal.

In subsequent years, we would conduct several more studies that FAIR published and released, including research on *The MacNeil-Lehrer NewsHour*, public affairs programming on PBS, the most widely circulating syndicated newspaper columnists, the classroom news program *Channel One*, and the political attitudes of Washington journalists (Hoynes and Croteau 1990; Croteau and Hoynes 1992; Croteau, Hoynes, and Carragee 1993; Hoynes 1997; Croteau 1998).

The *Nightline* study served as the foundation of a long-term researcher-activist collaboration. Exploring the experience of this collaborative relationship illuminates a great deal about the potential connections between scholarly research and activism. In particular, we can see both the ways that research can support activism and some of the tensions between scholarly and activist approaches to research and the presentation of research findings. Perhaps most important, we can see the difference between studying social movements and doing research in support of social movement goals.

Media Monitoring and Media Activism

The *Nightline* study was read and cited far more widely in activist circles than in the academic world. Indeed, our subsequent book, *By Invitation Only: How the Media Limit Political Debate* (Croteau and Hoynes 1994), which grew out of our studies for FAIR, was published by a progressive publisher (Common Courage Press) and circulated primarily among activists. We found that our research was useful to activists in the short term, allowing FAIR to build a campaign to pressure *Nightline* to include a wider range of perspectives on its program. Later, when FAIR focused attention on the shortcoming of the *MacNeil-Lehrer NewsHour*, after our study documented the narrow range of debate on that program, FAIR activists took a small measure of credit for the *NewsHour*'s subsequent inclusion of Erwin Knoll, editor of the monthly magazine the *Progressive*, as a regular on its roundtable discussions with journalists around the nation. And we heard from local media activists that critical media research—available in FAIR's magazine instead of a scholarly journal and written in a language accessible to nonspecialists—was a helpful resource as they developed and disseminated their own critique of the news media.

To the extent that activists found our research useful, it was in the context of a shift in the broader strategies of media activism. During the 1990s, systematic media monitoring emerged as a common approach for media activists who wanted both to mobilize new recruits and build a foundation for direct discussion with journalists about their performance. Rather than media criticism of a single article or news report, media monitoring gave activists a tool for analyzing the broader patterns of media discourse. Individual stories could be criticized for what they said or what they missed, but activists could provide a much more compelling critique by linking the problems of a single report to persistent patterns of inclusion and exclusion.

In the context of media monitoring, news that relied primarily and credulously on official statements was not just poor reporting, but a sign of the broader problems with how news is gathered and produced. And media research that identified these broader patterns proved to be a helpful resource for media activists facing a series of difficult challenges—building alliances with issue-based movements founded on a shared critique of the news media, mobilizing citizens to "talk back" to media when there are limited venues of such two-way communication, seeking access to journalists to explain their critique of the news and possible alternatives, and working to have the major news media do stories on the ideas and arguments of media critics.

For each of these challenges, media research in the form of media monitoring can provide valuable support to media activists. Media monitoring is often issue-specific, and this can provide a substantive basis for coalition building between media activists and organizations focused on other policy domains. In addition, media research can provide activists with a more in-depth critique when they send critical letters, e-mails, or make phone calls to their local media, and, just as important, the circulation of the results of media monitoring can serve as an opportunity to encourage activists to talk back to the media. Media monitoring can also help open channels of communication between activists and journalists. Rather than single out an individual story or reporter, activists sometimes find that research gives them a helpful, less blame-oriented approach to discussing journalistic performance with reporters and editors. And the findings of media research can be the basis for a publicity campaign that mainstream news outlets may occasionally cover—further circulating the research findings.

As media monitoring became a regular part of the repertoire of media activism, several other academics conducted research for FAIR and other media activist organizations (see, for example, Ryan 1993; Larson 1998; Lewis, Jhally, and Morgan 1991; Montgomery and Pasnik 1996; Soley 1997). It quickly became clear, however, that media activists could not rely on academics to carry out regular media monitoring, especially at the local level. While activist groups might find sympathetic academics to complete periodic research reports, it is not likely that university-based researchers will be available as regular research staff for movement organizations. (In contrast, well-funded conservative organizations such as the Media Research Center and the Center for Media and Public Affairs have paid staff researchers who provide regular media monitoring reports for conservative activists and politicians.)

Activists cannot rely on consistent research support from university-based academics due, in part, to the professional risks academics face when they join activists in collaborative research projects. One powerful risk revolves around the publication venue of such research projects. Publishing research findings in activist-oriented, independent media may be a valuable contribution to movement goals or public discussion, but it is likely to do little for one's academic career goals. Indeed, the likelihood that activist-oriented research will not be published in the kinds of prestigious professional journals that are the key to securing academic jobs and gaining tenure may weigh heavily on academics as they work on such collaborative projects.

While our *Nightline* study was widely read and discussed by media activists and media critics, we failed to publish the research in a prestigious scholarly journal, with one editor rejecting our research as "too interpretive." We did find a sociology journal that enthusiastically published our study of *Nightline*—and we were more successful at finding scholarly journals to publish subsequent studies, perhaps because we were more strategic in our submissions or because our research was better known—but the *Nightline* study was published in a small and marginal journal. While our *Nightline* study may have been read, cited, and even taught by other academics, our inability to publish this research in a prominent scholarly journal severely limited the academic value of this study for its two graduate student authors.

In this context, maintaining a long-term media monitoring project requires that the key researchers be activists themselves. In order to support such local media activism, I worked with FAIR to develop materials to help train activists to do their own media monitoring in hopes that activists would define monitoring projects that were consistent with their own specific needs and goals. In the early 1990s, I helped to train local activists in media monitoring in cities from Philadelphia to Phoenix, Chapel Hill to San Francisco. While most of these activists were initially intimidated by the idea of doing research on the news media, they commonly found that carefully analyzing media was an empowering experience that gave them a stronger foundation from which to criticize their local media. Rocky Mountain Media Watch, an organization that would go on to produce the activist-friendly guide to media, *Making the News* (Saltzman 1998), became a prime example of how local activists built a movement with media monitoring as a central component.

While monitoring and activism may be deeply intertwined, we should not confuse media monitoring with media activism itself. Studying media is not a form of political activism in its own right, but monitoring can be a critical component. Media monitoring became valuable to media activists precisely because research produces knowledge that has a cultural authority that activism often lacks. This status difference can be overcome in collaborative projects that are built on mutual respect and shared goals. But the different social positions of activists and researchers pose some real dilemmas for these kinds of activist-scholar collaborations, which place structural limits on the degree and forms of such projects.

Challenges of Activist-Academic Collaboration

Academics and activists neither occupy the same social space nor have precisely the same interests. Even politically active scholars and intellectually inclined activists will find that they face distinct incentives and constraints and have different resources. My experiences working on several collaborative projects with media activists suggest some of the challenges that make these projects difficult to sustain and yet, at the same time, why such projects can be mutually beneficial.

Activists and scholars bring different skills and resources to their collaborative projects. In fact, this is often the basis for such endeavors. Activists often have commitment, vision, and organizing skills. Academics are likely to have knowledge of scholarly literature, research skills, and the legitimacy of an academic institution. Combining these two sets of resources can be politically and intellectually productive, but collaborations can be perilous for both activist and academic. While activists face the challenge of veering too far from their core organizing goals by launching lengthy and resource-depleting research projects, academics face a potential challenge to their legitimacy as scholars.

When researchers work with activist organizations, we bring knowledge and skills that can be useful to activists. But we also bring a specific form of status to the table, one based in the authority of the university, and we should not deceive ourselves about the potential value of this status for movement organizations. Activist efforts to publicize the findings of research routinely invoke the signs of academic status of the author—PhD, professor, university or college affiliation—because this lends legitimacy to the research. There is nothing improper about this practice of emphasizing the academic status of the researcher, although it can be risky for activists to implicitly suggest that expert knowledge is more valuable than citizen knowledge.

Scholars face a different set of challenges when we lend the cultural authority of the academy to our activist partners. We risk being labeled "advocacy academics"—similar to the charge that journalists face ("advocacy journalism") when they report too frequently on the ideas and activities of social movements. Because the legitimacy of scholarly knowledge remains at least partially rooted in a definition of objectivity that emphasizes detachment from the object of study, scholars who work with social movements run the risk of being dismissed as politically motivated partisans. Younger scholars who are just starting their academic careers and those without a stable institutional home are likely to be the most vulnerable to such charges. But pressure to keep our work separate from our political commitments will be familiar to even the most senior scholars. This kind of disciplinary pressure undoubtedly elevates the potential costs of scholar-activist collaboration, making it likely that many academics will think twice before joining research projects with activists.

Even in this context, it would be foolish for academics to shy away from potentially productive collaborations. Scholars do research for and with a wide range of institutions—including government agencies and corporations—and research with a social movement organization is no different. While academics need to be careful to abide by the methodological and ethical guidelines of their professional field, we need to actively resist the notion that collaborative research with activist organizations is somehow less valuable or "scholarly" than other professional research. Perhaps academics inclined to work with activists could learn something from advocates of participatory action research, who have long argued for the benefits of designing and conducting research projects with organized community groups (Whyte 1991).

Scholar-activist collaborations face a new set of dilemmas once the research is complete. At this point, particularly if activists hope to distribute the research findings widely, framing the significance of the research, including decisions about which specific research findings to highlight, is an entirely new challenge. Most academics are likely to have little experience in publicity work—and, perhaps ironically, even academics who study media are likely to have a limited understanding of how to promote their research as a newsworthy story—but activists are often quite skilled at media work.

During our collaboration with FAIR, we found FAIR's core activists to be both strategically sophisticated and remarkably effective in publicity work. But it was not always easy to come to a mutual agreement about how best to pitch the research to journalists. When it came time to draft a short press advisory to promote the *Nightline* study, it became clear that FAIR's goal of maximizing mainstream media coverage of the study would influence how the study was framed. In this context, our quantitative findings—data on the most frequently appearing individuals and the demographic characteristics of the guests—was the most valuable. These numbers were easy to communicate to journalists, and they provided a useful overview of the study's broader argument about the narrow range of perspectives on *Nightline*.

However, the quantitative data were only a small part of the research report and provided a very broad view of our critique of *Nightline*. The bulk of the report was a series of more qualitative case studies that demonstrated the consequences of *Nightline*'s narrow guest list for the debates about several key issues. The qualitative components of the study were far more difficult to communicate to journalists, especially when trying to promote a story to an already busy reporter. And we later learned that even those journalists who read the full study found the quantitative findings—the numbers—to be more compelling and easier to cover than the lengthier and somewhat more nuanced case studies. The qualitative analysis was clearly less news-friendly than the numbers.

In the days following the study's release, I learned a great deal about how to talk with reporters—both print journalists preparing stories on the study and broadcast journalists hosting live talk radio programs. Although I had spent several years studying the news media and could provide detailed advice on strategies for talking with journalists, I quickly learned that FAIR activists had a much clearer vision of how to communicate with reporters and especially how to communicate effectively on live radio. They were skilled at talking about the study in clear, succinct, and unambiguous terms; they were able to talk in sound bites without oversimplifying too much. I found this much more difficult, and I often left interviews with the feeling that I had not been able to convey what I was trying to say.

The publicity phase of the *Nightline* study taught me an important lesson about the difficulty of communicating complex ideas to mainstream journalists. One of the costs of seeking widespread attention for research is the simplification required to effectively explain research findings to reporters who have only a few hundred words or a few seconds of air time. Given the broad media coverage of the research, FAIR's assessment of how best to promote the study was undoubtedly correct. But it quickly became clear that press reports about the study would focus on only the most dramatic and number-oriented parts of the study; we would need other outlets to disseminate the broader findings of the study.

More challenging than the dilemmas associated with how to frame the research findings was the question of defining a broad conceptual framework for talking about what research like the *Nightline* study tells us about the American news media. This may seem like a purely academic question, but the way one interprets the broader lessons of research is consequential for both activists and academics. It has been this issue—how to describe the meaning of the patterns identified in the *Nightline* study and other research we have done with FAIR—that has been the hardest to sort out. At the same time, this persistent dilemma has clarified both the benefits and the limits of academic-activist collaboration.

In a nutshell, the term "bias" has been the most problematic aspect of our collaborative relationship with FAIR. Since its founding, FAIR has focused on the problem of media bias and argued for news that is more fair and balanced—and bias-free. FAIR has characterized the *Nightline* study, as well as subsequent studies, as evidence of the fundamentally elite bias of the American news media. There are real political benefits to using a bias framework to describe the problems with the news media. Journalists are accustomed to this language and may be responsive to arguments using this terminology. And bias arguments are likely to resonate with activists who are often frustrated with what they see as the propagandistic nature of much news coverage. The bias framework may also make it easier to communicate a critique of the news media to the general public, particularly in short television or radio appearances, since the bias discourse is likely to be familiar to a wide range of citizens.

Over the years, however, I have become increasingly dissatisfied with the bias framework (see Croteau and Hoynes 1994). Bias is the same language that conservatives use to describe what they define as the problems with news media—leading to a situation where journalists and citizens can dismiss media criticism from both sides since conservatives and progressives can appear to be advancing mirror-image arguments of each other. Indeed, some journalists are explicit that persistent claims of both a "liberal bias" by conservative critics and a "conservative bias" by liberal critics effectively cancel each other out, leaving the news where it wants to be, right in the center. But the problem with the bias framework is more than just the political baggage that weighs it down. The bias framework is intellectually problematic and, ultimately, inconsistent with an understanding of news as an arena of cultural contestation—where the meanings of events and issues are framed and reframed. The bias framework too easily devolves to questions of whether news coverage is true or false and, as a result, emphasizes a kind of ideological uniformity that is the consequence of news that is supposed to be the singular, objective truth.

Our colleagues at FAIR have generally been quite careful in their use of the bias framework, working hard to distance their critique, which calls for the inclusion of more voices, from conservative claims of bias, which often call for the exclusion of "inappropriate" voices. And FAIR has consistently emphasized the importance of diversity in news coverage—a framework that I find far preferable than the bias framework. However, activists at FAIR consistently fall back on the term "bias," which remains a key component of their critique of the news.

The dilemma is quite clear. In this academic-activist collaboration, there has been a longstanding disagreement about the consequences of describing the collaborative research through the lens of media bias. After initially trying to use the term very precisely, we avoided it in later projects, stressing diversity as an alternative concept to bias. I was vigilant about avoiding the term in interviews with reporters, going so far as to correct journalists who used the language of bias in their questions about the study. In short, I have not used the bias framework to interpret the meaning of these collaborative research projects, but activists at FAIR have continued to employ the bias framework to discuss the same research.

Here is an example of when academic-activist collaboration can be productive and, at the same time, recognize the limits of that collaboration. FAIR activists find the bias framework to be a valuable component of their strategic repertoire; persuasive arguments about bias can help to mobilize outraged activists and can effectively speak to mainstream journalists. There are clear reasons why activists would prefer the language of bias. At the same time, I have found the bias framework to be increasingly unsatisfying as an explanation of the shortcomings of news reports, and I do not use the term to describe my work, even the collaborative work that I have done with FAIR. In this case, activists and academics share a political critique, and both find the collaborative research process useful. But, recognizing our different goals and the needs of academics and activists, we talk about the same research in somewhat different terms. There is no deep conflict here, but there is an implicit (although rarely articulated) acknowledgment that we occupy different institutional locations.

Lessons for Social Movement Scholarship

At various points in the 1990s, I thought about conducting a study of FAIR and the new form of media activism that it represented. As a sociologist trained in the study of social movements, I thought that a focus on FAIR's evolving strategy and tactical repertoire would provide useful insights for social movement theory and for activists, including FAIR itself. But as I became increasingly familiar with FAIR as an organization—its staff, understanding of media, and political strategy—it became clear to me that FAIR was not in need of organizational consultants or strategic assistance. They needed credible, current research on the American news media.

FAIR had a compelling critique of the news media, plenty of examples to cite, and articulate spokespeople to make their case. What they needed was the same thing that elites have—the support of legitimate experts, in this case scholars, who can provide technical assistance in the form of media research. Without high profile, well-funded think tanks to rely on, movement organizations like FAIR cannot count on the ongoing support of researchers to help them develop and disseminate their critique. This can put movement organizations at a distinct disadvantage in comparison to political actors who can draw from a steady stream of research reports and policy briefs.

Our collaborative work with FAIR was neither large nor constant—just six projects in ten years—but it provided modest research support for an ambitious movement organization, and our relationships solidified over time. In particular, our research provided FAIR with a series of studies that carried the stamp of approval of the academy. During the course of our collaborative research with FAIR, we saw the potential value of scholarly research for social movements. Academic researchers have skills and resources that are often unavailable to movement organizations. And just as important, academics have a form of cultural authority—our research findings have a distinctive legitimacy—from which movements can benefit. This is, of course, a two-way street. Researchers who work with movements can gain access to perspectives, and sometimes to hard-to-obtain data, that can enrich their work. And working with movements can provide an opportunity to do work that does more than contribute to a research literature and reaches readers who care deeply about the research questions.

When activists and researchers collaborate in a context that respects the knowledge and expertise of both partners, the benefits can extend beyond the participants in the collaborative project. Connecting activist and academic knowledge and publishing the results of such collaborative projects in both alternative publications and scholarly journals, while sometimes risky for both activists and academics, can help to enrich the dialogue between activists and scholars and may help to bridge the long-standing divide between these two worlds that have so much to gain from each other.

References

Croteau, David. 1998. "Examining the 'Liberal Media' Claim: Journalists' Views on Politics, Economic Policy, and Media Coverage." Research Report for FAIR.

Croteau, David, and William Hoynes. 1992. "Op-Ed Politics: The Lopsided Worldview of the Nation's Most Syndicated Columnists." *Extra!* 5, no. 4 (June): 22–26.

———. 1994. *By Invitation Only: How the Media Limit Political Debate.* Monroe, ME: Common Courage Press.

Croteau, David, William Hoynes, and Kevin M. Carragee. 1993. "Public Television 'Prime Time': Public Affairs Programming, Political Diversity, and the Conservative Critique of Public Television." Research Report for FAIR.

Douglas, Susan. 1987. *Inventing American Broadcasting, 1899–1922.* Baltimore: Johns Hopkins University Press.

Engelman, Ralph. 1996. *Public Radio and Television in America: A Political History.* Thousand Oaks, CA: Sage Publications.

Extra! 2003. "What's FAIR?" July/August, 2.

Ferree, Myra Marx, William A. Gamson, Jurgen Gerhards, and Deiter Rucht. 2002. *Shaping Abortion Discourse: Democracy and the Public Sphere in Germany and the United States.* New York: Cambridge University Press.

Gamson, William A. 1990. *The Strategy of Social Protest,* 2nd ed. Belmont, CA: Wadsworth.

———. 1992. *Talking Politics.* New York: Cambridge University Press.

Gamson, William, and Gadi Wolfsfeld. 1993. "Movements and Media as Interacting Systems." *Annals of the American Academy of Political and Social Science* 528 (July): 114–25.

Gitlin, Todd. 1980. *The Whole World Is Watching.* Berkeley: University of California Press.

Hoynes, William. 1994. *Public Television for Sale.* Boulder, CO: Westview Press.

———. 1997. "News for a Captive Audience: The Case of *Channel One.*" Research Report for FAIR.

Hoynes, William, and David Croteau. 1989. "Are You on the *Nightline* Guest List?" Research Report for FAIR.

————. 1990. "All The Usual Suspects: *MacNeil/Lehrer* and *Nightline*." Research Report for FAIR.

Larson, Gary O. 1998. "Fulfilling the Promise: Public Broadcasting in the Digital Age." Report for the Center for Media Education.

Lewis, Justin, Sut Jhally, and Michael Morgan. 1991. "The More You Watch, the Less You Know." University of Massachusetts Center for Studies in Communication.

McAdam, Doug, John D. McCarthy, and Mayer N. Zald, eds. 1996. *Comparative Perspectives on Social Movements*. New York: Cambridge University Press.

McChesney, Robert W. 1993. *Telecommunications, Mass Media, and Democracy*. New York: Oxford University Press.

Montgomery, Kathryn, and Shelley Pasnik. 1996. "Web of Deception." Center for Media Education.

Ryan, Charlotte. 1991. *Prime Time Activism*. Boston: South End Press.

————. 1993. "A Study of National Public Radio." Research Report for FAIR.

Saltzman, Jason. 1998. *Making the News: A Guide for Nonprofits and Activists*. Boulder, CO: Westview Press.

Soley, Lawrence. 1997. "The Power of the Press Has a Price: TV Reporters Talk about Advertiser Pressures." *Extra!* July/August, 11–13.

Starr, Jerold. 2000. *Air Wars*. Boston: Beacon Press.

Streeter, Thomas. 1996. *Selling the Air*. Chicago: University of Chicago Press.

Whyte, William Foote. 1991. *Participatory Action Research*. Newbury Park, CA: Sage.

7

Successful Collaboration: Movement Building in the Media Arena

Charlotte Ryan

This volume asks how bridging the academic-activist divide might change social movement theory and practice. I speak as a bridge worker: my job is to create and strengthen working collaborations between theorists and social movement organizations. Here I describe one episode of bridgework—a seven-year effort to establish a two-way learning relationship between the university-based Media Research and Action Project (MRAP) and the statewide advocacy organization Rhode Island Coalition against Domestic Violence (RICADV).

We wanted to collaborate to establish intentional framing practices within RICADV that would improve its communication with its diverse publics. Two stories entwine. First is the story of bridgework—how MRAP developed working relationships with collective actors. On this unfolds the second story—how MRAP and RICADV's collaboration helped us understand framing as a counterhegemonic practice.

My efforts to convey these lessons are complicated by the fact that social movement scholars and activists lack common language, much less chat rooms. At present, stories remain bridge workers' most reliable stock-in-trade—accessible to activists yet readable by academics as theoretically informed ethnographies (Burawoy et al. 1992).

Activist-intellectual Cynthia Peters urges social movement theorists to collaborate with activists to translate academic critiques of hegemony into effective counterhegemonic practices (ch. 3 this volume). Responding to Peters, I share how MRAP and RICADV's collaboration around framing practices strengthened our mutual ability to talk politics.

First, I define bridgework and review the academic literature on collective action frames. Then I briefly trace MRAP's origins, including my role, and describe how MRAP utilized collective action framing theory. I next describe a translational research project that involved MRAP and its partner, RICADV, in developing collective action framing practices. Reflecting on this case, I discuss lessons from our bridgework and how it magnified our understanding of collective action framing. I conclude by summarizing the mutual benefits of theorist-activist partnerships.

Bridgework

Bridging metaphors abound in social movement practice. They also permeate writings of feminists of color (Moraga and Anzaldúa 1983; Anzaldúa 1990), social movement theorists of color (Robnett 1997), and other feminist activist-writers (Albrecht and Brewer 1990; Gottfried 1996; Stout 1996). Morris highlights bridging efforts that succeeded in establishing freestanding institutional "movement half-way houses," such as the Highlander Folk School (1984, 139).

In a similar vein, I use "bridgework" as conceptual shorthand for working relationships, the intentional "patterning of social ties" (Diani 2000, 19) between social movement theorists and collective actors. Bridgework builds ongoing two-way learning relationships that grow from and facilitate the flow of information, language, concepts, practices, systems, services, and resources in the context of an articulated vision or mission. While an individual social movement scholar may engage with collective actors in specified projects, structural constraints make such work hard to sustain. Similarly, individual activists and ad hoc coalitions rarely muster the resources needed for sustained relation building. Typically, therefore, bridgework involves established collective actors capable of sustaining commitment.

Bridgework has a cousin in the political process model's concept of brokerage[1]—"the linking of . . . previously unconnected social sites by a unit that mediates their relation with one another" (McAdam, Tarrow, and Tilly 2001, 102). The term "brokerage," however, evokes market-influenced exchanges and fees, whereas "bridgework" evokes mutuality, sustained commitment, and resultantly broader measures of success: collaborators share ideas, emotions, experiences, visions, and history. Moreover, bridge workers take risks that brokers would hesitate to assume.

Bridgework is costly since collaborative relationships, on average, take several years to mature and produce results. For instance, Highlander, a movement halfway house playing a critical role in the civil rights movement, began in 1932 (Morris 1984). Start-up funds are especially problematic; one-year foundation grants throw bridging organizations into a constant grant-writing cycle and premature push for results. Even multiyear grants demand self-sufficiency in ways that can hurt the actual work.

Adding more risk still, bridgework increases social movement scholars' vulnerability within their home environment, the university; scholars suffer professionally if bridgework produces few immediate benefits or if it diverges from academic models of paradigm construction (see Croteau, ch. 2 this volume). The activist organization also risks losing scarce resources if bridging experiments prove unproductive. To make bridgework succeed, therefore, theorists and social movement organizations need clear goals, plans, and resources. In this case, our shared goal was to strengthen RICADV's ability to frame and influence political debates around domestic violence, building on MRAP's existing work on framing (Ryan 1991; Gamson 1992).

Collective Action Framing

A central part of collective mobilization is political discourse—how people "talk politics" (Gamson 1992). In making sense of their historical reality, people highlight some facts and events and ignore others, organizing their reading of the world into stories. Theorists often focus on framing contests, competing interpretations of reality that can be tracked via mass media, organizational documents, interviews, movement archives, and/or other historical records (Ferree et al. 2002; Gamson 1992; Steinberg 1999).

Of particular interest to social movement theorists are collective action frames sponsored by social actors intent on mobilizing both individuals and other social actors (Snow and Benford 1992). The study of collective action framing has sparked wide-ranging debates over the definition of a frame and its relation to ideology, emotion, hegemony, and power. Theorists further question whether methodological choices have sent frame research drifting toward positivism and reductionism (Snow and Benford 1988; Donati 1992; Benford 1997; Steinberg 1999; Oliver and Johnston 2000; Benford and Snow 2000; Snow and Benford 2000; Carragee and Roefs 2004). Carragee and Roefs (2004), citing the value of Donati's 1996 study of the environmental movement, further call for longitudinal studies to demonstrate how framing contests affect political discourse and political outcomes over time.

Many of these issues in framing theory would benefit from closer exploration of the historically embedded processes through which collective actors actually construct collective action frames (Carragee and Roefs 2004). Distanced from functioning collective actors, framing theorists cannot observe how the collective action frame responds to shifting historical conditions, rendering collective action framing processes more opaque.

In lieu of direct observation of framing processes, framing theorists have employed various qualitative and quantitative methods. Theorists analyze the collective action frames in texts—the *products* of collective action framers. Theorists study recorded discourses and historical records that document collective action framing contests. Historical exemplars become the best available substitutes for active collaboration with collective actors themselves (Steinberg 1999). While valuable, however, these studies do not substitute for explorations of framing processes as conducted by collective actors.

Others in this volume suggest many reasons why theorists work in isolation from functioning collective actors. Here the question of academic discourse—its content and its venues—warrants attention. Drawing from multiple literatures—resource mobilization, linguistics, ethno-methodology, political science, history, anthropology, semiotics, and other branches of communications and cultural studies—debates over framing in peer-reviewed journals have spawned a terminological growth industry; in addition to collective action framing, scholars speak of oppositional consciousness, political discourse, hegemonic and counterhegemonic scripts, causal stories, political narratives, political cultures of opposition, discursive repertoires of action, master frames, meta- and counternarratives. Even social movement paradigms previously focused on structural dimensions now call attention to the cultural/ideational mechanisms of dynamics of contention (McAdam, Tarrow, and Tilly 2001).

That social movement theorizing should generate specialized terminology and specialized venues—scholarly presses, conferences, and peer-reviewed publications—is neither surprising nor necessarily problematic. Specialization becomes problematic only if it produces isolation, i.e., if social movement theorists lose exchanges with collective actors regarding ideas, experiences, and needs. The problem is not that framing theorists debate concepts; the problem is terminological proliferation as a symptom of withering dialogue with activists. More troubling still, theorists do not seem to recognize that the dialogues they are missing are valuable.

Consequently, *as currently organized,* academic-based framing theory focuses on frames as fossils—the products or remnants of political discourse. Framing theorists rarely involve themselves in a sustained fashion with working framers, the processes framers employ, or the audiences they mobilize. As activists and their constituencies perceive framing theorists' disinterest, the activist-theorist gap grows.

Aware—at least superficially—of these barriers, graduate students and faculty launched the Media Research and Action Project in 1987. Almost twenty years later, MRAP still works to accomplish what we initially planned as a summer foray into bridgework—translating collective action framing into popular language accessible via popular venues. I turn now to this saga and to one tale of success.

A Short History of How MRAP Began

Hungry to reflect on my experiences as a labor and community organizer, I became one of a dozen graduate students joining William Gamson to create the university-based, activist-oriented Media Research and Action Project in the mid-1980s. For the last fifteen years, I have eaten Wednesday breakfast with MRAP, an ongoing group of scholar-activists and activist-scholars that shares an interest in how social movements grow and communicate. And from MRAP's tenuous location, I have worked with community, labor, and other social movement organizations to strengthen communication for social change, the ability of marginalized groups to talk politics. MRAP's attempts to bridge the activist and academic worlds now compete with the *Odyssey* in duration; our tale merits telling.

To bridge the gap between social movement theorizing and practice, we fashioned MRAP quite intentionally along the lines of a "movement half-way house" (Morris 1984, 139). We prioritized establishing collaborations with dominated groups, "excluded from one or more of the decision-making processes that determine the quality and quality of social, economic and political rewards that groups receive in a society" (282). MRAP's trainings began with a one-page summary of Morris's indigenous model of organizing, stressing not only the structural nature of inequality but the capacity of marginalized groups, *when organized,* to make change.

What we offered activist groups was our understanding of how frame analysis could enhance political discourse. MRAP's mission, we decided, was "to work with under-represented and misrepresented communities to identify and challenge barriers to democratic communication, to develop proactive messages and strategies and to build ongoing communications capacity" (MRAP 1997). Recognizing mass media as the "master forum" (Gamson 1998) of our historical times, we used social movement organizations' resultant attraction to media as an entry point that allowed MRAP to explore political discourse and movement building while being of use.

The role of mass media as the convening forum for political discourse was heightened for other historical reasons as well. While conservative movements are often explicitly ideological, U.S. progressive social movements are not. Facing the complex legacy of McCarthyism, the crises in socialism, and the rise of identity politics, progressive collective actors often coalesce around constituency or program rather than explicit ideology. The resulting single-issue, coalitional structures reflect both the pragmatic compromises and unresolved conflicts of U.S. social movements that talk politics primarily when they prepare to step into the media arena.

In carrying out this mission, MRAP evolved over time into a collective actor in its own right; while many MRAP members were located within traditional academic departments, in our collective persona as MRAP we worked for social movements, forming partnerships to bridge the usual university-community divides. We were more than an aggregate of individuals with shared interests; we became a small collective actor defining and implementing a mission and a social practice—thinking, listening, speaking, collaborating, and reflecting as a conscious change agent. While MRAP has never achieved financial stability as a halfway house, it has served a steady stream of collective actors and social movement theorists.

MRAP Begins Framing Collaborations

In summer 1986, Bill Gamson funded me, MRAP's future field director, to distill framing theories for popular use. Informally, I began talking with activist-friends about how they talked politics. In 1987, MRAP launched its first framing workshops with social movement groups—national student environmental coalitions, regional anti-intervention groups, labor organizations, and groups organizing around quality of life issues in working-class and poor communities. MRAP placed high priority on working with communities of color. Furthermore, women and women's issues were strongly represented in all groups. On average, 80 percent of workshop participants were women, and welfare reform was a dominant issue.

Our first workshops drew from my and Sharon Kurtz's preexisting activist contacts with labor and housing groups. These workshops were sweat-equity arrangements; activist groups would find a space, do photocopying, and provide child care and food. MRAP's initial office was a box in the corner of Bill Gamson's office. In a phone interview for our first grant, the foundation asked if MRAP had an office. "I'm standing in it," I said, stepping into the box.

By 1988, MRAP had simplified framing into three key questions activists should ask themselves:

- What is the main issue or problem?
- Who is responsible?
- What are the viable solutions?

After helping groups focus on a core message or frame, we worked together to identify emotion-laden symbols or anecdotes that could illustrate the frame/story line (Gamson and Lasch 1983). Given my own Irish American working-class upbringing, I used stories as popular carriers of collective action frames. As modern parables, stories were favored by labor and community activists alike; in storytelling activists linked their lived experience to their shared collective action frame. Moreover, stories met journalistic norms for news whereas explicit frames reside in editorials.

During the next five years, we conducted workshops for over two hundred organizations. For the workshops, we translated core teachings into metaphors, drawings, sayings, stories, and games. From workshop participants' reactions, we developed more insights and stories to plough back into the presentations. Then, from stories told by workshop veterans, I began documenting the movement group's best framing practices and outstanding problems (Ryan 1991).

These experiences led us to see that activists operated within a truth/falsehood logic. Many activist groups—except legal advocates trained to prepare cases—believed that facts should "speak for themselves." To them, preparing spokespersons with a preframed message felt dishonest. Similarly, they were uncomfortable practicing responses to challenging questions that might be posed by opponents. Implicitly, activists thought of themselves as representing a repressed truth while their opponents represented slick misrepresentations.

As such, they expected content to take care of itself. It was simply the truth. They focused on form, assuming that good visuals and clever sound bites would ensure access. When media coverage failed to materialize, activists tended to dismiss their chances of breaking into mass media, seeing the power inequalities as insurmountable.

Watching activists slide into despair, MRAP realized that the key to strengthening collective action framing rested not in the frame—the fossil of political discourse—but in strengthening the framer, the collective actor. We began to help groups integrate framing as a component of strategic planning. In workshops we would say, *"There is no communication strategy without an organizing strategy."*

To move the work forward, we focused on longer-term partnerships. Picking ten groups committed to sustained collaboration, we established a more intensive program to build their capacity to talk politics, stressing the ties between leaders' growth and organizational infrastructure. The groups learned to use framing to engage in internal political dialogue and external coalition building. And we developed translational and collaborative research projects focused on talking politics. Our work with the Rhode Island Coalition against Domestic Violence is a case in point.

Translational Research—RICADV Develops Collective Framing Practices

MRAP's relationship with the Rhode Island Coalition against Domestic Violence grew from prior framing workshops. In 1996, housing and welfare rights organizer Karen Jeffreys assumed a new position as communications director for the RICADV, a statewide coalition whose mission is to end domestic violence in Rhode Island. The organization was just developing its communications systems, and Jeffreys asked me/MRAP to collaborate. Jeffreys was skeptical of academic social sciences, yet conversant in its lingo. She had attended MRAP's framing workshops, and we were friends.

A working relationship with RICADV offered some major advantages over MRAP's prior collaborations. First, the coalition had sufficient resources to undertake a serious communications initiative; Jeffrey's hiring represented that. Second, as a statewide initiative, RICADV sponsored legislative policy initiatives as well as direct organizing; our collaboration would allow us to experiment with integrating communication strategies with political strategies. Finally, in Rhode Island's midsized media market, forty-third largest of the United States' two hundred media markets, RICADV's modest resources could bankroll communications campaigns as regular components of organizing and policy campaigns.

From the outset, RICADV and MRAP agreed to take a multiyear approach to improving communication; over seven years, we developed a full set of communications systems and established RICADV as Rhode Island's leading source regarding domestic violence. RICADV began by establishing clipping files that provided a robust introduction to the Rhode Island media market. Through the clippings, RICADV familiarized itself with the existing political discourse vis-à-vis domestic violence and started what became a comprehensive media database of reporters and outlets. As relations with reporters deepened, RICADV created a handbook for journalists highlighting best practices and offering advice from multiple perspectives—advocates, court officials, survivors, journalists, and framing theorists (RICADV 2000).

RICADV Systematizes Framing

With RICADV, MRAP had an opportunity to share its understanding of framing, then watch as RICADV elaborated its own approach. I had told RICADV that some activists, if alone when the media calls, phone someone to talk through their framing before returning the media call. RICADV's Jeffreys took this idea to its logical consequences, creating a routinized process through which RICADV activists could work together—caucus—to frame messages. Jeffreys adapted the questions MRAP posed in workshops, translating them into a work sheet format. The media caucus helped RICADV's staff and members frame messages quickly using the caucus sheet as a structure. This led to the formalized practice of caucusing whenever the coalition faced unfolding events. After each caucus, the caucus forms were archived for future reference, becoming part of RICADV's collective memory.

Jeffreys called the first caucus in November 1998. Construction workers found Betty Sue Gillespie's body in an attic crawl space at her home. She had been missing for a month. Her husband was charged and later convicted of strangling her to death and hiding her body. Upon hearing of the murder, Karen Jeffreys called all available RICADV staff and members to frame a joint message. The staff remembers this first caucus:

KAREN: When we heard about the Gillespie murder, we held our first formal caucus to prepare what we were going to say. We were coming out with "Domestic violence is bad, and blah, blah, blah" . . . a talking head, no feeling when someone had just been brutally murdered.

ANGELA: We were sitting there brainstorming about what we would say, just throwing around sound bites.

KAREN: At first we had said, "Act now. Stop the violence! Get answers, get help, get involved." . . . All the things you'd say at the end of a flyer.

ANGELA: And I thought, "Wait a minute. To me, we're not connected."

KAREN: And Angela stopped and said, "You know what? We have to say that we give a damn. This woman just died! We need to say, 'Our hearts go out to her family.' Our reaction is, 'We are horrified!'" The caucus gave us time to step back and think about what we were saying, and one of the things we wanted to say was that we were sad for this family.

ANGELA: We were doing all these sound bites, when we needed to be thinking about the family watching this, that these are not just words, that these are stories about someone's life and be aware of how hard emotionally it is.

KAREN: And the very first question the reporter asked us was, "What is the Coalition's reaction to hearing about this?"

ALICE: Our response was perfect. After someone's been stuffed in a closet for a month, it would have been inappropriate if not disrespectful to say, "Get answers, get help, get involved!" It just would not work. (RICADV 2003)

After its first trial caucus, RICADV drew several lessons, the most basic being that framing a message collectively was infinitely superior to previous arrangements in which a spokesperson and perhaps a second person labored in isolation. The experience of framing messages in real time—in response to actual situations—also reinforced other insights into the framing process. Messages are dialogues with specific audiences debating historical events. Nonverbal elements—visual and emotional—are essential. Visual and emotional elements include picking a messenger with whom the targeted audiences will identify easily.

Over the next three years, the caucus became increasingly sophisticated as the organization set clear strategic priorities and developed written cultural agreements spelling out the group's core values as respect, equality, and diversity. Every available staff person or member was expected to drop what he or she was doing to join the caucus. The caucus became a recurring opportunity for staff and members to discuss how their shared values, mission, and strategy could be forwarded by responding to events not of their own making, such as domestic violence murders.

The coalition's careful record keeping and community outreach further enhanced the framing effort. From its files, coalition staff could pull the work sheet of every caucus held, past news coverage of comparable situations, past writings of specific reporters. Legislative lobbying developed RICADV's understanding of state political dynamics, and its trainings for school, police, and emergency room and court personnel strengthened and expanded its networks. As its networks and infrastructure grew, RICADV entered each media caucus with more information—from reporters, police, its clipping files, and its notes on prior caucuses. In the caucus, they framed this information to promote their strategic perspective.

Caucusing as a group increased RICADV's message consistency—each staff member learned how the others thought. In collectively framing their actions, RICADV staff and members reaffirmed the connection between happenings in the world, their core values and daily efforts, and their mission of ending domestic violence. Caucuses became moments of political sharing in which the collective staff thought as a whole, framing a message that used the historical moment to convey via the mass media the organization's core values/ideology and its strategic priorities. Caucuses felt important. They represented a lived experience of simultaneous movement building and movement extension as they shared their framings with wider audiences.

A Typical Media Caucus

By 2000, the caucus had evolved into a routine organizational practice. If a reporter calls while communications staff are unavailable, others initiate the caucus. Typically, a staff member pre-interviews the inquiring reporter to find out as much as possible about the crisis at hand and the reporter's angle on that crisis. Then a caucus is held: "Everyone comes in whether you are an intern, executive director; we all sit down and we all talk about the message" (Mao Yang, in RICADV 2003). The caucus has three parts—thinking through message framing, identifying and answering the hard questions that reporters might ask, and practice.

> During our media caucus, we think both about message and positioning the message—what's the hook, what's the angle? We also ask ourselves what questions the reporter might ask, the obvious questions as well as questions that are hard to answer. And we prepare answers as a staff. We think through visuals as well. (Mao Yang, in ibid.)

Then the actual practice begins. RICADV separates the task of developing the message from the task of selecting and preparing the messenger. Everyone contributes to the message, but the group chooses a spokesperson most likely to connect to the audiences being prioritized for this event or issue. The caucus and spokesperson think about the emotions to be conveyed along with the frame/story:

> The caucus gives us a change to step back and think about what we are saying—nonverbal messages as well as verbal ones. To convey emotion, I think about the emotion I want to convey—that these are not just words—these are stories about someone's life. If someone's been murdered or killed, it's particularly important to pay attention to feelings. (Angela Wade-Nash, in RICADV 2003)

After the action unfolds, coalition staff and volunteers debrief. They evaluate media coverage, reflect on its effectiveness, and plan any changes.

Framing training gradually extended outward, with workshops established for survivors, then with local member organizations. As the coalition grew in staff power, it also offered to maintain basic systems for member organizations, extending the resources of the central staff to other organizations in the coalition such as SOAR (Sisters Overcoming Abusive Relationships), an organization of domestic violence survivors. Hand in hand, framing capacity grew as RICADV grew in strength as a collective actor capable of thinking collectively under pressure. As domestic survivor and SOAR member Gretchen Nelson put it, "I went from being talked about to being involved in the talk" (RICADV 2003).

Nelson's distinction, "being involved in the talk" as contrasted to "being talked about," captures the transformation that RICADV caucus participants experience. Even those caucus participants who never become spokespersons reiterate that their participation in RICADV's message caucuses made them feel part of a collective actor, and thus they feel larger than themselves. In telling their story, they contribute to the organization's change goals by providing spokespersons who can link policy concerns to direct experience. SOAR also develops survivors as leaders and public spokespersons by providing framing preparation and post–media event support for speakers. In sum, as organized by RICADV, the caucus represents not simply a collective action frame but the collective actor framing.

Message development and dissemination becomes a collective process in which many participate. Backed by policy supports, training supports, and media and court infrastructures, survivors who could have felt that they were being used as token poster children for domestic violence stop feeling that their story has been stolen, expropriated. Instead, they feel that in telling their story, they have appropriated/repossessed their own lives.

The meaning grows out of the story being attached to a call for change; survivors repeat their stories because they believe they will have an effect, that their experience will benefit and protect someone else. RICADV, in systematizing its work, illustrates MRAP's saying, "If it takes a whole village to raise a child, it takes a whole movement to raise an issue." Through the media caucus, RICADV's spokespersons benefit from everyone's ideas, and everyone learns how to frame a message, and the resulting framing respects the entire collective actor. "This system helps everyone learn. It means that everyone owns a piece of the story and a piece of the message" (Karen Jeffreys, in RICADV 2003).

An intern explains:

> It was cool how everyone was kind of involved; they all focused on what they were going to say. They all came to work together; it wasn't like a bunch of people shouting things at one another. It was very organized. . . . I had wondered, "How do these people know what to say on camera?" Then I saw, "Oh, they have a media caucus!" (Sarah De Cataldo, in RICADV 2003)

The process deepened the political unity of the group. Caucus conversations would spill over into lunch conversations, and reflection became embedded in the organization's culture. Once the caucus had been institutionalized, the learning exploded: "After the caucus we would debrief and realize they had asked almost all the questions that we had prepared. Debriefing came naturally as part of being systematic—once we had a caucus, we had a system!" (Angela Wade Nash, in RICADV 2003).

One intern captures how the media caucuses reinforce participants' commitment to the mission and to the domestic violence movement:

> I knew I wanted to change the world. Working here, I learned to connect my heart and my words. RICADV had a clear message: domestic violence—it IS your business. Here I learned about the work and heart and knowledge that lie behind the message. It's not just about the message. It's about all the people who put it together, all the work they put into it, all the time—everything that creates the message. It's about so much more than that one phrase. It's the heart and work behind the message—all the ideas, values, discussions, training, and work to disseminate the message, all the outreach. (Sarah De Cataldo, in RICADV 2003)

As a conscious, intentional practice, the caucus can be transferred easily to other counterhegemonic battles. RICADV interns now staffing other organizations apply the caucus to these settings with similar results:

> The best part is this: We run this conflict resolution program with kids at the middle school, and the kids wanted to propose all these changes to make the school safer. So two days after I had learned to do a media caucus, we did a media caucus with the kids to prepare them to talk to the principal. And the kids loved it. They were so well prepared. After the kids left the principal said, "Wow, the kids were so eloquent, so prepared." (Titus Dos Remedios, in RICADV 2003)

The caucus, along with other participatory practices, transformed RICADV's communications work: from being invisible, RICADV became the preeminent source in its state for domestic violence. Moreover, it shifted the framing of domestic violence (Ryan, Anastario, and DaCunha forthcoming) and successfully moved its legislative agenda (RICADV 2004).

MRAP's Bridging Role with RICADV

I have yet to describe how I, representing MRAP, contributed to RICADV's evolution. Over time, MRAP and RICADV's collaborative partnership had deepened. Initially, I served as an unpaid consultant; RICADV public relations director Karen Jeffreys would phone when she wanted a second opinion. Sometimes, at RICADV's request, I conducted framing workshops and trainings similar to those described above. Then, at RICADV's request, MRAP interns and I used RICADV clipping files to analyze news coverage. We began to help on other studies and projects; on some RICADV took the lead while MRAP led others. For instance, RICADV led and MRAP participated in creating *A Handbook for Journalists: How to Cover*

Domestic Violence (2000). MRAP then led and RICADV participated in an evaluation of the handbook's impact (Ryan, Anastario, and DaCunha forthcoming).

From early on, we've maintained an open-phone policy; Karen calls, I sit at my computer and type as we talk; our conversations represent an ongoing journal, a log of crises, unanswered questions, and future projects. While at first I was the teacher, over time, teaching became increasingly two-way: Jeffreys and other RICADV staff began to join me in other settings to share what we've learned. Now RICADV teaches framing workshops across the nation.

As RICADV and SOAR have developed critical insights into the framing process, my discussions with them have become far more central to my own learning. At RICADV's urging, I began taping long conversations with RICADV staff and SOAR. The interviews increased RICADV's internal awareness of the learning they had consolidated. Transcribing the tapes, I realized that my paraphrased renditions of their framing practices were poor substitutes for their own words; my writing began to include longer and longer quotations from our interviews. The more I listened, the more I learned.

My role had evolved over time from an itinerant teacher of framing techniques into a regular collaborator. RICADV had grown and changed over time as well; reflection was now built into many of its practices. As an outside listener, I encouraged, but by no means created, the space for reflection. RICADV restructured itself as a learning organization (Linnell, Radosevich, and Spack 2002), consolidating its learning through routine cycles of thinking, listening, speaking/acting, and reflecting. In fact, MRAP has adopted RICADV's organizational culture, making our bridging two-way: always sharing mission—communication for social change— we now share tools, language, core values, and rules of engagement. The flow of ideas, resources, people, and projects between our two locations is fluid, and both parties see our collaboration as valuable and empowering.

RICADV and I now collaborate to share its practices beyond its immediate networks. We have just finished a story-filled manual documenting how RICADV organizes and communicates (RICADV 2004). Two years in the writing, the manual involved group discussion of main lessons, workshops attended by coalitions from thirty-seven states to test RICADV's framing methods, thirty interviews with key participants, and three drafts read by committee. With RICADV joining in theorizing, the flow across the bridge becomes increasingly two-way.

Discussion

So what have I and MRAP learned from the entwined sagas of bridgework and the framing experiments that the bridge supported? I've learned that bridgework is a sine qua non if we are to build counterhegemonic theories and practices that help collective actors challenge inequalities. I've learned that bridgework needs to be two-way, horizontal, and sustained as contrasted to one-way, hierarchical (researcher/subject), and fragmented, all common problems in academic-activist joint ventures. Moreover, RICADV and MRAP's success depended on our amassing sufficient infrastructure to establish consistent collaboration over an extended time period.

Bridgework Needs Infrastructure

It seems obvious in retrospect that, to sustain its work, MRAP would have to develop infrastructure, to become an institution in its own right. Thinking primarily in terms of breaking the isolation by building working relationships, however, we initially underestimated the need for a separate bridging institution (see Goodson, ch. 12 this volume.) Naively, I expected to function like a modern Friar Tuck; as a contingent academic in a secularized information age, I would funnel social capital to movement groups just as the mendicant monk Friar Tuck, a similarly marginal character in church-driven medieval England, slipped resources to Robin Hood (Kern 2000). Bill Gamson was my modern equivalent of Friar Tuck's sympathizing abbot; an established scholar, his participation eased access to university resources—computers, Internet, phones, libraries, space, and so on. Paying minimal attention to institution building, we focused on bridging the divide by sharing what we knew best—framing theory.

I also learned that my success as a bridge worker rested on the good will of respected, well-established residents of the disparate social worlds I proposed to bridge. I needed someone to create entry points for me as a bridge worker and for my companions from the other world. In MRAP, we came to call those who provided entry "edge walkers," masters at functioning within their existing culture and yet open to exploring new vistas. Edge walkers resemble Robnett's bridge leaders (1997), but are institutional insiders; they open their institution and its resources to others. Edge walkers and bridge workers counsel, shelter, and push each other.

Gamson functioned as an edge walker to make MRAP viable; his academic credentials opened the opportunity of running a weekly seminar committed to both social movement scholarship and movement-theorist engagement. Once established, the seminar attracted more edge walkers, bridge workers, and travelers. Similarly, within collective actors, someone plays edge walker, the person willing to invest labor and resources in exploring the merits of collaboration with other worlds. Within RICADV, Karen Jeffreys was the edge walker who solicited MRAP's involvement.

Bridge established, I described how MRAP and RICADV undertook to develop RICADV's intentional framing practices as undertaken from an indigenous perspective. Working with RICADV, I learned that collective action framing is not only about developing a product—a frame for dissemination. In the framing process, the collective actor creates and consolidates itself: the collective actor's individual members read the world and forge a shared response to their particular historical conjuncture. Individual participants' life experiences, cultures, and values fuel the collective action framing process. The framing's focus, however, comes from the collective actor's strategy. Strategy emerges as individuals operating in the persona of the collective actor apply a shared worldview and mission to their reading of the historical circumstances. Through the prism of this strategy, collective actors frame their organizational message.[2]

My collaboration with RICADV was especially valuable in exploring framing as a process through which a collective actor addresses internal differences. While creating this collective action frame/counternarrative, the collective actor must be attentive to its own internal multiplicity of values, views, interests, and oppressions. Structural inequalities of citizenship status, language, class, race, sexuality, gender, and age create countercurrents within the collective actor and must be addressed. Hegemony is not just "out there." This point holds true for activists and for social movement theorists; awareness of the social construction of reality does not release us from hegemonic constraints: history binds us.

I also came to appreciate Steinberg's (1999) insight that framing is an innately dialogic process; individual participants in the collective actor dialogue about differences as they frame a public message. The dialogue continues as the collective actor uses the mass media to intentionally extend its external communications. Dialogue and more dialogue ensues as the collective actor uses frames to consolidate members, strengthen alliances, woo supporters, and/or isolate opponents. Mass media outlets are not ends in themselves but conduits to dialogue with their desired audiences. Collective action framing, in short, is an exercise in movement building, not merely an exercise in crafting a standpoint.

Many valuable studies of collective action frames focus on frames as products created and disseminated in historical time and space. While valuable, these insufficiently capture collective action framing as a lived process in which the framer, the collective actor conscious of its mission and world-view, develops and promotes a strategic response to structural barriers. As such, framing is both process and product (Carragee and Roefs 2004). Framing becomes an iterative practice through which a collective actor creates its strategy-laden message, mobilizes support for that strategy, and, in doing so, trains new generations of members and allies to do likewise. In connecting "heart and mind and action" (Sarah DeCataldo, in RICADV 2003) through the prism of conscious collective strategy, RICADV caucus participants experience counterhegemony lived; through counterhegemonic framing practices, they transform patterns of social ties (Diani 2000).

This case is strongly reminiscent of the work of Belenky et al. (1997). Working with rural working-class women in an adult education context, they stress the synergistic potential of learning that connected heart, mind, and action. This "really talking," they suggest, is life changing for those involved:

> "Really talking" requires careful listening; it implies a mutually shared agreement that together you are creating the optimum setting so that half-baked or emergent ideas can grow. "Real talk" reaches deep into the experience of each participant; it also draws on the analytical abilities of each. Conversation, as constructivists describe it, includes discourse and exploration, talking and listening, questions, argument, speculation and sharing. . . . The capacity for speaking with and listening to others while simultaneously speaking with and listening to the self is an achievement that allows a conversation to open between constructivists and the world. (Belenky et al. 1997, 143)

Belenky, Clinchy, Goldberger, and Tarule's description of the social construction of knowledge as highly relational runs parallel with the process of a collective actor engaged in framing. Their insights rooted in U.S. women's movements also resonate strongly with Italian social movement theorist Mario Diani's urging that framing theorists attend to the importance of relationships (2000).

Applied to collective actors, connected learning—"really talking"—explains what collective actors do when they create frames and enter political discourse. RICADV's experiences illustrate this relation-centered, materially grounded understanding of collective action framing—collective actors framing—as a life-changing, counterhegemonic practice.

The phrase "really talking politics" captures these essentials of collective action framing. First, talking—unlike text as product of discourse—is embodied; concrete actors located in historical time and space engage in dialogue. Second, the focus is politics—citizens, usually groups of citizens organized into parties and/or social movements, take sides as they negotiate their relationship to governance. By governance, I mean not formal power alone but rather "the human ability to transform existing reality and create a new one . . . men/women as social beings [exercising] the right and the power to intervene in the social order and change it through political praxis" (Freire 1994, 12).

In describing "real talk," Belenky et al. focus on *individual* growth through connected learning. Social movements accomplish the same on the level of a collectivity: if "real talk" is conversation between individuals that matters, "real talk" about politics is political discourse that matters. Really talking politics acknowledges power and its inequalities—*whose accounts count.* In really talking politics—for RICADV, talking politics through the media caucus—the collective actor forms and promotes collective action frames that represent its strategic intervention in the existing hegemonic order.

Like "real talk," RICADV's framing practices are collaborative and respect each individual's contribution. While "real talk" described a learning culture that mobilizes individuals to take charge of their individual lives, RICADV's caucuses function as part of a collective learning culture through which the collective actor, RICADV, mobilizes its staff, members, their bases, and other allies.

The two experiences—really talking and really talking politics—coexist. For RICADV, collective action framing via the media caucus is a counter-hegemonic practice; through it individuals forge a collective actor that engages in "connected knowing"—"really talking politics." As explained by SOAR member Gretchen Nelson (RICADV 2003), they become part of the action—their individual account counts in the collective account. Personal transformation and social transformation reinforce each other.

In forming a collective actor, individual activists jointly interpret how power or, more precisely, inequalities of power shape their life chances. They discuss the sources of and their responses to those inequalities of power. And they seek eagerly to win others to their vision. Through collaboration with RICADV, I began to see how some debates in the academic framing literature could be resolved, and in MRAP I began to describe collective action framing as "really talking politics."

MRAP's collaborations have taught us respect for the framer; collective actors create and sponsor the collective action frames produced by their political discussions and analyses. Individuals may be silently or vocally disenchanted with their reality. Many complain to friends and coworkers. They dream of other possibilities but can enter the political process proactively only when they form a collective actor, an organization sharing values, mission, and strategies. Without an organization, individual impact on political discourse is limited. Challenging modern mass media systems takes serious and sustained resources. The ability to create and disseminate a shared reframing of social reality distinguishes collective actors from individuals.

For social movements, collective action framing practices create a counternarrative that forwards a counterhegemonic worldview: collective actors challenge existing social arrangements by establishing new affirmative relationships and offering counterhegemonic interpretations of current events. Pressing for new advantage within existing discourses and institutions, framing contests resist and challenge existing inequalities of power. Tentatively, provisionally, participants in the framing process experience counterhegemony lived.

Thus, the collective actor functions simultaneously within an existing culture and an imagined better world. With each crisis and responsive framing process, the collective actor positions itself to play within the dominant culture and yet break with it in significant ways. Through its members' actions and stories, it tells audiences steeped in that dominant culture about possibilities imagined but not yet real—"What life would be like if it were fair," explained community activists in another MRAP collaboration (City Life/Vida Urbana 1999).

The Limits of This Discussion

In painting our bridgework in broad strokes, I underplay its messiness; bridges are construction sites before they become shining landmarks. Even in our success, MRAP and RICADV are hounded by resource constraints, hostile political winds, and recurring tensions between academia and activism. Working against the current has its rewards, but our bridgework lacks a safety net. The realization that MRAP's permanence is not assured heightens my responsibility as a bridge worker to share the lessons we have learned.

Conclusion

To illustrate our best bridging practices, I have described how a small group of framing theorists (MRAP) developed collaborative working relationships with a collective actor, Rhode Island Coalition against Domestic Violence. MRAP's seven-year collaboration with RICADV blossomed practically and theoretically. RICADV changed news coverage of domestic violence in Rhode Island and diffused its model throughout the nation. Both groups deepened their understanding of counterhegemonic collective framing processes, how a collective actor challenging inequality in a particular historical conjuncture taps all its cultural resources—its members' lives, shared values, mission, and strategy. Moreover, we came to see how collective action framing could function as a recurring experience of counterhegemony lived; through the media caucus and other organizational practices, RICADV participants create routines that embody the fairer life they imagine and work for.

Despite its tremendous potential, our collaborative relationship remains compromised by existing institutional constraints—the inequalities of power that shape both our social locations. Our existing relationships, pressures, routines, and cultures keep us in check. For both MRAP and RICADV, hegemony is lived (Bourdieu 1977; Williams 1977). But within these relations we find room for change: counterhegemony is also lived.

I have argued that theorists, like activists, are socially bounded and must work consciously and strategically to create and maintain counterhegemonic practices from within their academic habitus. This work—bridgework—cannot be sustained by individual academics, nor will occasional collective acts suffice. To transform the academic habitus, i.e., to live counterhegemonically, theorists, like activists, need to build collective actors.

Notes

For extensive feedback, I thank editors David Croteau and Bill Hoynes, and the Media Research and Action Project; Eitan Alimi, Kevin Carragee, Bill Gamson, Adria Goodson, Sharon Kurtz, Jeff Langstraat, Sarah Pabst, Jordi Trullen, Owen Whooley, and Matt Williams.

1. Eitan Alimi noted this similarity (personal correspondence, May 15, 2004).

2. I thank Eitan Alimi for helping me articulate this.

References

Albrecht, Lisa, and Rose Brewer, eds. 1990. *Bridges of Power: Women's Multicultural Alliances.* Philadelphia: New Society Publishers.

Anzaldúa, Gloria. 1990. "Bridge, Drawbridge, Sandbar, or Island: Lesbians of Color Haciendo Alianzas." In *Bridges of Power: Women's Multicultural Alliances,* ed. Lisa Albrecht and Rose Brewer, 216–31. Philadelphia: New Society Publishers.

Belenky, Mary, Blythe Clinchy, Nancy Goldberger, and Jill Tarule. 1997. *Women's Ways of Knowing: The Development of Self, Voice, and Mind.* New York: Basic Books.

Benford, Robert. 1997. "An Insider's Critique of the Social Movement Framing Perspective." *Sociological Inquiry* 67: 409–30.

Benford, Robert, and David Snow. 2000. "Framing Processes and Social Movements: An Overview and Assessment." *Annual Review of Sociology* 26: 611–37.

Bourdieu, Pierre. 1977. *Outline of a Theory of Practice.* Cambridge: Cambridge University Press.

Burawoy, Michael, Alice Burton, Ann A. Ferguson, Kathryn J. Fox, Joshua Gamson, Nadine Gartrell, Leslie Hurst, et al. 1992. *Ethnography Unbound: Power and Resistance in the Modern Metropolis.* Berkeley: University of California Press.

Carragee, Kevin, and Wim Roefs. 2004. "The Neglect of Power in Recent Framing Research." *Journal of Communication* 54, no. 2 (June): 214–33.

City Life/Vida Urbana. 1999. Comments in workshop. December 12, 1999.

Diani, Mario. 2000. "The Relational Deficit of Ideologically Structured Action." *Mobilization: An International Journal* 5, no. 1: 17–24.

Donati, Paolo. 1992. "Political Discourse Analysis." In *Studying Collective Action,* ed. Mario Diani and Ron Eyerman, 136–67. London: Sage.

———. 1996. "Building a Unified Movement: Resource Mobilization, Media Work, and Organizational Transformation in the Italian Environmentalist Movement." *Research in Social Movements, Conflicts, and Change* 19: 125–57.

Ferree, Myra, William Gamson, Jürgen Gerhards, and Dieter Rucht. 2002. *Shaping Abortion Discourse: Democracy and the Public Sphere in Germany and the United States.* Cambridge: Cambridge University Press.

Freire, Paolo. 1994. Foreword to *Participatory Communication: Working for Change and Development,* ed. Shirley White with K. Sadanandan Nair and Joseph Ascroft, 12–14. New Delhi: Sage.

Gamson, William A. 1992. *Talking Politics.* Cambridge: Cambridge University Press.

———. 1998. "Social Movements and Cultural Change." In *From Contention to Democracy,* ed. Marco Giugni, Doug McAdam, and Charles Tilly, 57–77. New York: Rowman and Littlefield.

Gamson, William. A., and Kathryn E. Lasch. 1983. "The Political Culture of Social Welfare Policy." In *Evaluating the Welfare State: Social and Political Perspectives,* ed. Shimon E. Spiro and Ephraim Yuchtman-Yaar, 397–415. New York: Academic Press.

Gottfried, Heidi, ed. 1996. *Feminism and Social Change: Bridging Theory and Practice.* Urbana: University of Illinois.

Kern, Maurice. 2000. *The Outlaw of Medieval Legend.* New York: Routledge.

Linnell, Deborah, Zora Radosevich, and Jonathan Spack. 2002. *Executive Directors Guide for Successful Nonprofit Management.* Boston: United Way of Massachusetts Bay.

McAdam, Doug, Sidney Tarrow, and Charles Tilly. 2001. *Dynamics of Contention.* New York: Cambridge University Press.

Moraga, Cherríe, and Gloria Anzaldúa. 1983. *This Bridge Called My Back.* New York: Kitchen Table Press.

Morris, Aldon. 1984. *The Origins of the Civil Rights Movement.* New York: Free Press.

MRAP (Media Research and Action Project). 1997. "Mission Statement." Unpublished.

Oliver, Pamela, and Hank Johnston. 2000. "What a Good Idea! Ideologies and Frames in Social Movement Research." *Mobilization: An International Journal* 4, no. 1: 37–54.

RICADV (Rhode Island Coalition against Domestic Violence). 2000. *Domestic Violence: A Handbook for Journalists.* Providence: RICADV.

———. 2003. Interviews by Charlotte Ryan, September–December 2003.

———. 2004. *Putting the Public in Public Relations: Participatory Communication for Social Change.* Providence: RICADV.

Robnett, Belinda. 1997. *How Long? How Long? African-American Women in the Struggle for Civil Rights.* New York: Oxford University Press.

Ryan, Charlotte. 1991. *Prime Time Activism: Media Strategies for Grassroots Organizing.* Boston: South End Press.

Ryan, Charlotte, Michael Anastario, and Alfredo DaCunha. Forthcoming. "Changing Coverage of Domestic Violence Murders: A Longitudinal Experiment in Participatory Communication." *Journal of Interpersonal Violence.*

Snow, David, and Robert Benford. 1988. "Ideology, Frame Resonance, and Participant Mobilization." *International Social Movement Research* 1: 197–217.

———. 1992. "Master Frames and Cycles of Protest." In *Frontiers in Social Movement Theory,* ed. Aldon Morris and Carol Mueller, 133–55. New Haven, CT: Yale University Press.

———. 2000. "Clarifying the Relationship between Framing and Ideology." *Mobilization: An International Journal* 5, no. 1: 55–60.

Steinberg, Marc. 1999. "The Talk and Back Talk of Collective Action: A Dialogic Analysis of Repertoires of Discourse among Nineteenth-Century English Cotton Spinners." *American Journal of Sociology* 105, no. 3: 736–80.

Stout, Linda. 1996. *Bridging the Class Divide and Other Lessons for Grassroots Organizing.* Boston: Beacon Press.

Williams, Raymond. 1977. *Marxism and Literature.* Oxford: Oxford University Press.

8

Feminist Research and Activism: Challenges of Hierarchy in a Cross-National Context

Myra Marx Ferree, Valerie Sperling, and Barbara Risman

Organizational hierarchies and differences in the social power and material resources that participants bring to a group are familiar sources of problems for social movements. Both scholars and activists in a variety of movements have noted the conflicts among participants and the shifts in movement goals that can result from power struggles. Differences among participants or between members and leaders in an organization have been the primary focus of attention (Michels [1910] 1998; Polletta 2002). In this chapter, we shift the lens slightly to look at the power relationships between nonlocal academics, who want both to study and to collaborate with local social movements, and local activists, who may also be academics but who are more directly engaged in building the movement. We see this as a matter of strategic interaction, where all parties have multiple interests and identities that are under negotiation. These interactions can be especially complicated, as they were in this case, by differences among the parties in nationality, political culture, and material resources.

We begin with a brief discussion of the politics underlying the emergence of a transnational women's movement. We proceed to reflect on the context of research with women's groups in post-totalitarian Russia. As feminist researchers who also consider themselves activists, our experiences lead us to investigate the complicated ways that hierarchies manifest themselves in social movements where the identities of activist, researcher, and "expert" are continually reassessed. We then discuss some of the general theoretical questions we bring to the analysis that follows. We finally move to an exploration of what our encounters with the Russian women's movement taught us about hierarchies, power, and inclusive learning in social movements, focusing especially on how local grassroots work can and should expand a culture of conversation in which participants learn to see themselves as expert and take ownership of making social change.

Transnational Women's Movements

Negotiations over the meaning of a movement and the specific nature of movement goals have been very evident in the debates over feminism that have been happening transnationally. The UN-sponsored World Conferences on Women and their associated forums of nongovernmental organizations involved tens of thousands of women from all over the world. While the first UN conference, held in Mexico City in 1975, produced confrontations between participants from the global South and those from more affluent countries, intervening decades saw a gradual process of increasing consensus that women's rights and status were inevitably tied to issues of development and social justice that were not gender-specific. In the 1990s, the issues of what feminism means, who would call themselves feminists and why, and how gender equity relates to other social movements for justice and rights remained core debates within the increasingly transnational women's movement.

How effective this emerging transnational women's movement has been in legitimizing gender equality as a political goal is unclear. On the one hand, the 1995 governmental and nongovernmental organization conferences on women held in Beijing drew approximately thirty thousand women, and the Plan for Action that was formulated there was endorsed by the majority of the world's governments. This suggests that demanding gender justice has become normatively acceptable across the globe (Naples and Desai 2002). Even countries far from realizing this goal sometimes accepted strategies for empowering women as a legitimate form of politics. On the other hand, the collapse of communism, the fission of the USSR into Russia and a number of smaller successor states, the transformation of Eastern European governments, and the redrawing of the national boundaries in the former Czechoslovakia, Yugoslavia, and Germany were frequently accompanied by rollbacks in the political representation of women and controversy over whether feminism was just a "Western import" (Einhorn 1993; Funk and Mueller 1993; Gal and Kligman 2000). The stigma attached to feminism and the marginalization of women from political institutions was still powerfully evident in this transformation.

The end of the Soviet Union was also a watershed in the development of democratic politics. The overbearing influence of the Communist party and

Soviet Army had blocked the emergence of multiparty democracies and participatory forms of civil society throughout its sphere of influence. The end of totalitarianism in so many countries at once created enormous interest in the West in what kind of new democracies would be constructed in Russia and Eastern Europe. Western experts, often economists, frequently came as consultants to governments, and foundations in the United States and Western Europe invested in supporting a variety of emerging nongovernmental organizations in these countries. A key interest was in helping local groups form, both to be advocates for the interests of their members with government and to be the direct providers of social services and support to citizens, from training them to run businesses to counseling victims of domestic violence. Although the Western investment in developing free markets and an active civil society applied to both men and women, quite a few of these interventions were specifically designed to empower women as entrepreneurs and activists. Because the post-totalitarian societies of the USSR and Eastern Europe lacked a fund-raising infrastructure for nonprofit organizations such as those found in the West, these resources played an important role in supporting many women's groups in the region (Sperling 1999).

The Context of Our Research

As American feminist academics with activist backgrounds and inclinations, we began a collaborative study of Russian feminist mobilization in 1994. In partnership with the Moscow Center for Gender Studies, Barbara had gotten funding for an exploratory meeting on possible collaborative social science work on gender in Russia from the National Science Foundation in 1992. At that exploratory meeting, Barbara and Myra met a former leader of the American Association of University Women (who was then working in Moscow on training seminars for women activists), some of the Russians the leader was working with in Tver and other cities around the country, and several Russian feminists active in the Moscow Center for Gender Studies, one of the first and most strongly institutionalized of the new feminist organizations springing up like mushrooms in Russia in the early 1990s. Barbara and Myra found interest there in starting some research on feminism in Russia. Valentina Konstaninova, from the Moscow Center, was particularly interested in research on the emerging women's movement, though she was quick to say that such research should serve the needs of the movement and not become "the tail wagging the dog." Valerie, who at that time was conducting fieldwork for her dissertation on the Russian women's movement, also joined our research team.

Our initial intention was to study the emergence of a women's movement and to help in any way we could to assist its birth. We wanted to understand what was bringing Russian women to feminism (or not), how it spoke to their needs or aspirations, what organizational strategies for recruitment to activism were working, and what specific impediments they faced. Our actual research focused on a series of seminars on women's civic activism that the American organizer and her Russian coleader conducted in Zhukovsky, Obninsk, Cheboksary, Tver, Novocherkassk, Izhevsk, and Ekaterinburg in 1995–96 (Ferree et al. 1999; Sperling, Ferree, and Risman 2001). These seminars were pitched as creating a "Women's Agenda," and were designed to educate local women in largely Western techniques for promoting women's interests through civic activism, such as lobbying, media outreach, and so on. With the seminar leaders' cooperation, Valentina and Valerie were allowed to attend the seminars, although the constraints placed on their participation varied at different times, as we will later discuss. We conducted surveys (collaboratively developed by the research team) of participants at some sites, had focus group discussions at some sites, and had a participant-observer taking field notes at some sites, but we never had all three types of data together at any one site, since the research also needed to fit into the schedule for training. We ended up focusing our research on the interactions between the activist seminar leaders and the local activists who participated in the seminars because that is where our data was best. However, we could also describe and differentiate among the groups of women who presented themselves (and were selected) for training in this seminar context.

There were three different subgroups of activists attending these workshops. The first described themselves as "long-time activists in the women's movement," and they were veterans of the Soviet *zhensovety*, or women's councils. They had been subordinate to the Communist party but specifically assigned to work with women on "women's issues." Mostly their work had been defined as mobilizing women for party goals, and while some could express this work in terms of challenging gender relations, for many it was more about mobilizing women than making any kind of change. The second were the self-described "feminists" who were active in new, autonomous feminist groups. They drew a considerable amount of their self-image and sense of support from contacts with feminists elsewhere in the world but also looked to Russian forebears for models and legitimation. The third were women active in mobilizing women in civil society, and thus part of what we would call the women's movement, but who were not focused on challenging gender relations as a goal and thus not feminist as we would define this term, at least when they came to the seminar initially (Ferree and Mueller 2004). They worked on all sorts of issues within the new Russia, from expanding women's opportunities in business to trying to clean up environmental problems to confronting drunkenness and opposing the war in Chechnya. Unlike the veterans of the *zhensovety*, they were part of the new civic culture that challenged party hegemony and was very much oriented to democracy, but their goals were to engage women as women in the general tasks of building a certain kind of new social order, not to question the gender relations inherent in that order.

Theoretical Issues

In this chapter, we discuss the strategic interactions among these diverse activists, the seminar leaders, the research team (ourselves and Valentina) that had come to study and to support the women's movement emerging in Russia, and several Russian and non-Russian experts who were invited to various of the seminars to address issues of goals, strategies, and tactics for the movement. We focus particularly on the ways in which the interactions among these different parties revealed new dimensions of power to us. We try to tease out the implications of power differences among groups like these for the development of social movements and civil society in general and for the transnational growth of feminism specifically.

We suggest that issues of hierarchy are particularly interesting in relation to four specific themes. First, we analyze the interactions between "locals" and "outsiders" in the development of political theory and the construction and legitimation of particular movement goals in relation to such theory. Second, we discuss the negotiation of the identities between "activist" and "expert" in relation to each other and in relation to academic credentials, local movement involvement, and particular forms of knowledge and skill that people bring to this interaction. Third, we propose that the cultural infrastructure of civil society that is necessary to support democratic participation and that is produced through the process of such participation is a culture of conversation rather than a culture of lecture. Fourth, we show how the material infrastructure available for movement building, the struggles over who possesses what goods that the movement needs, and who benefits directly from the material resources and organizational frameworks that are being generated in this process create complicated relationships between activists and researchers, locals and outsiders.

In our conclusion, we attempt to apply the insights from this particular case study of movement interaction to better understand the overall nature of social movements in countries where civil society is now developing, to place our Russian experience in the context of the larger dynamics of transnational feminism, and to analyze doing gender politics in post-totalitarian settings.

The Role of Locals and Outsiders in Defining Women's Interests

The variety among types of activists we observed reminded us initially of the distinctions that Maxine Molyneux (1985, 1998) drew between what she called "practical (or pragmatic) gender interests" rooted in the context of women's existing social relations and helping women to better meet their needs within that context and so-called strategic gender interests that would target the subordination of women as a social issue and attempt to transform gendered social relationships so as to reduce or eliminate women's gender disadvantages. But when we looked more closely at the activists and what they said they wanted, what they did at the seminars, and what they found most rewarding in the training, we began to question the framework for thinking about political theory and gender interests that Molyneux offered.

First, Molyneux suggests that strategic gender interests arise from the outside, based in a theory about what is good for women and how to achieve it. This would suggest that the transnational and Moscow-based activists leading the seminars would be primary vectors for carrying a wider and more challenging view of gender relations to the local activists. This was not typically what we saw. Instead, in the seminars, the leaders often had a predefined view of what women's interests might be, whether that was increasing women's representation in the Duma through more active participation in party politics or using the media and local lobbying of city and state officials to get more attention paid to children's needs and family policy. While these leaders clearly saw these interests as strategically feminist, in that these would be ways to improve women's collective status and power, the local activists were dubious about the agenda, not because they did not think strategically but because they saw these methods as not well suited to the conditions that needed to be changed. They questioned the use of media when the media were not free but in the control of oligarchs, of lobbying politicians who could not be held accountable in the absence of real party competition, or of running for office if women were co-opted into doing "dirty politics" just like the men.

For many local activists, the priority was first to strengthen the institutional basis of civil society and then to work on the more specific goal of women's equality. As they put it, the leaders were trying to teach them "to ride a bicycle" when the problem was that the skill was not yet relevant. As one participant put it, in America "the bicycle is already made. But somebody (in Russia) has to begin to make the bicycle from the beginning" before anyone could learn to ride it. Or as another said, women's projects were like "the buttons on the dress," but the dress needed to be made first. Thus, rather than not being strategic about gender interests, the local activists were differently strategic. As one activist argued, "the point is to create a basis for the rule of law. . . . without solving this problem, without constructing a law-abiding state, women's social problems cannot be solved." Thus, mobilizing women as women was part of their strategy for creating a participatory democratic state, and only then did they think that using the state to challenge gender relations could be considered pragmatic.

By stressing their local conditions, these activists reminded us that a strategy that may work within the context of established democracies is less useful in the context of a fragile and possibly failing new democracy, and leaders were pressed to offer more suggestions for how to construct a general civic infrastructure. In a sense, the local activists were being both practical and strategic simultaneously, while the seminar leadership seemed at times more committed to the general set of issue goals than to any concrete way of getting there in the immediate and particular context.

This is the essence of the second problem we see in Molyneux. Her model seems to us to reflect the idea that movement strategy derives from a grand theory such as Marxism, making strategic feminism into an already formulated set of priorities that people with access to theory would know more about and could help others to grasp. Outsider feminists, with privileged access to transnational theorizing about women's position in society, would thus be able to help the locals connect the dots and see how specific issues connect into a larger whole of gender oppression. How useful this model is for feminists should be questioned, not only because the means need to be locally appropriate but also because the perceived significance of the overall goal is the result of a complex mix of cognitive and emotional experiences.

What we observed was that local activists had concrete insights about the gender oppressions that they encountered in their own lives, including in their organizing work. One of the most valuable aspects of the seminars for them was the opportunity to network and share these experiences with women who were facing similar challenges. "To know you are not alone," they said, was a significant emotional experience that "gave you the strength to keep fighting." Rather than a cognitive-theoretical analysis, the participants sought and valued an emotional experience of solidarity and community, reminiscent to us of consciousness-raising group experiences. This in turn supported a visceral sense that gender was important and helped to legitimate the priority they gave to gender as an issue.

The seminars thus fostered a feeling of identification with the goal of challenging gender stereotypes and oppressions, but did not necessarily encourage adopting a particular theory or even the identity "feminist." Those who came to the seminar as feminists already had a complex agenda that connected challenging gender relations with adopting nonhierarchical and autonomous organizational forms such as are often used by grassroots feminists, especially radical feminists, in the West. But the other participants did not see any need to take up this sort of organizational style, which they identified with feminism, and they urged the group as a whole to stay away from the label, which they saw as carrying negative baggage and stereotypes rather than a useful analytic framework. The external, theoretically consistent, prepackaged concept of feminism could be rejected, however, without giving up a deep commitment to challenging gender inequity as a central goal. In Zhukovsky, for example, one Russian participant argued against the use of the term "feminism" because of its negative connotations, saying, "other words need to be used . . . 'feminist' should be avoided." Yet even in avoiding the word, she argued for a feminist definition of issues, saying:

> From my point of view the main priority is to change the stereotypes of social consciousness that still push women to the back of social and political life, and that do not allow her to take a single step. That is, we are dealing with a vicious circle. Breaking it is the main task, the main priority.

Finally, Molyneux's emphasis on strategic feminism as the more developed, theoretical, and abstract form toward which "practical" and local feminism needs to develop assumes a single direction of growth and change. This was contradicted in our experience of the seminars, where struggles over the targets of change were ongoing, not only among the differently located participants who were recruited but also between the local participants and the seminar leadership. Sometimes there was a compromise; sometimes the goals were changed in the direction that the participants wanted. At one seminar in the southern Russian city of Novocherkassk, for example, local activists placed ending the war in Chechnya at the top of their agenda; for them, this was a prerequisite for any specific focus on women's needs or oppressions as women. Outsiders come into a situation on the basis of some cause or issue that makes a particular identity salient for them, but this does not actually mean that this is the only identity that matters.

As local activists make clear, all women have multiple identities simultaneously. Consequently, women's movement organizations with diverse goals, such as those at these Russian seminars, play key roles as bridge builders, and their focus on multiple, concrete needs in their communities makes them central in grassroots mobilizations, as is also the case in American cities (Naples 1998) and African villages (Tripp 2000). Movements and activists with already formed feminist identities, if involved in local politics, may learn to take on these wider agendas no less often or importantly than local activists with a wide range of social change goals may learn to use a specific feminist rhetoric or adopt a particular theoretical model that privileges gender oppression alone. We suspect that the dialogue between local and outsider versions of needs, interests, and identities will be most productive if change takes place on both sides and in both directions. Fortunately, at least in this case, such mutual influence, rather than one-sided development toward some theoretically defined strategic feminist priorities, seems to happen in practice.

Overall, our experience suggested that Molyneux's widely influential strategic/pragmatic model is problematic in three important regards that reflect its privileging of outsider perspectives. First, it assumes that there is some external, overarching theoretical model that will permit judging the correctness of the analysis that guides the movement and makes it "strategically" address the "true" roots of gender inequality or not. In that sense, it replaces the grand theoretical claims of Marxist social analysis with equally comprehensive, but competing, claims for objective feminist truth. Second, it establishes a hierarchy between the strategic and the pragmatic, in which it is better when knowledge comes from theory rather than experience, and when extra-local experts lead and direct local activists. Particularly for feminists who found locally situated direct experience to be a potent source of criticism of established theoretical paradigms, the value system (vanguardism) thus embedded in the analytic categories is troubling. Finally, it suggests a single direction of change, in which "pragmatic" activists grow more strategic over time as they learn to adopt more explicit and more exclusive claims about gender inequality. This disallows the alternative dynamic, where theory-inspired feminists also learn to address gender issues in more locally specific, pragmatic ways or to adopt a more intersectional and less exclusively gendered analysis over time.

Such common forms of local, grassroots, intersectional politics are, as Linda Christiansen-Ruffman (1995) has argued, "in the closet"—not openly claiming to be political—because they are more distanced from state institutions. Women doing this political work do not usually name it as "politics" (Naples 1998; Roth 2003; Tripp 2000). The welfare mothers and ethnic-Acadian women that Christiansen-Ruffman studied in Canada (1995), the grassroots activists in the War on Poverty that Nancy Naples interviewed in

U.S. urban neighborhoods (1998), and the women dissidents in the former East Germany that Ingrid Miethe studied (1998) all said emphatically, "I don't do politics; I work for my community." Women, especially women in some degree of opposition to their governments, do not always see their local, practical resistance as politics. Just as housework is made invisible as work even to its own practitioners, civil society's practical grassroots politics is made conceptually invisible as politics. Bringing such work "out of the closet," to name it and own it, is part of what the trainers in these seminars were doing. Yet this process also raises questions about the identity and role of the "expert" doing "training" of the activists, and it is to these issues we now turn.

Negotiating Expert and Activist Identities

Although Molyneux's schema would tend to invest "experts" with a special theoretical role, we also found that, in practice, the negotiations over expertise and the lines between academics and activists were far more fluid than her model would have suggested. The idea of expertise is important and can often be constructed as the opposite of activist commitment. The reality is more complex than that.

In the seminars we studied, few, if any, of the women participating were without any higher education, since the Russian women's movement drew particularly strongly from among university-educated urban women, and many had postgraduate training, even if not necessarily in the social sciences. The American seminar leader had a background in university administration and her Russian counterpart was a physical scientist. Valentina Konstantinova was both a leading activist in the Moscow Center for Gender Studies and a feminist historian. We three outsider-researchers were social scientists (in sociology and political science), but our identity was also as feminist activists, and our engagement in this project was motivated by a mix of scientific research and feminist social change goals.

Within the research team, the questions of who was perceived as an activist and who as a researcher were actively negotiated in the course of the project, in part through conflicts over whether the goals of the research were serving or potentially interfering with the goals of the seminars. The seminars were based on a coalition-building model drawn from IAUW experience, with dot voting used to identify priority issues around which individuals and groups might coalesce. These issues were then used as examples to teach political lobbying and other social change techniques and so to produce "activists." The seminar leaders had obtained grants from the Eurasia Foundation and the Peace Foundation to support these training seminars, which made it possible to bring these Russian women together, and had invited "experts" to come and speak to the participants formally. These experts included both American activists, such as Gloria Odell, a U.S. politician/activist who once ran against Bob Dole, and Russian women politicians, such as Nadezhda Bikalova, a state parliamentary deputy from Chuvashia. Their speeches were a complex mix of formal theories of political mobilization, effectiveness, and influence and some more or less specific suggestions of how to organize, lobby, and act politically.

Both in our own manuscripts and in the grant proposals we (the research team) were initially described as activist researchers and sometimes as evaluators. As researchers, we were granted access to the seminars but were asked to take a low-visibility role that would not compete with the experts. While this was something that suited our interest in not having an impact on what we were observing (which we felt might compromise our ability to describe a process of mobilization for which we were not the responsible organizers), we found our role increasingly under debate. We could not avoid answering questions posed by the participants, and we were also interested in nonhierarchical give-and-take discussion with them. Over time the interaction between the research team and the seminar participants became problematic to the seminar organizers, and they eventually requested that we cease data collection entirely. We negotiated a compromise where we were allowed to stay as researchers but not activists, with the proviso that our team should be as noninteractive "as a fly on the wall."

We were willing to do this in principle, but in practice this was not possible. Valentina Konstantinova's role, as both a leading activist in the Moscow Center for Gender Studies and as a fieldworker who was taking notes as part of the research team, was particularly complex and open to constant challenge and renegotiation. Valerie was sometimes asked what feminism was like in the United Stataes, but was not supposed to (and did not want to) take on the role of expert to offer specific theories and strategies of movement development to the local activists, the way that the invited experts were doing. Although our goal was to help build the Russian women's movement, we found ourselves not able or willing to be the sort of consultants who could do so, for this would have been at the cost both of challenging the seminar leaders' control over their events and of undermining our own separation from leading the process that we wanted to observe.

In the end, we concluded that expertise is a valuable commodity in the context of building a social movement but that the negotiation over what it is and who has it is open-ended. In this particular setting expertise was socially constructed by the intentions of the participants more than it was given by their degrees, skills, or identities in general. Power relations, in defining whose seminars these were and whose funding was responsible for them, were also involved in defining the roles of academic and activist, even apart from the specific skills and goals of the actors involved. As women who see ourselves as feminists, academics, and activists, we found ourselves eventually identified by the workshop leaders as researchers and sometimes by local activists as experts, and we were constantly negotiating our role.

In sum, drawing a sharper line between the academics and the activists in these seminars than we perceive to ever have been really there was part of the social context being constructed in the organizing process itself. Both culture and material conditions framed the construction of expertise in particular ways. It is to a further analysis of the cultural and material infrastructure of that context that we now turn.

The Cultural Infrastructure for Mobilization

The interactions among participants in the physical setting of the seminars themselves evidenced certain cultural assumptions about how information is transmitted and how organizations work. We draw on studies of participation in learning to make a distinction between what we call "cultures of conversation" and "cultures of lecture" (Applebee 1996; Wink 2000). In a culture of conversation, learning happens through simultaneous engagement with the material and with others, all of whom are treated as already knowledgeable and as learning and teaching each other. In a culture of lecture, information is provided in a top-down way that defines the "expert" as teaching the passive and presumably wholly ignorant learner, whose role at the time is to merely absorb what he or she is given, reciting it back or applying it in a separate process later.

The seminars provided considerable evidence of how the Soviet Union had successfully inculcated a culture of lecture even in these activists who were, atypically for the bulk of the population, engaged in political mobilization and organization building in post-Soviet Russia. Whenever speakers had the floor, they tended to fall into a lecture mode, which often made the round of introductions with which the leaders began seminars interminable. The idea of taking turns and allowing everyone just a brief moment in the round was not familiar, and rather than a short and mutually considerate self-introduction, a lengthy speech often ensued. The American seminar leader occasionally deployed a whistle or timer to indicate that their time was up (after four minutes). Although we are sure this would have been experienced as deeply offensive in a U.S. context, here it had the function of teaching and enforcing a participatory rule that would have been self-evident in the United States and was simply not part of the normative repertoire of these Russian activists. It is paradoxical—and somewhat amusing—to reflect how such a hierarchical gesture as setting a timer could be part of the process of developing an antihierarchical culture of conversation.

The culture of lecture also allowed participants to simply disregard the speaker when they were bored (a phenomenon not unknown to university lecturers confronted with students whispering among themselves, reading newspapers, or passing notes in class). In these seminars, participants would turn to each other and relatively openly and audibly begin conversations with each other when they were no longer interested in listening to what the expert in the front of the room was speaking about, or sometimes when engaged by the topic and wanting to share and voice their interest or to privately disagree with the speaker. For their part, the experts themselves typically gave lengthy, nonparticipatory lectures, not pausing to ask questions or to do the sorts of exercises that might engage their listeners with the material or encourage interaction. The gulf between the front of the room and the audience was thus very large, even though, as we noted earlier, the actual spread of expertise among the various types of activists and academics present was quite mixed and the boundaries between them in what they might know and be able to contribute were really indistinct.

Part of what the seminar leaders were trying to teach were skills for carrying on a more effective learning process and engaging the entire group in a collective process of setting goals and deciding on strategies. They imported specific strategies that had been developed in U.S. social movement contexts, such as the AAUW's method of dot voting, which apportions points to specific goals by each person placing their limited number of dots on a collectively brain-stormed list of possible goals. They insisted on norms such as beginning with a round of self-introductions even when these were time-consuming and difficult to manage. They broke the bigger group into smaller discussion groups and asked for reports back to the whole. Yet the organization of the workshops presented mixed messages about the value of lecturing versus group process. Along with classroom practices that tend to share voice, the leaders also organized the seminars in terms of practices that affirmed the necessity and value of being lectured to, deferring to experts' knowledge, and thinking of what they were offering as discrete packages of knowledge, which could be passed around and carried back to the local settings in which these activists were working, rather than generalized skills for eliciting and using local knowledge more effectively.

If one thinks of a culture of conversation as transmitting the set of skills that help participants to work nonhierarchically to build political will and inform political judgment, it seems evident that a well-functioning civil society requires such an investment in developing individual actors' voices, and that social movements in particular are both the means and the outcome of this process. However, these seminars tended to be quite limited by how little of the culture of conversation the women brought with them to the setting and, to a certain extent, by the power relationship between the experts and local participants that contributed to sustaining the culture of lecture.

Nonetheless, the participants themselves were often most enthusiastic about what the seminars had offered them as ways to run a meeting in a more participatory way and to network with others nonhierarchically. A good part of the "bicycle" of a functioning civil society, they seemed to feel, was emerging in these skills. The activists were highly attuned to learning the specific skills of organizing, whether how to run a meeting or how to constructively listen to each other, as well as how to construct more formal coalitions. If social movement theory assumes that all that has to be done for organizations is raise funds or get politically noticed, it may be taking for granted the actual way that organizations function internally to empower their members, give them a sense of ownership of a social problem, and encourage them to develop the skills in a culture of conversation necessary to sustain an activist identity to work in a social movement over the long run (Shemtov 1999; Polletta 2002).

This engagement, arising from the active participation in talking about and acting in response to a social situation of injustice, can develop both emotional and cognitive skills. Robnett calls passing on engagement through a participatory process of goal setting at the local level "bridge-building leadership" and sees this work as something that women in the American civil rights movement did frequently and well (2000). In another article, we have called this the "housework of politics" because, like housework, it is naturalized as being "women's work" and scarcely recognized as being work at all, and when it is noticed, it is not valued as much as it deserves (Sperling et al. 2001). Yet constructing a culture of conversation is an important part of what keeps democracy alive at the grass roots, and it is recognized as critical by activists, such as those we worked with in Russia.

Without having such an infrastructure for empowering participants to take ownership of a problem, talk is more difficult and less valuable for building a social movement. This is not to say that social movements in long-standing democracies escape the pitfalls of power hierarchies and the way such hierarchies disrupt the culture of conversation. Yet, social movement scholars who are more accustomed to studying mobilizing practices in long-term democracies—where the culture of conversation has not been additionally stifled by generations of top-down, authoritarian leadership that actively instilled fear of speaking out—may not notice the importance of this cultural resource as much as the activists in Russia did. Building communicative skills and enabling a democratic process create a basis for civil society on which social movement organizers rely, no less than on resources, when mobilizing people to act.

The Material Infrastructure of Mobilization

In addition to communicative skills, activists need material resources if they are to build a movement. Especially when a society, like Russia in the early 1990s, is in the midst of massive social dislocations, the time, space, computers, travel money, food during meetings, and other necessities for holding a seminar can scarcely be taken for granted. Funds from outside Russia, in the form of grants, were critical to making the seminars happen. Bringing financial and logistical support to the Russian women's movement in the form of computers and stipends to activists as research assistants was no small part of our own assessment of how our research project could help contribute to the movement.

In this case, the notion of who "owned" specific parts of the women's movement was contested in various ways. The tendency of groups to split into ever smaller organizations with their own formal leadership, producing a huge number of very tiny groups, was inadvertently encouraged, for example, by the process by which Western funders allocated money, often providing a minimal stipend only to a single leader of an organization. Since affiliation as "the" local branch of a transnational organization like the International Association of University Women could be a route for potential future access to trips or funds, local groups battled over the naming rights to be recognized as affiliated. The legal ownership or physical custody of equipment like a computer or an operational phone line was a valuable asset not only for an organization but also for the individual who had it. Thus there were significant jealousies and pitched arguments over issues of organizational structure and names as well as office-holding and membership rules, some of which were actively played out in the context of the seminars, and for access to the very meager resources available from our project.

Even less obviously high-stakes issues could be bones of contention when it came to control over material resources. The grants to run and to study the seminars brought power to the individuals who held them. Being the grant "owner" conferred a great deal of decision-making authority in setting the rules for what could or should happen, and the potential for getting future grants was a source of negotiating power within the movement. Within the seminars, this was apparent in terms of the occasional conflicts of authority between the American seminar leader and the research grant holders, but it was also manifested in the power differentials between those who were paying the bills and those whose active participation was producing the movement. Sometimes, the authenticity of apparently earnest participation seemed questionable because it might also have been generated by the desire to get something out of the grants. Sometimes the grant holders were able to set rules and ask for forms of participation (like filling out questionnaires) that activists went along with without any commitment to the process. Without the external funding, the unquestionably valuable and much appreciated opportunities of the seminars for networking and acquiring social support and organizational skills could never have happened; with outside funding, the dynamics of interaction were inevitably skewed toward appeasing the powerful and trying to win more material support.

However, the dynamics of vying for access to funds and competing for recognition are hardly unique to transnational organizing nor limited to social movements that are relying on funding from cross-national sources. Similarly, possessiveness over a movement organization, fragmentation into smaller groups that are more closely tied to individual leaders, and unwillingness to pass along an office by an orderly means of succession are not only found in social movements in poor countries that rely on donors in affluent ones, but can be an expression of the sense of ownership that movement "entrepreneurs" feel in relation to an organization anywhere in which their labor and emotion has been invested. And questions of donor control and the possibility of distortion in the organizations' priorities or strategies arise in many contexts other than that of transnational support for feminist groups. Yet to consider the way that movement members interact with each other and construct their organizations without acknowledging the powerful role that material resources play in shaping these dynamics would be naive. Activists in the Russian women's movement and the specific groups involved in these seminars are working in and through a material infrastructure that is deeply affected by the inequalities of control over international, national, and interpersonal economic assets, however much they may wish to be nonhierarchical and participatory in form and style.

Conclusions

Our experiences in studying the seminars conducted for women's movement activists in Russia led us to think more about the many ways that hierarchies operate to separate academics and activists to the detriment of both—and at the cost of failing to construct a more effective and vital communicative culture in politics. Some of this is a matter of academic privilege, which too often goes unnoticed relative to other forms of social and political advantage.

For example, academic theories, such as Molyneux's distinction between strategic and pragmatic gender interests, have tended to privilege the academic as the expert knower in the situation, to emphasize purely cognitive types of insights, and to assume that the direction of movement growth is toward a more abstract strategic theory of the academic type. Although individuals may enter a movement setting with an identity as both academic and activist, the structure of interaction in the movement context is likely to place each person in a role that privileges the disengaged academic or the committed activist aspect of their identity, separating their cognitive and emotional selves.

The material and cultural infrastructure of a movement can work to heighten or reduce these and other forms of privilege in practice. To the extent that the movement has a culture of lecture rather than a culture of conversation as its characteristic style of transmitting information, the line between the academic and the activist is going to be sharpened along with the privilege inherent in being the one seen as having expertise (whether experientially based or academically based) from which to lecture others. And when material advantages are disproportionately distributed among participants, struggles over who is in control of what aspects of the organization are accentuated, whether that is between those with the activist grants and those with the academic ones, or between the donors and the recipients.

A particular insight that we derived from studying these Russian women's movement seminars is that there is a real body of skills that goes into running a social movement organization, particularly doing so in the more engaging manner that develops a sense of ownership and commitment in the participants and enables them to find a political voice in which to express themselves. These skills involve participants both cognitively and emotionally. We have called these organizational skills necessary to construct a democratic process a culture of conversation, and suggest that social movement scholars take such skills for granted—the invisible infrastructure of democratic political cultures that make civil society function—in part because they are often naturalized and devalued as "women's work." They are at the grass roots of political organizing and stand in contrast to the high-profile speech making, theory writing, and office holding that men in movements tend to monopolize and that are called leadership.

Such "women's work" at the grass roots, whether done by women or lower-status men, is vital in weaving the fabric of civil society. The activists we studied realized this and expressed it as needing to build the fabric of the "dress" in Russia before they could sensibly put on the "buttons" of particular movement projects. Constructing such fabric, through building a culture of conversation that incorporates previously excluded groups and individuals, is a much more radical and important step in a post-totalitarian society than it might appear at first glance. Social movement analysts should pay attention to those who build the culture of conversation that allows civil societies to develop, as well as to those who monopolize more conventional forms of leadership. Looking more closely at the local work done by grassroots activists is important because this work is vital for movement success.

Developing a culture of conversation might be good not only for building a movement in general, but also for blurring the lines between academic and activist that we found so pronounced and hard to navigate in Russia. By taking expertise away from the front of the room and developing more strategies to empower every participant to recognize their own expertise and develop their personal ownership of the issue, these learning strategies might make talk more valuable in a variety of activist/movement settings, be they conferences or strategy meetings or more hybrid forms like the seminars we studied. Rather than beginning from the assumption that epistemologically privileged academic theory can provide the "answers" for the movement, the culture of conversation encouraged in grassroots organizing practice starts with the idea that participants will have to define their own needs and form their own answers.

Constructing a culture of conversation in the face of so many hierarchies—international differences in control over income and wealth, gendered disparities in the value given to certain kinds of work, cultural advantages given to academic forms of expertise over those acquired in practice, with interpersonal differences in material resources and skills compounding all of these in ways that are structured by gender, class, and age—will never be easy work. But we think that blurring the lines that divide theory and practice, activists and academics, and the front of the room from the rest will contribute to making this culture of conversation more widespread and vital, and so to enriching the nature of democracy in the United States no less than in Russia.

References

Applebee, Arthur N. 1996. *Curriculum as Conversation: Transforming Traditions of Teaching and Learning.* Chicago: University of Chicago Press.

Christensen-Ruffman, Linda. 1995. "Women's Conceptions of the Political: Three

Canadian Women's Organizations." In *Feminist Organizations,* ed. Myra Marx Ferree and Patricia Yancey Martin, 372–95. Philadelphia: Temple University Press.

Einhorn, Barbara. 1993. *Cinderella Goes to Market.* Los Angeles: Verso.

Ferree, Myra Marx, and Carol McClurg Mueller. 2004. "Feminism and the Women's Movement: A Global Perspective." In *Blackwell Companion to Social Movements,* ed. David A. Snow, Sarah A. Soule, and Hanspeter Kriesi. Malden, MA: Blackwell.

Ferree, Myra Marx, Barbara Risman, Valerie Sperling, Tatyana Gurikova, and Katherine Hyde. 1999. "The Russian Women's Movement: Activists' Strategies and Identities." *Women and Politics* 20: 83–109.

Funk, Nanette, and Magda Mueller, eds. 1993. *Gender Politics and Postcommunism.* New York: Routledge.

Gal, Susan, and Gail Kligman. 2000. *The Politics of Gender after Socialism.* Princeton, NJ: Princeton University Press.

Michels, Robert. [1910] 1998. *Political Parties: A Sociological Study of the Oligarchical Tendencies of Modern Democracies.* Somerset, NJ: Transaction Publishers.

Miethe, Ingrid. 1998. "From Mothers of the Revolution to Fathers of Unification." *Social Politics* 6: 1–23.

Molyneaux, Maxine. 1985. "Mobilization with Emancipation? Women's Interests, the State, and Revolution in Nicaragua." *Feminist Studies* 11: 227–54.

———. 1998. "Analyzing Women's Movements." *Development and Change* 29: 219–45.

Naples, Nancy A. 1998. *Grassroots Warriors: Activist Mothering, Community Work, and the War on Poverty.* New York: Routledge.

Naples, Nancy A., and Manisha Desai, eds. 2002. *Women's Activism and Globalization: Linking Local Struggles and Transnational Politics.* New York: Routledge.

Polletta, Francesca. 2002. *Freedom Is an Endless Meeting: Democracy in American Social Movements.* Chicago: University of Chicago Press.

Robnett, Belinda. 2000. *How Long, How Long? African American Women and the Struggle for Freedom and Justice.* Oxford: Oxford University Press.

Roth, Silke. 2003. *Building Movement Bridges: The Coalition of Labor Union Women.* Westport, CT: Praeger.

Shemtov, Ronit. 1999. "Taking Ownership of Environmental Problems: How Local NIMBY Groups Expand Their Goals." *Mobilization: An International Journal* 4, no. 1: 91–106.

Sperling, Valerie. 1999. *Organizing Women in Contemporary Russia.* Cambridge: Cambridge University Press.

Sperling, Valerie, Myra Marx Ferree, and Barbara Risman. 2001. "Constructing

Global Feminism: Transnational Advocacy Network and Russian Women's Activism." *Signs* 26: 1155–86.

Tripp, Aili Mari. 2000. *Women in Politics in Uganda.* Madison: University of Wisconsin Press.

Wink, Joan. 2000. *Critical Pedagogy: Notes from the Real World.* New York: Addison-Wesley Longman.

9

Building the Movement for Education Equity

Cassie Schwerner

"Eighth grade is not enough! We are not so big and tough," chanted fifty middle school students as they marched during the Manhattan kickoff of New York City councilman Robert Jackson's 150-mile trek to the Albany courthouse where his decade-old lawsuit for fair public school funding finally came to a dramatic conclusion in June 2003.

Councilman Jackson's claim against the state of New York, charging that New York City school children did not receive the "sound basic education" required by the state constitution, would eventually be upheld by the state's highest court in Albany. But education advocates understood that a lawsuit was only one element of a necessary strategy to build a broad social movement to fight for fiscal fairness for New York's students.

Many involved in the litigation believed that the lawsuit would, first and foremost, generate media attention spotlighting the crisis and resulting inequities. A simultaneous goal was to spark a social movement. In this goal, as with the first, Campaign for Fiscal Equity (CFE) and its allies proved successful. Movement actors knew that the court case was a key lever of political opportunity, but without a simultaneous grassroots movement the case would not have the power to force the legislature's hand. It was important to win in the courts, but also important to show politicians that CFE and its allies had won over the public as well.

As author of this article I have multiple perspectives. My academic training is in social movement theory; in addition I have specialized in media analysis and concepts of frame analysis. But I am also a participant-observer in this movement. For the past seven years, I have been a program officer at the Schott Foundation for Public Education, directing its New York work, which focuses, essentially, on how New York State funds its public schools.

As a funder of this movement, I have been greatly impressed with its participants' ability to create and sustain a major mobilization without drawing on much of what social movement theory has to offer. For all of our analysis as researchers, many of our insights have not trickled down to the activist and movement leaders on the front lines. Yet much of what New York's education activists have learned about movement building and framing debates to move public opinion is of direct relevance for social movement theory. The problem is that the innovative social movement mobilizing going on today is not being adequately captured for reflection and learning.

I must confess to learning more about social movements as a funder than I did as a scholar. At the Schott Foundation we have developed a theory of change regarding public policy reform that I will detail. After providing some background to New York State's school finance movement, I will explore how this movement engaged the media to help move its case and build public and political power. In doing so I will illustrate how the foundation's theory of change was operationalized.

Despite my skepticism of the academy's role in support of social movement building, academics have played several very important roles in this movement and, in taking a step back, it is possible to identify many other roles they could have played—and may yet still—to help build this movement. I will discuss this further in the conclusion.

The Schott Foundation's Theory of Change

Like most foundations, Schott developed an interest in evaluating and measuring its outcomes. Unlike most foundations, however, Schott was less interested in measuring its grantees than its own effectiveness. This led the foundation to develop a logic model and through that process uncovered the theory of change that is used to inform its grant-making practices. To accomplish the foundation's main goal of having the New York State legislature reform the state's public education funding formula, the logic model suggested Schott would need to provide funding within four key pillars that would lead the way to the final goal.

The first pillar was termed *media and public will*. The logic maintained that in order to generate a broad-based public movement on the fairly arcane issue of school finance policy, the media would be a key location of the contest. The media's portrayal of the issue would be critical in reaching a large and diverse statewide public.

The second pillar of the logic model was *statewide campaign*. A statewide campaign would be needed to sponsor a major mobilization, with actions located in each of the regions of New York, to mass the political power needed to convince Albany to make a change on a very controversial and politically dangerous subject. Whereas school finance was not a key issue with the public, it was seen as a bread-and-butter issue for legislators—money they brought home for schools could make or break a career.

Schott called the third pillar *movement support;* the logic was that many organizations providing key data, research, or technical assistance were needed to make the first two pillars strong.

The final pillar was termed the *funding community.* Schott was well aware that its own resources were far from sufficient to fully fund a statewide movement calling for a challenging political reform. Many funders and sources of revenue would be critical for the movement to be sufficiently powerful.

New York's Movement for Educational Equity

Councilman Jackson's personal journey began in 1992 when, as a concerned parent and president of Community School Board 6, he urged the school board's counsel Michael Rebell to sue the state of New York on behalf of New York City's 1.1 million public schoolchildren. To undertake the suit, Rebell founded the Campaign for Fiscal Equity (CFE) in 1993.

The Lawsuit

CFE lawyers, supported by a coalition of parents, advocates, and community school board members, filed the lawsuit in 1993 in New York State Supreme Court. This suit is what is known in the school finance litigation field as an adequacy case. School finance suits have been filed in forty-five of the fifty states. In the earlier years of litigation, these suits were known as equity cases. These cases did not have a successful track record because state constitutions did not promise equity. However, most constitutions did provide language offering children the right to an adequate education (Rebell 1999). In New York's case, the Education Clause of the state constitution offers what has been defined by the courts as "the right to a sound basic education." Thus CFE's suit claimed the schoolchildren of New York City were being denied their right to an adequate education. Oral arguments began in the fall of 1999.

During the seven months of testimony, Justice Leland DeGrasse heard arguments from the country's leading experts on a range of issues, including overcrowded classrooms, crumbling school facilities, and insufficient and inexperienced teaching staff. The plaintiffs' experts maintained that all children can learn with proper resources, whereas the defendants argued that the state had provided ample funds and the New York City education department simply wasted money. The years of determination and preparation paid off when, in January 2001, DeGrasse ruled in favor of the plaintiffs. The decision stated: New York State has over the course of many years consistently violated the state constitution by failing to provide the opportunity for a sound basic education to New York City public school students (see www.cfequity.org). In a major setback to advocates, however, Degrasse's decision was overturned in June 2002, when state appellate court justices issued a shocking ruling interpreted by education advocates as upholding racial and class divisions and denying equal opportunity. The justices argued that the state was obligated to provide only a minimally adequate education, the equivalent of "eighth or ninth grade" (*CFE v. State*, 295 A.D.2d 1 [2002]).

New York's public schoolchildren finally won their victory in June 2003 when the court of appeals, the state's highest court, ruled in favor of the plaintiffs. In the decision Chief Justice Judith Kaye wrote that all New York students deserve a "meaningful" high school education and that New York City's schools were severely underfunded (*CFE v. State*, 100 N.Y.2d 893 [2003]).

Enter the Alliance for Quality Education

At the close of 1999 a statewide grassroots campaign emerged, in part as a reaction to the state of the schools and in part due to a realization that political change could not rely on a legal strategy alone. Advocates knew that the court case was a key political opportunity, but without a simultaneous grassroots movement, the case would not have the political power needed to persuade the legislature to act in accordance with a court victory. It was critical to win in the courts, but also important to arouse the grass roots to let their government representatives know that they understood how school funding had become subsumed under politics and that they supported CFE's efforts to restore education funding as the priority in the legislature's state budget process. Other states, such as neighboring New Jersey, had won important legal victories, but it often took decades, if ever, for the legislature to create budgets that implemented the court's rulings.

Advocacy groups, principally ACORN and Citizen Action, lent their support to CFE's effort by drawing on their network of community activists to build a grassroots coalition calling for equitable funding. Moreover, these organizing groups were building an alliance with the United Federation of Teachers (UFT), New York City's powerful teacher's union.[1]

Those three groups, additional unions, and community organizations came together to plan a kickoff conference in March 2000, with the intention of creating a new statewide grassroots coalition to ensure that every child in New York State received a quality education. By 2001 sufficient funding was in place to open two offices in the state, one to cover upstate areas and the other for New York City and the surrounding downstate suburbs. After conducting a poll of New York voters, Alliance for Quality Education (AQE) refined its message and developed a platform calling for: (1) small class size; (2) qualified teachers; (3) universal prekindergarten; and (4) safe, sound, and technically up-to-date buildings. AQE expanded its base of support rapidly, building a statewide coalition with over 230 organizations. A steering committee with representation from major regions and organizations was established, and organizers developed a cohesive mission and message. By 2003 AQE had opened six offices located strategically throughout the state. AQE generated hundreds of media stories, organized local forums, educated local and state policy makers, released relevant research reports, and mobilized parents and students across the state.

Public Opinion and the Battle for Media: How CFE and AQE Generated Extensive Media Coverage

In this section I explore the "framing contest" that ensued between the various actors to illustrate the multipronged components of Schott's theory of change. I argue that all four of the pillars that Schott focused on were critical for the coalition to successfully reframe the media's discussion of school finance over several years.

Before CFE went to trial in the fall of 2000, organization leaders realized they needed to maximize the trial's media potential to communicate and control the message. As Gamson, Croteau, Hoynes, and Sasson state, "Participants in symbolic contests read their success or failure by how well their preferred meanings and interpretation are doing in various media arenas" (1992, 385). Similarly, Ryan, Carragee, and Schwerner contend that "news media represent critical arenas of social struggle" (1998, 166; also see Ryan 1991).

When considering the needs of New York City's schools, the public held many dominant frames simultaneously. One frame was the waste frame, which maintained, "If New York City receives more money, these new dollars will simply fall down a black hole like the funds in the Board of Education's bloated budget." Of course, racism was a factor here. New York City schools are 86 percent students of color and educate 70 percent of the state's students of color.

A second frame was what might be called the Robin Hood frame. This stated, "Additional money for New York City will come from our share." This frame pit the city against the rest of the state, upstate rural and sub-urban school districts especially, further fueling long-standing downstate-upstate tensions. (Like many large states, New York has a historic tension in the legislature between what is known as upstate and downstate. There are legislators from upstate communities, even those suburbs just outside of New York City, who are disinclined to "send more money to the city.")

A third dominant frame was the "no new taxes" frame: "New York City may need more funding for the schools but we simply do not have the money." Prior to trial, many stories regarding CFE and the litigation often stated, "Of course, if CFE is successful, it will mean the state would have to raise taxes." For example, an August 1999 article from the *New York Times* inserted frames two and three into the fourth paragraph of a lengthy article: "If successful," warned the *Times*, "the lawsuit, which is scheduled to be tried in October, could force New York State to raise taxes to provide more funds for the city schools or to shift hundreds of millions of dollars in state aid from suburban and upstate school districts to New York City to make up the shortfall" (Hartocollis 1999, B1). Both frames were very dangerous to movement participants, and here the *Times* posited only two possible solutions. In fact, at the time New York actually had revenue surpluses that could have absorbed much of the additional funding to high-needs districts throughout the state, but this was never mentioned.

CFE needed to reframe this debate, and due to the fluid nature of media discourse it would have such an opportunity. "The undetermined nature of media discourse," submits Gamson and his colleagues, "allows plenty of room for challengers such as social movements to offer competing constructions of reality and to find support for them from readers whose daily lives may lead them to construct meaning in ways that go beyond media imagery" (Gamson et al. 1992, 373).

So how did CFE successfully reframe the debate? It wasn't luck; it was resources. CFE acquired financial resources at a key moment and was able to make two organizational changes to best prepare them for the media contest that lay ahead: (1) CFE hired a public relations firm with excellent contacts at the New York City daily papers, and (2) CFE hired an internal staff person to manage media relations throughout the trial.

These steps, combined with the press-savvy lead plaintiff, Councilman Jackson, made for a winning combination. Jackson, for example, decided to march from his home in Washington Heights, a neighborhood at the northern tip of Manhattan, to the courthouse in lower Manhattan on the morning that the first trial began. CFE and its allies mobilized approximately one hundred people to march with Jackson, evoking scenes of the southern civil rights movement of the 1960s. The participants marched the fifteen miles from Washington Heights to the courthouse, arriving just in time for the pretrial kickoff rally. The morning the trial began, Bob Jackson and his daughter, Sumaya, were on the front page of *New York Newsday*. The following day, local and national newspapers carried a photo of an exuberant Jackson and daughter during the march. More significant, the stories that ran with the photo did not contain the dominant frames used in past discussion about the lawsuit. New York City papers, and a surprising number of papers around the state, ran positive editorials in support of the case. Eight months later, after the decision was announced, within the immediate two-week period, roughly 150 news articles on the case and the issue of school funding were published across the state.

As the trial began, media frames shifted from concerns over waste, redistribution, and taxes to issues of fairness and rights. As stated earlier, the lawsuit initially challenged that the state denied New York City students the right to a "sound basic education." New frames emerged. A civil rights frame and a fairness frame became dominant. The day before the trial began *New York Newsday* ran an article with the headline, "Fight for Equity: Suit Contends State Has Shortchanged City Schools." There was a large picture of a dilapidated school with a corresponding caption that was "on message." A picture ran of the school's chancellor, Rudy Crew, an African-American, who was quoted as stating, "My interest is in doing for these kids what in the first wave of the civil rights movement lots of folks did for me and others" (Willen 1999, A7). That same day, the *New York Times'* Bob Herbert wrote an op-ed column titled "Cheating the Schools," decrying the grossly inadequate funding to New York City schools, as evidenced by 8 computers per 100 students versus twice that number in the suburbs and 90 library books per 100 students versus 235 books per 100 students in the suburbs. "The numbers are stark," Herbert wrote. "The system is unfair" (1999, A19).

During the seven months of the trial, 269 stories were placed, most of them "on message" as far as CFE was concerned. Positive press coverage continued through the initial verdict in the case finding in favor of the plaintiffs. One week before the verdict was issued, the governor, the lead defendant in the case, called the school funding formula a "dinosaur" that deserved to be buried "on the ash heap of history" (Goodnough 2001, B6). Why did the governor take this stand? Perhaps we'll never know for sure. But those familiar with Albany politics believe that the press coverage during the trial had been so effective sponsoring the CFE fairness frame that the governor wanted to "come out in front" of the likely decision favoring the plaintiffs. Taking the moral high ground first would mean the governor could save face if he lost in the court.

Around the state, press coverage of Justice DeGrasse's decision was so positive that even the plaintiffs were stunned. *Newsday*'s headline read, "Unconstitutional: At Last the Court Orders Reform of the State's Unconscionable Ways of Distributing School Aid" (*New York Newsday* 2001, A42). The *New York Times* ran many favorable stories, including one in Sunday's Week in Review (Zielbauer 2001, sec. 4, 3). Even the *Daily News,* which had run a negative editorial about the case the day it began, ran a supportive editorial immediately following the decision. "In ruling that Albany's school aid formula cheats New York City students of a sound basic education," the paper wrote, "a Manhattan Supreme Court justice did more than restate the obvious. He handed the legislature a blueprint for setting things right" (*New York Daily News* 2001, 38).

Roughly one month later Governor Pataki filed papers to appeal the decision. On June 25, 2002, the unthinkable happened. The appellate division overturned the case. As stated above, the decision maintained that the state was obligated to provide only an eighth- or ninth-grade education. CFE and other advocates were taken aback but not caught off guard.

Instantaneously, CFE developed a message and drew in its allies across the state. These efforts resulted in a near-unanimous outpouring of print support for CFE. The local New York City press was as appalled as CFE. Even the upstate media were shocked. "A cruel ruling," cried the editorial page of the *Buffalo News* (2002). The *Westchester Journal News* blasted, "Not nearly good enough . . . An appeals court ruling that accepts an eighth-grade education as the constructional standard for a 'sound basic education' for New York's students leaves most people, regardless of their own education, speechless" (2002). The *Syracuse Post-Standard* editorial page ran the headline, "Leaving Kids Behind: Ruling Sets the Cause of School Funding Equity Back a Generation" (2002). Michael Casserly, executive director of the Council of Great City Schools in Washington, DC, got it right when he said, "The decision is so bad that it's good" (phone conversation with the author, summer 2002). Had the decision simply overturned DeGrasse as "going too far," which many in the legal community expected, it might not have generated such unanimous outrage.

In fact, the press coverage so consistently offered CFE's framing that once again the governor was forced to distance himself from the decision as he ran for reelection in the fall of 2002. "Anybody who thinks an eighth-grade education is adequate is 100 percent wrong," said the governor. "That will never be the policy of this state as long as I am governor" (Becker and Katz 2002, 5). (Again, we can't know for sure why the governor offered this rhetoric. He made the comment at a press conference with the UFT, the powerful New York City teacher's union—who went on to endorse him in his reelection campaign. One suspects that the mean-spirited manner in which he fought the lawsuit suggests it was public pressure and/or union pressure during an election season rather than a change of heart.)

As Gamson writes in *Talking Politics,* critical discourse moments are times when "discourse on an issue is especially visible. They stimulate commentary in various public forums by sponsors of different frames, journalists, and other observers" (1992, 26). Critical discourse moments offer challengers ongoing opportunities to insert their frame or message into the discourse. Therefore, the litigation strategy was key to the overall success of the movement because a protracted legal struggle offered multiple moments to engage the media contest.

One such moment was the 2002 gubernatorial campaign. For Carl McCall, the Democratic candidate who challenged two-term governor George Pataki in the fall of 2002, the critical discourse moment that centered on the appellate division's decision was decisive for his campaign. Understanding the importance of public education to voters across the state, McCall took up the slogan of "eighth grade is not enough," which he used throughout his campaign. Referring to the governor's apparent flip-flop on the appellate division's ruling, McCall stated, "Gov. Pataki can't be trusted. He says one thing in the school house, he says something else in the courthouse and something else in the statehouse" (Becker and Katz 2002, 5). As Ryan, Carragee, and Schwerner state, "News stories, then, become a forum for framing contests in which political actors compete in sponsoring their preferred definitions of political issues" (1998, 168).

The Schott Foundation's pillar of *media and public will* suggested that the first site of the contest, on the road to winning a legislative victory, was taking the message of school finance to the public. The media coverage of CFE's lawsuit suggests that movement actors can effectively engage in a framing contest with a successful outcome. It does take considerable resources, as CFE's case demonstrates, but barriers to this framing contest are not insurmountable.

Moreover, CFE was not alone in the battle over public opinion. As Schott's theory contends, CFE was important because it provided the structural vehicle to raise awareness around school finance. As stated previously, Schott's theory of change submits that this is insufficient for promoting lasting legislative change. There must be a statewide campaign as well. In a statewide campaign grassroots (and also grasstops) mobilization becomes critical. The public must bring this demand to legislative leaders. And the public must be diverse and representative of the public as a whole. Therefore, Schott felt racial diversity representing all public school constituents was key but that it would also be important to represent clergy, business leaders, community/civic leaders, and other respected figures. Thus, the mobilization needed to focus on both grass roots and grass tops. The history of social movements has demonstrated that this type of multicultural coalition is very difficult to build and sustain. A coalition of this type must be well organized and, I would argue, well funded. In this case, AQE quickly mobilized grassroots constituents from around the state due to participants' decades-long track record of organizing. But the coalition also encountered some early luck in finding unlikely and powerful messengers.

Cynthia Nixon, star of HBO's *Sex and the City,* sends her daughter to one of New York City's public schools. One day, when picking her daughter up from school, Nixon spotted a small rally outside the building organized by AQE. She took a flyer and told the lead organizer she'd like to help. That simple beginning led to a significant involvement with AQE. Nixon began speaking at rallies, offering testimony at hearings of the New York City Council, and speaking out publicly against budget cuts that were being threatened in the spring of 2002. AQE launched a major protest over these cuts and found sufficient parental outrage to support a new and more aggressive tactic than had been used up to this point in the movement. They planned a weeklong demonstration, which included protests and blocking the entrance to City Hall. Twelve protesters were arrested in the civil disobedience; among them was Cynthia Nixon. Nixon's arrest turned this dramatic staging into news, thereby getting coverage for the arrests when it may have otherwise gone unnoticed. This was the first time New Yorkers would get arrested over the funding of public schools.

That spring *New York Times* political reporter Michael Cooper pondered the question of how organizers fighting budget cuts, an action "not exactly novel" could capture the "attention of the public, the press and the city's many newly elected to make the case that this year the cuts will hurt, and that they are not crying wolf" (2002, B1). Cooper continued:

> One way is to tap star power. Have Cynthia Nixon, a star of "Sex and the City" with a daughter in public school, speak out against school cuts. Have Ms. Nixon hold a news conference in favor of raising taxes, accompanied by other New York celebrities, like the playwright Eric Bogosian

and the singer Audra McDonald. Plan a weeklong series of protests. Have Ms. Nixon, parents, advocates for public schools, and other celebrities get arrested for blocking a gate at City Hall.

The spillover effect of Nixon's arrest was immediate. Renowned rap mogul Russell Simmons watched as this white woman was arrested on behalf of kids of color (Allah 2002). He was deeply impressed and mobilized immediately, reaching out to the local teachers' union and AQE, offering the services of his national youth network, the Hip-Hop Summit Action Network. The three organizations planned a rally to fight the proposed budget cuts. A massive rally was organized for June 4—complete with a who's who of hip-hop with musicians from Alicia Keys to LL Cool J to P. Diddy. The press estimated that there were twenty thousand people in attendance, but rally organizers maintain that there were between fifty and one hundred thousand people—many of them students and teachers. Through Simmons's contacts and resources, public service announcements ran on several of the local hip-hop radio stations for the week before the rally—listening to the radio, it seemed that they ran almost every hour.

Another rally highlighting Nixon organized by AQE featured the Republican movie superstar Bruce Willis. Willis's participation put AQE in the national media again, with a spot on *Entertainment Tonight*. Due to Simmons's and Nixon's involvement, AQE ended up in publications such as Oprah Winfrey's *O* magazine, *Redbook, In Style,* and *Money.* Even before celebrity spokespeople entered the debate, AQE and CFE had successfully reached thousands of New Yorkers. Newspaper editorials drew readers from Brooklyn to Buffalo to the issue of school finance. But with this new access to celebrity power, hundreds of thousands of people around the country would learn about New York's battle for school equity. Let me be clear, celebrities and other unlikely messengers are important, but a movement can only expect to enjoy this type of participation if it is well-organized and effective in its own right. I do not want to suggest that all a person with an agenda needs to do is book the latest superstar and the legislative package will flow from there. There must be a visible and sustained movement first and foremost. But, I maintain, movements will be furthered when they utilize celebrity participation because those individuals have the ability to reach a vast public to which most of us typically do not have access.

Aside from the litigation, which was raising public will and awareness in the press, and a statewide campaign mobilizing voters across the state, there was a third important sector—what the Schott Foundation refers to as *movement support organizations.* In Aldon Morris's landmark study, *The*

Origins of the Civil Rights Movement, he introduces the term "movement halfway house." Understanding this concept and how fundamental it has been to the New York movement is key to understanding the range of resources needed in building this comprehensive movement.

> A movement halfway house is an established group or organization that is only partially integrated into the larger society because its participants are actively involved in efforts to bring about a desired change in society. The American Friends Service Committee, the Fellowship of Reconciliation, the War Resisters League, and the Highlander Folk School are examples of modern American halfway houses in their relative isolation from the larger society and the absence of a mass base. This generally means that such groups are unable to bring about wide-scale change or disseminate their views to large audiences. Nevertheless, in their pursuit of change movement halfway houses develop a battery of social change resources such as skilled activists, tactical knowledge, media contacts, workshops, knowledge of past movements, and a vision of a future society. (1984, 139–40)

Although none of the movement support organizations that functioned in the education equity movement fit Morris's definition precisely, there were a few groups that functioned in a similar capacity. Several organizations, such as the Education Priorities Panel (EPP), the Fiscal Policy Institute (FPI), and the Institute for Education and Social Policy (IESP), all served to significantly strengthen CFE and AQE's mobilization and framing efforts. EPP, FPI, and IESP were all academic-like organizations that provided key movement support.

The Institute for Education and Social Policy, based at New York University, was key to training and providing technical assistance to many of the grassroots and traditionally marginalized organizations advocating for parents—particularly parents of color. IESP staff played two key roles. First, they trained and supported organizers in several communities across New York City. Prior to IESP's founding, many organizing groups existed, but as of the early 1990s only three focused on school reform; within a few years that number would increase to a dozen. IESP staff helped organizers make the transition to education issues because they understood organizing principles and strategies as well as the infrastructure of New York City's education arena (Hirota, Jacobowitz, and Brown 2004).

Second, IESP staff assisted in data analysis that bolstered the organizers' recruitment, mobilization, and strategy. The Institute's Community Involvement Program offers extensive technical assistance, including the following activities:

- Convening and facilitation of meetings to assist groups in exploring schooling problems and possibilities for working together
- Training on schooling issues and organizing/leadership development strategies
- Data analysis and presentation on school performance and expenditures
- Policy analysis and development of reform proposals
- Strategy and organizational development consultation to assist organizations in carrying out the organizing work
- Brokering relationships to other sources of information and support
- Assessment and feedback on progress, barriers, and overall strategy
- Coordination and administration support for citywide organizing activity (Zachary and olatoye 2001, 3)

Both FPI and EPP offered research analysis and provided key data to principal movement organizations such as AQE and CFE. For example, in 2003 FPI produced statistical runs for each of the seven hundred school districts in the state, demonstrating how their budgets would be affected by the governor's proposed cuts. Through press conferences across the state, AQE communicated how these budget cuts would be harmful and, moreover, provided a direct reframe to the "money doesn't matter" argument. AQE did not have the technical resources to produce this type of analysis; an outside think tank was needed. One of EPP's most striking contributions was a video produced in 1997. The EPP video, titled *Listen to the Children,* documents with striking visuals and narrative the stark inequalities of the New York public education system. As CFE toured the state in its public engagement process, it was able to show audiences exactly what was meant about New York City and rural New York schoolchildren being denied their right to a "sound basic education." Movement support organizations were clearly vital to the movement.

The final of Schott's four pillars is the *funding community.* Promoting a statewide movement, regardless of the issue, is extremely expensive. On top of the costs for well-trained and, ideally, well-paid organizers, there is the matter of media and a communications strategy. Even without the use of professional public relations firms, this is extremely expensive.

Resource mobilization (RM) theory emerged in the 1970s as a fundamental way to understand social movements (Gamson 1975). RM, "writes Mueller, offered a viable alternative to previous traditions in scholarship concerning collective behavior, mass society, relative deprivation, and political sociology" (1992, 3). Social movements were not composed of "irrational" actors, engaged in unfocused activities with rapidly shifting targets, as mass society theory explained (Hoffer 1951; Kornhauser 1959). Rather, movements succeeded when the appropriate resources were available to build social change—resources, moreover, that consisted of more than funding. "They include formal and informal organization, leaders, money, people, and communication networks," writes Morris (1984, 27).

Resources were central to the mobilization of the movement for education equity in New York. And, yes, money was a significant element within the resources required for success. Money was not the only resource this movement had going for it, but as those immersed in progressive education reform know, money matters. Having a well-funded movement was critical to its success.

Many funders were part of this movement, in fact, too many for me to discuss them all, but I do want to highlight a funding source that was vital to the movement—the Donor's Education Collaborative (DEC).[2]

Donors' Education Collaborative

In 1995, twenty-one local, national, and corporate funders came together with the mission of achieving "policy reforms that will make the New York City public school system more responsive to the needs of all children. DEC members share a belief that an informed, organized, and empowered constituency of parents, educators, businesses and community leaders is required to formulate policy and advocate for change" (DEC n.d.).

When it began making grants in 1996, DEC planned a four-year life span, and expected to disband in the summer of 2000. However, two important reasons for DEC to continue emerged. First, the increased public attention that focused on education at the local and state levels made this a propitious time for the kind of community engagement in public education that DEC sought to build. Second, after four years of progress by the grantees, accompanied by careful monitoring by DEC and an intensive evaluation, it became clear that the kind of lasting policy changes that DEC sought takes many years to develop and sustain. DEC is currently in its seventh year of funding and plans to run a total of nine years, raising and disseminating approximately $9 million.

With their pooled resources DEC funded four sets of coalition partners. One of the groups was the Equity Reform Project—the lead partner being CFE. While DEC did not specifically fund the litigation, it funded what became known as CFE's Public Engagement Process. "The goal of the public engagement campaign was to build a broad-based constituency for the fiscal reform and help develop a community-supported remedy for achieving that reform" (DEC n.d., 2). Another DEC grantee was the

Parents Organizing Consortium, whose goal was to build a citywide network of grassroots organizations composed mainly of parents who would work for education reform. "The project's partner focused on bringing parents' voices into educational debates and decision-making by exerting pressure on public officials and politicians through direct action campaigns" (ibid.). This network of parent groups, many of them trained and supported by IESP, was critical to developing AQE. In addition to funding the four coalition partners, DEC also made the decision to use a portion of the funds raised to offer a variety of forms of technical assistance to the grantees. These included:

- Media and communications training
- Assistance with survey construction and data analysis
- Advice on goal setting, strategic planning, and evaluation
- Capacity building on organizing and coalition building
- Advice on long-term fundraising (DEC n.d., 15).

Conclusion

I began this chapter critiquing the role of academic scholarship regarding social movement building. While I do not believe social movement theory has sufficiently assisted activists on the ground, there are numerous ways in which academics interested in social movement can be extremely helpful.

Translation. If movement scholars wish to continue theorizing about social movements in the manner in which we have done for the past forty years, that is clearly a personal choice. These scholars, however, must recognize that their work is not being used by activists who need their insights the most. If academics could translate writing for academic journals or books that they need to publish for their own careers into publications for laypeople, it would be an important first step. I believe there would be an interested audience from the nonprofit sectors where there are many individuals who would use this work in a variety of ways. To be utilized, the writing would have to be jargon free, not a style we in the field are accustomed to using.

Relevant research. Many foundations are squeamish about funding direct advocacy; although they need not worry, many funders believe supporting advocacy jeopardizes their tax status. Funding research is something foundations are willing to do. Researchers in the field of education could document such subjects as the benefits of small class size, the economic consequences of dropping out of high school, and the benefits of a high-quality prekindergarten education—all valuable for education campaigns. And, of course, there are many scholars around the country engaging in this research. I believe that many academics who would like to have their research used directly by a social movement they support would do well to meet with movement leaders directly and find out exactly what research would be most valuable. Related to *translation* is the dilemma that academics often—whether they are sociologists or economists—write in such a style that their data and arguments cannot easily be translated to movement groups. Frank Mauro, executive director of the Fiscal Policy Institute, is an exception, Fred Frelow from the Rockefeller Foundation argues, in his ability to provide user-friendly data to activists. Activists in many states, maintains Frelow, do not have access to someone like Mauro. Though great universities and researchers exist in every state, there are few individuals who can simultaneously conduct their academic work and offer movement support.

Use of intermediary organizations. Movement organizations often are not even aware of what access to data and resources academics might have. Academics who wish to study the social movement process and create theoretical concepts around movement building may indeed uncover valuable insights for movement activists. Aside from translating this work, another option is to present theoretical concepts and data to intermediary organizations. These institutions, like NYU's Institute for Education Social Policy, are, in this regard, invaluable. Academic papers and lectures presented to the institute's staff would surely be one audience where academic insights would trickle down to activists.

Strategic frame analysis. The work of scholars such as Ryan (1991), Gamson (1992), Iyengar (1994), and Entman (2003) in frame analysis has been extremely helpful to activists who are learning to develop an organizing agenda that integrates media as a central component of their quest for policy reform. This work has been furthered by Susan Bales through her nonprofit organization FrameWorks Institute. FrameWorks Institute uses a variety of academic approaches, borrowing from the fields of communications, sociology, anthropology, linguistics, and social psychology, among others, offering insights to progressives in developing communication campaigns using framing strategies designed to move the general public on a given issue. Strategic frame analysis, write Bales and Gilliam, "is a multi-disciplinary, multi-method approach that pays attention to the public's deeply held worldviews and widely held assumptions" (2004, 33). Many foundations in the last few years have made large grants to FrameWorks to assist grantees in their communication efforts. This work, however, is extremely expensive; it is not work that grassroots organizers can generally afford. Nor, some argue, is it work that supports capacity building of the organization to engage in their own efforts of strategic communications. If media scholars could partner with activists on the grassroots level and work with them at considerably reduced rates, it might further the activism and at the same time provide research opportunities for scholars. Through the Boston College's Media Research and Action Project (MRAP), Charlotte Ryan worked with ten organizations in Boston's communities of color to cultivate a leadership development program that trained board members and key activists to develop effective communications strategies that furthered their organizing efforts. Ryan's efforts were successful in that those who participated had the media skills to enhance their work long after she was gone (Ryan, ch. 7 this volume).

As for the movement for school finance equity, the ten-year-long battle is not over. Although victorious in the courts and in the New York press, CFE and AQE still have their work cut out for them. As I write, the New York legislature is about to pass a 2004 budget that does not include a CFE remedy, despite the movement's demands and the public's support. The suit will likely return to the courts seeking a court-imposed remedy. The landscape, however, as activists move forward, is forever changed. Editorial pages, for example, are growing weary and suggesting that voters elect new politicians into office to accomplish the job, since those currently in office seem utterly ineffective.

Notes

I'm indebted to Jennifer Kramer-Wine for research assistance and to Matthew Goodman and Aimee Frank for critical feedback on the initial draft of this chapter. I am also grateful for the many insights provided by editors William Hoynes, David Croteau, and Charlotte Ryan.

1. The UFT has a troubled relationship among many communities of color in New York City due to its stance in the Ocean Hill/Brownsville community control debate of 1968. This history has continued to haunt the union, and thus the fact that the UFT was also a key player in the coalition offered a unique moment for organizing efforts in the city.

2. Rockefeller Foundation deserves special mention because of their vision of statewide public policy change and the enormous amount of resources they have put into the statewide approach. The New York Community Trust deserves special credit for being CFE's first funder and for housing DEC.

References

Allah, Dasun. 2002. "Hip Hop Hollas at City Hall." *Village Voice,* June 18.
Bales, Susan, and Franklin D. Gilliam Jr. 2004. *Communications for Social Good.* Practice Matters Series. New York: Foundation Center.

Becker, Maki, and Celeste Katz. 2002. "McCall Rips Pataki on Ed Funding." *New York Daily News,* September 13, 5.

Buffalo News. 2002. "A Cruel Ruling." Editorial. July 2, B10.

Cooper, Michael. 2002. "What's the Ostrich For? Politics: Budget Protests Use Street Theater and Star Power." *New York Times,* May 18, B1.

DEC (Donors' Education Collaborative). N.d. *Lessons Learned about Effecting Public School Reform.* New York: Donors' Education Collaborative.

Entman, Robert M. 2003. *Projections of Power: Framing News, Public Opinion, and U.S. Foreign Policy.* Chicago: University of Chicago Press.

Gamson, William A. 1975. *The Strategy of Social Protest.* Homewood, IL: Dorsey.

———. 1992. *Talking Politics.* New York: Cambridge University Press.

Gamson, William A., David Croteau, William Hoynes, and Theodore Sasson. 1992. "Media Images and the Social Construction of Reality." *Annual Review of Sociology* 18: 373–93.

Goodnough, Abby. 2001. "Pataki's Criticism of School Aid, and Its Timing, Is Questioned." *New York Times,* January 4, B6.

Hartocollis, Anemona. 1999. "Justice Dept. Supports Suit on School Aid." *New York Times,* August 26, B1.

Herbert, Bob. 1999. "Cheating the Schools." *New York Times,* October 11, A19.

Hirota, Janice, Robin Jacobowitz, and Prudence Brown. 2004. *Pathways to School Reform: Integrating Constituency Building and Policy Work.* Chicago: Chapin Hall Center for Children, University of Chicago.

Hoffer, Eric. 1951. *The True Believer.* New York: Harper & Row.

Iyengar, Shanto. 1994. *Is Anyone Responsible? How Television Frames Political Issues.* Chicago: University of Chicago Press.

Kornhauser, William. 1959. *The Politics of Mass Society.* New York: Free Press.

Morris, Aldon D. 1984. *The Origins of the Civil Rights Movement.* New York: Free Press.

Mueller, Carol McClurg. 1992. "Building Social Movement Theory." In *Frontiers in Social Movement Theory,* ed. Aldon D. Morris and Carol McClurg Mueller. New Haven, CT: Yale University Press, 1992.

New York Daily News. 2001. "Final Judgment on School Funding." Editorial. January 11, 38.

New York Newsday. 2001. "Unconstitutional: At Last, a Court Orders Reform of the State's Unconscionable Way of Distributing School Aid." Editorial. January 11, A42.

Rebell, Michael. 1999. "Education Adequacy Litigation and the Quest for Equal Educational Opportunity." *Studies in Judicial Remedies and Public Engagement Series* 2, no. 2: 7–9. Campaign for Fiscal Equity.

Ryan, Charlotte. 1991. *Prime Time Activism.* Boston: South End Press.

Ryan, Charlotte, Kevin Carragee, and Cassie Schwerner. 1998. "Media, Movements, and the Quest for Social Justice." *Applied Communication Research* 26, no. 2: 165–81.

Syracuse Post-Standard. 2002. "Leaving Kids Behind: Ruling Sets the Cause of School Funding Equity Back a Generation." Editorial. June 30, C2.

Westchester Journal News. 2002. "Not Nearly Good Enough." Editorial. June 27.

Willen, Liz. 1999. "Fight for Equity: Suit Contends State Shortchanged City Schools." *New York Newsday,* October 11, A7.

Zachary, Eric, and shola olatoye. 2001. *A Case Study: Community Organizing for School Improvement in the South Bronx.* New York: Institute for Education and Social Policy, School of Education, New York University.

Zielbauer, Paul. 2001. "The Courts Try to Get City Schools Their Fair Share." *New York Times Week in Review,* January 14, sec. 4, 3.

10

Sweatshop Labor: (Re)Framing Immigration

Robert J. S. Ross

Thirty years ago Ross and Staines (1972) began to think about the phenomenon we now call framing as a matter of "social problem definition," the most central feature of which was causal attribution. The ideas of a media frame from Gitlin (1980) and an issue frame from Gamson (1975) both address the same problem: the ways in which contextualizing material influences prognosis and political action.

This chapter focuses on the application of these concepts in relation to the problem of labor abuse in the apparel industry (sweatshops) and to the discourse used by and applied to the antisweatshop movement. The frames used by the antisweatshop movement at the beginning of the twenty-first century may have had some unfortunate influences on policy, action, and perception among the broader public. My approach to the framing issue is virtually the same as Benford and Snow's (2000). In addition, I argue that diagnosis predisposes prescription. Similar to Oliver and Johnston (2000), I understand that frames *implement* ideologies. Once elaborated, however, frames do not necessarily manifest or reveal the entire ideology that called them forth. Another main point addresses the primary issue of this volume—the role of the expert within and alongside social movements.

Briefly, my experience is that the key to influence in social movements is ongoing relationships rather than the power or importance of an expert's analytical ideas. This chapter is only in part a report of a systematic or experimental application: it is largely a report of a certain kind of ongoing political practice—the expert in and around a social movement—about which some preliminary comments are in order.

Academics in all branches of knowledge share a well-known tendency to look down on "applied" research in contrast to theory or otherwise "purely" scientific work. There is in addition a deep caution, at least in the culture of Anglo-American scholarship, which distrusts scholarship that is motivated by value or political commitments. Yet every policy is a hypothesis: by proposing to do A in order to get effect B, a policy proposal suggests that the lawful nature of the universe will cause B to happen if A occurs. By extension, social movements create similar propositions in their demands: condition A needs correction; do B to correct it. From the point of view of framing or attribution theory (and practice), the act of defining A—the thing that needs correction—is a critical analytical step that Benford and Snow have called "diagnostic framing" (2000). One might, for example, propose that excessive supply of cheap or undereducated labor supplied by immigration erodes labor standards and therefore causes sweatshops (a labor supply theory of labor abuse). To use Benford and Snow's language, this *diagnosis* might lead to a *prognosis* of restricting immigration (or at least increasing the penalties for the employment of illegal immigrants) to control the problem. In the 1990s, at least one interest group did just that (Jencks 1997), while the public discourse assumed the partial accuracy of the proposition without necessarily thinking through the consequences.

One implication of seeing policies and movements as making propositions that have implicit scientific content is that those who have analytical skills, substantive knowledge, and values engaged about a given issue—experts—have much to offer to social movements.

Framing Immigrants

The new (that is, post-1940s) sweatshops began to be noticed in the late 1970s in journalistic and academic work on abuse of labor and human rights and extreme economic exploitation in the U.S. apparel industry (Buck 1979; Ross and Trachte 1983; Wong 1983; Weingarten 1981). At least one theoretical orientation (which I share)—the political economy of global capitalism—leads to doubts that the labor supply view of sweatshops, i.e., the availability of immigrants—adequately explains the reappearance of this phenomenon after forty years of decency in the industry (see R. Ross 2002). By 1997 this was elaborated in an argument that used Puerto Rican migration to New York in the 1950s as the counterexample of high immigration but no sweatshops (R. Ross 1997).

In 1997–98 a new social movement appeared among college students. The "sweat-free campus" campaign became visible with a wave of sit-ins in 1999–2000. United Students Against Sweatshops (USAS) was formed in the summer of 1998, sparked the movement that demanded collegiate codes of conduct for licensed insignia apparel, and grew to two hundred campuses by 2003 (Featherstone 2002; R. Ross 2004).

The development of a social movement around a problem to which I had previously decided to devote my scholarly and political energies was quite exhilarating. A relationship of some duration and sporadic intensity developed between my work and political energies and USAS and at least one other major NGO in the field—the National Labor Committee for Labor and Human Rights. For example, USAS groups in the Northeast invited me to address regional meetings and campus organizing events on a score of occasions, presenting what one USAS activist at my own university called "Sweatshop 101."

Among the features of my research on the apparel issue was my development of an estimate that in the 1990s over 400,000 American workers toiled under sweatshop conditions; given drastic shrinkage in the industry (but no improvement in rates of abuse) that number is, I estimate, now about 250,000 (R. J. S. Ross 2004).

From these many contacts with campus and other civic groups, a pattern appeared: the most frequent referents, the subjects of abuse, in the campus sweatshop movement imagery, were people in other places. In a group interview with Brown University students in 1998, the response to an inquiry as to why this was so was that advocating for workers in developing countries was more "hard core" than taking up the cause of U.S. workers.[1]

In consequence, the campaign rhetoric of USAS was in that period almost exclusively about workers exploited in poor countries. It should be noted, though, that the apparel workers union UNITE has sponsored USAS and worked with them on multiple occasions. Altering their discourse to include more people in the United States would make alliance with U.S. workers easier and better—and draw more of the activists to future roles in the U.S. labor movement. (In spring of 2004, and responding to UNITE's appeals for support, USAS mobilized its chapters to support laundry worker organizing and local campus workers as well.) Others have called this strategy "rationale" (Oliver and Johnston 2000) or "motivational framing" (Benford and Snow 2000). This rearticulation would also make legislative and other solutions to the problems of exploitation in the U.S. apparel industry easier to attain if thousands of energetic college students were available on their behalf.

The Mass Media Discourse: Framing Immigrants

Students were not the only ones in the nineties for whom the sweatshop problem happened only to some externalized Other—people abroad or the special problem of immigrants to America (R. J. S. Ross 2004).

Consider the report of a tragic factory fire in Hamlet, North Carolina, on September 3, 1991. The September 4 headline in the *Washington Post* read, "25 Die As Fire Hits N.C. Poultry Plant; Locked Doors Are Said to Add to Toll" (Taylor 1991a). The story continued:

> Fire broke out near a deep-fat fryer fueled by natural gas at a chicken-processing plant in this rural community, killing at least 25 people and injuring at least 49 others this morning, authorities said.
>
> Friends, relatives and coworkers of victims at the Imperial Food Products plant said locked doors at the one-story brick and cinderblock building contributed to the death toll. Most of the victims suffered from smoke inhalation, not burns, fire officials reported.
>
> "I don't see how people can lock doors in a plant where you know something like this can happen," said Thomas Brown, 25, whose cousin was flown to a hospital in Durham, about 100 miles north, to be treated for smoke inhalation.

The twelfth paragraph of this article, the first-day story, was composed of this sentence: "'You couldn't tell if the bodies were black or white, because everybody was black from the smoke,' [Hamlet police lieutenant] Downer said." It was not until the second day of the story cycle that readers of the *Washington Post* learned that "Imperial employees are non-union, and most work for near-minimum wages of between $4.90 and $5.60 an hour. Most are black, and an even larger majority are women" (Taylor 1991b). This information came in the twenty-fourth paragraph of a thirty-four-paragraph story.

These stories created a context, a frame, for their readers. In this context the fire causes the tragic death of twenty-five workers; the workers were jeopardized by bad conditions; and their deaths were in some sense caused by a locked back door and, thus, by the negligence of the owners. By invoking "one frame or set of meanings rather than another," the journalist predisposed public perception about the prognosis, i.e., what to do about the problem (Oliver and Johnston 2000, 8). The race of the workers is not a central part of the story.

The story of the locked exits that contributed to the twenty-five deaths in Hamlet stirs, in any human who recalls the Triangle Factory Fire, a heavy-hearted sense of déja vu. Exploited workers, a locked door, negligent conditions, death by smoke and fire. Do things ever change?

Indeed, things do change, some for better and some for worse. The owners of the Triangle Shirtwaist Factory were acquitted of manslaughter; the owner of the Hamlet factory was jailed (*Washington Post* 1992). One thing that did not change in reporting these fires is the relative insignificance of the ethnic or racial attributes of the victims.

The *New York Times* story of March 26, 1911, had the following head-line and lead:

141 Men and Girls Die in Waist Factory Fire; Trapped High Up in Washington Place Building; Street Strewn with Bodies; Piles of Dead Inside

Three stories of a ten-floor building at the corner of Greene Street and Washington Place were burned yesterday, and while the fire was going on 141 young men and women at least 125 of them mere girls were burned to death or killed by jumping to the pavement below.

In the fifth paragraph of the story, readers were told:

The victims who are now lying at the Morgue waiting for some one to identify them by a tooth or the remains of a burned shoe were mostly girls from 16 to 23 years of age. They were employed at making shirtwaist by the Triangle Waist Company, the principal owners of which are Isaac Harris and Max Blanck. Most of them could barely speak English. Many of them came from Brooklyn. Almost all were the main support of their hard-working families.

And in the twenty-sixth paragraph of the story:

The victims mostly Italians, Russians, Hungarians, and Germans were girls and men who had been employed by the firm of Harris & Blanck, owners of the Triangle Waist Company, after the strike in which the Jewish girls, formerly employed, had been become unionized and had demanded better working conditions.

So, back in 1911 the immigrant character of the victimized workforce is not in the lead paragraph; their gender and age—"mere girls"—is appar-ently more relevant. When the reader is informed of the ethnicity of the "girls," he or she learns, literally in the same sentence, that employees of the Triangle firm had led the famous strike of the year before. In these stories the *frame* is about working conditions and owners' accountability.

Consider by contrast the headline and lead paragraphs of the *Los Angeles Times* first-day story on the El Monte slave labor workshop. Raided at dawn on August 2, the story ran on August 3:

Workers Held in Near-Slavery, Officials Say

State and federal agents raided a garment factory in El Monte early Wed-nesday that allegedly held dozens of Thai immigrants in virtual slavery behind barbed wire for years, forcing them to labor in servitude to sup-posedly pay off creditors.

The pre-dawn raid by a multi-agency team headed by the California Department of Industrial Relations discovered more than 60 Thai nationals living and working at a gated apartment complex ringed with barbed wire and spiked fences.

The raid exposed conditions that seemed to belong to an earlier era.

Workers told government agents and *The Times* that they had been held against their will and that they were forced to toil day and night for less than $2 an hour. Some said they were told they must repay the cost of transporting them from Thailand, yet the detention continued after the "debt" was repaid. One worker—who provided only her nickname, "Yat"—said she has not been allowed to leave the complex in the 2 1/2 years she has lived there, even though her debt was repaid long ago. (White 1995)

In three of the first four paragraphs the *LA Times* told its readers that the El Monte workers were Thai and were immigrants. The *San Francisco Chronicle* did not wait for the lead paragraph: its headline was "70 Immigrants Found in Raid on Sweatshop/Thai Workers Tell Horror Stories of Captivity" (Wallace 1995). In the *LA Times* second-day coverage there were two stories. One was headlined "Thais"; both were framed about Thai immigrants in the first sentence (see Torres 1995; White and Lee 1995).

The reporting of the El Monte case was sensational, and it shaped public opinion by telling people the case was about immigrants. Others have found that the kind and context of information received helps shape public opinion (Pritchard 1994; Salmon and Moh 1994). Research has shown that slight alteration in the context within which an issue is presented can lead to a different impact on audiences (Cappella and Jamieson 1996; Nelson, Clawson, and Oxley 1997; Domke, Shah, and Wackman 1998). The way media attention is focused on events may spark policy decisions by officials (Doppelt 1994; Pritchard 1994). One local example from sweatshop research: shortly after the Kathie Lee Gifford affair, in which child labor was found to be involved in the Wal-Mart Kathie Lee line in El Salvador, a Boston union official complained to the local U.S. Department of Labor about a contractor shop that was a sweatshop. The official went in and then reported to the union fellow: there were no kids there, so no problem. The issue du jour was child labor.

These ideas suggest the potential impact—the stakes—in framing sweatshops in an immigrant or foreign context. The framing of stories on subminimum working conditions may deflect the attribution of these conditions onto the ethnic or immigrant groups or individuals described rather than other factors such as employer greed, industrial structure and power, the trade structure of global capitalism, or the lack of government regulation. This is the distinction Ross and Staines called "person blame" versus "system blame," widely used by sociologists in the form of individual versus social attribution.

Simon and Alexander (1993) examined the portrayal of immigrants in newsmagazines since 1880, concluding that it led to attitudes in favor of immigration restriction on the grounds of job displacement and an unwanted addition to the "culture of poverty."

Table 1 shows the incidence of the immigrant/foreign frame in major newspapers, the *New York Times* and the *Los Angeles Times*. Between 36 percent and 51 percent of the sweatshop-related stories in the time period selected used this frame. I chose May 1997 to May 1998 to avoid the effects of the El Monte and Kathie Lee affairs, as well as the USAS student sit-ins of 1999. Alerted by the high incidence of the immigrant/ethnic frame, I turned to explore its consequences. With the cooperation and advice of William Gamson, Lisa Grandmaison (a student of mine) and I performed an experiment using 233 student respondents from four different campuses (Clark University, Wellesley College, Boston College, and Keene State, NH), employing news stories that described sweatshops as populated by (undocumented) immigrants. The experimental stories were expurgated, removing ethnic and immigrant identifiers. The statistical results showed that those who read the original immigrant/ethnic stories were more likely to see immigration restriction and related views as the solution and less likely to adopt what was called a pro-labor index (R. J. S. Ross 2004, ch. 10).

Attempting to Reframe

I discussed this issue—the lack of inclusion of U.S. sweatshop workers—with the students with whom I had contact, and aggressively continued to discuss the issue in the context of American workers as victims. My public speaking was generally to small audiences, but very frequent—twenty-five to thirty times per year for five or six years. In addition, I attempted to ally myself with the apparel workers union, UNITE. I explicitly adapted and talked about the idea of a frame—and tried to shift the frame from one of ethnicity and immigrant status to class and worker status. I would have measured success by observing a shift in student movement rhetoric and some more agitation about cases and issues in the United States. This did not occur at that time.

My connection with the participants—both the union and student participants—was as a freelance "expert" intellectual, not as a coparticipant in the sense of ongoing organizational participation. So there was no on-

Table 1. Sweatshop newspaper stories from May 5, 1997, to May 5, 1998.

Newspaper	"Sweatshop" in headline or lead paragraphs	"Sweatshop" plus "immigrant" reference in headline or lead paragraphs*
Lexis-Nexis news search	400 (100%)	145 (36%)
New York Times	37 (100%)	19 (51%)
Los Angeles Times	29 (100%)	12 (41%)

Note: These are raw numbers that do not correct for the fact that the Nexis news database includes numerous non-U.S. newspapers. Also, duplicates of stories appear when they are carried in separate editions of metropolitan papers (e.g., the home edition of the Los Angeles Times and its final sports edition may both carry slightly reedited versions of the same story, and both are listed here in the story count).

* "Immigrant reference" means that one of the following words specifically appeared in headline or lead paragraphs, along with "sweatshop": immigrant, immigrants, undocumented, Mexico, Mexican, China, Chinese, Philippines, Filipino, Thailand, Thai, Korea, Korean, Dominican, Haiti, Haitian, Vietnam, Vietnamese.

going relationship or context that brought my perspective into steady dialogue with actors. The union did not make very much of my overtures, and the students I lectured or spoke to could go on doing what they were doing without confronting the matter again. By contrast, on my own campus where I have more of a continuing relationship with activists, while the rhetoric privileging developing countries continues, they were quite stalwart in doing solidarity work on local labor issues. There is a conclusion, tentative, built as it is on one person's experience, but it is consistent with other things we know about personal influence and group process: the professor who tells the movement the facts is not as influential as the ally in an ongoing relationship.

There is a very important qualification to the propositions stated. However much the language of the antisweatshop and newly termed global justice movement privileges developing world workers, USAS and other groups within the antisweatshop movement do respond when unions ask for their assistance. This new global justice movement utilizes a master frame, an overarching common thread among social movements. The global justice master frame is similar to the environmental justice master frame, and both are derivative of the civil rights frame (Capek 1993, 8). USAS, for example, did respond when the Communications Workers asked for help in a contract dispute with the maker of baseball hats in Buffalo, New York. Since the apparel workers union (UNITE) is now organizing industrial laundries and uniform firms, and not focusing on small shop garment makers, it has not made many direct appeals for help with American campaigns among fashion clothing workers. It has, however, repeatedly asked for and received student support (demonstrations, letter writing) for its organizing campaigns. In the last big campaign on American sweatshops, the Guess jeans case in the mid-1990s, before USAS was formed, there was a great deal of campus support. If union behavior had been different, it is possible student movement behavior would have been different as well. As distinct from my outside expert role, UNITE personnel are in close touch with USAS leadership (and help fund the organization).

Shifting Geography: South-South

Having failed to make a difference at a national level, it seemed appropriate for me to fail at something even more global. There is another *reframing* enterprise that focuses on an aspect of a related issue, and the barriers reveal yet another problem. Largely unnoticed by most American activists, in particular the global justice critics of the international financial institutions (IFIs), is contention over the idea of incorporating labor rights into international trade agreements. Some Western governments lukewarmly support considering labor rights issues in the World Trade Organization, labor movements in the global North do so almost without fail, and many labor unions in the global South do as well. Making labor rights guarantees part of trade agreements is sometimes called working toward a "social clause" (Ross and Chan 2002; Chan and Ross 2003). Not only do market-oriented governments in developing countries oppose the social clause, but many critics of global capitalism reject it as well.

A careful consideration of the history of the working class in the older industrial regions, however, leads to the conclusion that universalistic standards and large geographic areas of application will most protect and enhance the position of workers around the world, including those in both rich and poor countries. Absent such standards, the competition between developing countries for access to rich country markets may exacerbate a race to the bottom that deprives workers in poor countries of the fruits of growth in their own countries. Mexico and China's competition for the North American apparel market are examples of this.

The social clause is usually framed as a North-South contention: the rich North (governments and unions) wish to protect markets against the poor South (Bhagwati 2000, 2002). The purpose of reframing the argument is to point out that it has an important South-South dimension: a social clause could help regulate the rules of the game among poor or developing countries themselves.

The maiden voyage of this argument took place at a conference in Beijing. Western labor rights advocates—both academic and NGO—were present, as were Chinese and Asian labor activists and NGO representatives. In this context another entire layer to the frame became apparent: some actors did not want to incorporate labor rights into World Trade Organization (WTO) arrangements because they do not want to reform it: they want to destroy it. They oppose activity that will legitimate the WTO, and they interpret attempts to reform it in this light.

This has caused the reframing argument to evolve from "do it in the WTO" to "if not in the WTO, propose a way to protect labor rights that is enforceable." The whole idea of contextualizing material—frame—is plastic: historically malleable and open to artistic reinterpretation. The larger frame of the social clause is seen by some not as North-South, but revolution versus reform. The reframing enterprise is itself a discursive one that evolves. This problem is certainly not unique to antisweatshop activism; frame disputes are a documented characteristic of social movements (Benford and Snow 2000). Responding to the revolution frame requires seeing the social clause as part of a historical effort that empowers the working class—whatever the dominant ideology of systemic challengers at that moment.

Reflections on Reframing

While theoretical perspective and empirical research lead to the belief that framing and reframing are critical for social movement success, experience and observation lead to a broader form of skepticism about the influence of the expert theorist. Reframing as an enterprise is but another form of political persuasion. Expert knowledge is not an active form of intervention, of persuasion, within a social movement.

The limits of the expert are not just those that apply to the problem of framing. On other matters as well, I discovered my "expertise" had no impact on highly embedded ideas of even the movement participants with whom I was closest. As a veteran of SDS I was accorded respectful attention when I discussed organization and process. None of my reflections on the errors of leaderless democracy were influential at all—local global justice activists, in a way similar to the general trend around the country, adopt a highly stylized consensus decision-making model and eschew the creation of organizations with strong national centers. Cultural and political trends more profound than my advice determine those matters.

In these and all other forms of persuasive communication, reframing is subject to all of the forces and constraints on that form of interaction. Frames don't have their own legs. As attempts at political persuasion, they have the same requirements: source credibility, interest compatibility, repetition, and access.

A good idea is not enough.

Notes

Timothy D. Sweetser, an undergraduate student at Clark University, made major contributions to the editing and revision of this paper.

1. "Hard core," apparently derived from hip-hop and ska slang, means more committed, more worthy of one's effort, tougher, i.e., stronger (more macho?), and braver.

References

Benford, Robert D., and David A. Snow. 2000. "Framing Processes and Social Movements: An Overview and Assessment." *Annual Review of Sociology* 26: 611–39.

Bhagwati, Jagdish. 2000. "Economic Sense and Nonsense." *Harvard International Review* 22, no. 3: 78+.

———. 2002. "Coping with Antiglobalization: A Trilogy of Discontents." *Foreign Affairs* 81, no. 1: 2+.

Buck, Rinker. 1979. "The New Sweatshops: A Penny for Your Collar." *New York Magazine* 12, no. 9: 29.

Capek, Stella M. 1993. "The Environmental Justice Frame: A Conceptual Discussion and an Application." *Social Problems* 40, no. 1: 5–24.

Cappella, J., and K. H. Jamieson. 1996. "News Frames, Political Cynicism, and Media Cynicism." *Annals of the American Academy of Political Social Science* 546: 71–85.

Chan, Anita, and Robert J. S. Ross. 2003. "Racing to the Bottom: International Trade without a Social Clause." *Third World Quarterly* 24, no. 6: 1011–28.

Domke, David, Dhavan V. Shah, and Daniel Wackman. 1998. "Media Priming Effects: Accessibility, Association, and Activation." *International Journal of Public Opinion Research* 10 (January): 51–74.

Doppelt, Jack C. 1994. "Marching to Police Beats: The Media-Source Relationship in Framing Criminal Justice Policy." In *Public Opinion, the Press, and Public Policy,* ed. J. David Kennamer, 113–21. Westport, CT: Praeger.

Featherstone, Liza. 2002. *Students against Sweatshops: The Making of a Movement,* with United Students Against Sweatshops. New York: Verso.

Gamson, William A. 1975. *The Strategy of Social Protest.* Homewood, IL: Dorsey Press.

Gitlin, Todd. 1980. *The Whole World Is Watching.* Berkeley: University of California Press.

Jenks, Rosemary. 1997. "Identification Document Fraud." Testimony by Senior Fellow, Center for Immigration Studies, Washington, DC, prepared for the U.S. House of Representatives Committee on the Judiciary, Subcommittee on Immigration, Border Security, and Claims. May 13. At http://www.cis.org/articles/1997/jenks51397.htm (accessed July 10, 2003).

Nelson, Thomas E., Rosalee A. Clawson, and Zoe M. Oxley. 1997. "Media Framing of a Civil Liberties Conflict and Its Effect on Tolerance." *American Political Science Review* 91: 567–84.

Oliver, Pamela E., and Hank Johnston. 2000. "What a Good Idea! Frames and Ideologies in Social Movement Research." *Mobilization* 5, no. 1: 37–54.

Pritchard, David. 1994. "The News Media and Public Policy Agendas." In *Public Opinion, the Press, and Public Policy,* ed. J. David Kennamer, 103–12. Westport, CT: Praeger.

Ross, Robert. 1997. "Restricting Immigration: A Sweatshop Nonsolution." In *An Academic Search for Sweatshop Solutions: Conference Proceedings,* ed. Janice McCoart, 32–45. Arlington, VA: Marymount University.

———. 2002. "The New Sweatshops in the United States: How New, How Real, How Many, and Why?" In *Free Trade and Uneven Development: The North American Apparel Industry after NAFTA,* ed. Gary Gereffi, David Spener, and Jennifer Bair, 100–122. Philadelphia: Temple University Press.

———. 2004. "From Antisweatshop to Global Justice to Antiwar: How the New New Left Is the Same and Different from the Old New Left." *Journal of World Systems Research* 10, no. 1: 287–319.

Ross, Robert, and Kent Trachte. 1983. "Global Cities and Global Classes: The Peripheralization of Labor in New York City." *Review* 6, no. 3 (Winter): 393–431.

Ross, Robert J. S. 2004. *Slaves to Fashion: Poverty and Abuse in the New Sweatshops.* Ann Arbor: University of Michigan Press.

Ross, Robert J. S., and Anita Chan. 2002. "From North-South to South-South: The True Face of Global Competition." *Foreign Affairs:* 81, no. 5: 8–13.

Ross, Robert J. S., and Graham Staines. 1972. "The Politics of Analyzing Social Problems." *Social Problems* 20, no. 1:18–40.

Salmon, Charles T., and Chi-Yung Moh. 1994. "The Spiral of Silence." In *Public Opinion, the Press, and Public Policy,* ed. J. David Kennamer, 145–62. Westport, CT: Praeger.

Simon, Rita J., and Susan J. Alexander. 1993. *The Ambivalent Welcome: Print Media, Public Opinion, and Immigration.* Westport, CT: Praeger.

Taylor, Paul. 1991a. "25 Die As Fire Hits N.C. Poultry Plant; Locked Doors Are Said to Add to Toll." *Washington Post,* September 4, A1.

————. 1991b. "Ashes and Accusations; Charges Fly over Factory Fire Deaths." *Washington Post,* September 5, A1.

Torres, Vicki. 1995. "'Slave' Shop Generated Few Suspicions." *Los Angeles Times,* August 5, D1.

Wallace, Bill. 1995. "70 Immigrants Found in Raid on Sweatshop; Thai Workers Tell Horror Stories of Captivity." *San Francisco Chronicle,* August 4, A12.

Washington Post. 1992. "Poultry Producer Gets 20 Years in Deaths of 25 Workers in Fire." September 15, A12.

Weingarten, Randi. 1981. "The Reemergence of the Sweatshop in the Downstate New York Area." *Industrial and Labor Relations Forum* 15, no. 2: 61–120.

White, George. 1995. "Workers Held in Near-Slavery, Officials Say." *Los Angeles Times,* August 3, A1.

White, George, and Patrick Lee. 1995. "Of Neighbors and Fences: Officials, Industry Express Anger over El Monte Case." *Los Angeles Times,* August 5, D1.

Wong, Morrison G. 1983. "Chinese Sweatshops in the United States: A Look at the Garment Industry." *Research in the Sociology of Work* 2: 357–79.

III
Implications for Theory and Scholarship

11

Scholarship That Might Matter

David S. Meyer

The wave of social movements that defined the 1960s shook not only the governments and societies of Western nations but also the academic study of social movements. Earlier scholarship had emphasized the irrationality and danger of social protest movements, casting a critical eye toward fascism in particular. In contrast, some who were pounding away at typewriters in university offices during the 1960s turned their attention to what was going on outside their windows. And it was quite a lot: it was the heyday of the civil rights and antiwar movements, and student movements were sweeping college and university campuses across the advanced industrialized world. The activities in the streets—and on the quads—challenged the received wisdom about social movements and raised fundamental questions about social movements, politics, and democracy.

In orientation, many of these early scholars were sympathetic to the movements of the day; in effect, their work often supported those movements, most significantly by validating their efforts. The early empirical work focused on basic questions, applying then-state-of-the-art methods to taken-for-granted assumptions about protest movements. Challenging preexisting conventional and scholarly wisdom, researchers found that protest was a reasonable politics for those otherwise poorly positioned to make claims (Lipsky 1970), that protest organizers were sane and better adjusted psychologically than nonparticipants (Keniston 1968), and that organizers helped people to recognize injustice and the possibility of collective action and, thus, to rebel (Gamson, Fireman, and Rytina 1982).

At the same time, the establishment of social movements as a legitimate field of inquiry in the academy hasn't necessarily generated very much new information that has percolated out to the people who are actually making social movements, creating something of an ongoing rearguard criticism within the academy (e.g., Flacks, ch. 1 this volume) and much forced discussion of activism and academia. Although such dialogues have been useful, more useful, I argue, is to resurrect the spirit of *praxis,* that is, theoretical reflection based on action and tested in further action. We should apply scholarly methods and tools to questions that come from engagement in social movements. This piece makes a tentative first step in setting a foundation for activism-oriented scholarship. I begin by considering, briefly, why prevailing social movement scholarship generally disappoints critics whose sympathies lie outside academia. I then suggest a series of questions drawn from activist dilemmas that might animate a more usable social movement scholarship.

Making Social Movements or Studying Social Movements

The social movements of the 1960s accompanied an expansion of the university in America and propelled a large number of people into academic study of sociology, history, and political science in general, and into the study of social movements in particular. Activists went into the academy for a variety of reasons. At bare minimum, it afforded the opportunity to stay on campus, a place that seemed so vital, volatile, and even important. Indeed, one line of analysis held that students were the new vanguard for social change, and many activists wanted to stay close. Others went into the academy to make sense of the activity they'd already engaged in and, moreover, to learn to be more effective. But how could studying social movements help to make them more effective?

Not a few critics have charged that the move into the academy was, at best, an individual solution to making a life, and at worst, a distraction for individuals and a diversion for movements. Russell Jacoby (1989) has powerfully and polemically argued that when activists went into the academy the academy went into them, transforming their concerns and reorienting their organizing efforts from movements and politics to careers. Their thoughts and research would be directed to a community of scholars, such as it is, the profession, rather than a broader public audience.

At the same time—outside the academy—there is no shortage of writing dedicated to activists. Naomi Klein's successful text for the movement against corporate globalization, *No Logo* (1999), offers something like an all-purpose manual for activists, heavily weighted toward materials that document the negative consequences of corporate globalization on health, democracy, and justice. The book also includes enthusiastic reports on activist efforts against the emerging economic order, highlighting successful strategies for political action, and deriving lessons for the next wave of activism. Klein's book is only a relatively recent entry in a well-established category of manuals for activists that offer how-to approaches to political activism and, often, useful contacts (e.g., Alinsky 1971). Such works, however, are rarely written by people who study social movements academically, nor are they generally valued in academic scholarship; there seems to be a growing distance between activist thinking and the contributions of those who study activists.

On one level, this shouldn't be all that surprising. Academia, like any other large institution, has rules and norms, reinforced by incentives and sanctions, that channel behavior—and not toward social change. Being an academic is a different job than being an activist. The young professor who forgets this risks compromising performance in both roles, to say nothing of losing a means of livelihood. Moreover, while both roles demand a kind of intellectual honesty, the different venues call for faith in different activities and time for reflection on very different matters. One likely outcome of the separation of intellectual inquiry about political activism from activism itself is that activists or scholars who try to do both jobs at the same time do neither well; there is another, perhaps more common outcome: diversion. Activism and academic study of activism become dichotomous, such that activists don't have time to think beyond the instrumental demands of the current campaign, and scholars veer into theoretical abstractions that, while potentially useful to building basic knowledge, are so far removed from often urgent contemporary questions that their works are easily ignored with no risk but to those who may have initially inspired them.

That said, it is possible for the study of social movements to be more useful to activists if framed around the passionate pursuit of answers to questions that are important to people trying to change the world. It is not so much that existing research traditions have avoided such pursuits as that they haven't been primary goals. Successful scholars have pursued the development of broad-gauge theory about social movements and social change or microlevel interactions among activists and authorities, and/or developed new methods of analysis and sought data sets with which to road test them. Nonetheless, much of the work that has gone on provides a foundation for a useful, activist-oriented social science, which will develop when the questions that confound activists are put at the center of academic research. Here, I want to suggest some of those questions and ways to pursue their answers. Most to the point, I want to provide a window into an academic world in which scholars would put the concerns of activists at the center of their scholarship.

Perhaps natural science provides something of a model. Cell biologists who study cell growth and differentiation maintain contact with other scientists who study disease, and even physicians who treat diseases. The zoologist who studies, say, particular strains of rodents can offer helpful insight on how to keep those rodents alive in captivity, how to breed a threatened species, and perhaps what sorts of habitats need to be designed or preserved to ensure species survival. While she may not be spending a lot of her professional time cleaning cages, her efforts are not completely divorced from those who do take care of the animals. With a target of developing useful knowledge, scholars can start with commitments that generate questions, not answers. Collectively they draw material from the world, as well as from laboratories and computer simulations. Most significant, they want honest answers to their research, feeling glad to get better information on questions of critical concern. The concept of praxis, that is, action with reflection, not in much favor in the academy, can provide a model for thinking about the utility of scholarship. To take time to think analytically about decisions typically made on the fly could enable scholars to come up with meaningful answers to important questions about actually staging social movements. Reflection follows action, and is then tested in subsequent action.

I want to suggest a variety of ways in which scholars can be useful to social movements. Let me start by recognizing that there are all sorts of social movements that many of today's scholars will have little interest in supporting. When Max Weber ([1919] 1946) warned against allowing politics into the classroom or scholarship, student politics in Germany was mostly nationalist, conservative, and anti-Semitic. (His less-than-inspiring vision of the scholar pursuing progressively narrower and more arcane issues must be considered in the context of available alternatives at the time.) We should not blindly endorse helping social movements altogether as a goal, nor should we confine honest research to those groups with which we identify. Indeed, research on the despicable is underrepresented in the modern scholarly canon and may be very important, both politically and in providing a broader understanding of protest politics (see, e.g., Blee 2002; Berlet and Lyons 2000). That said, I now turn to ways in which social movement scholarship can serve social movement activism.

A first broad distinction between ways in which scholarship can serve activism and, dare I add, ultimately democracy is between those who concern themselves with the grievances activists address and scholarship that focuses on the ways in which activists organize and make claims. In the first category, many scholars look at the effects of actual and intended policies, and analyze and report on their findings and their opinions. Knowing the likely effects of different standards of regulating toxic discharge, for example, is of obvious use to environmental activists, and clarity and honesty are always assets. Social justice advocates want to know with as much reliability as possible about the effects of changing tax rates and systems, offering Head Start programs or housing subsidies, or considering race as a factor in university admissions. The efforts of Amory Lovins and Hunter Lovins (1981), for example, as intellectuals organic to the environmental movement, or Randall Forsberg (1994), Mary Kaldor (2001), or Alva Myrdal (1982), who wrote in the service of the peace movement, were critical. These movement intellectuals legitimated and, to a certain degree, shaped the concerns of activists, laying out both criticisms of contemporary policies and suggesting alternatives.

Such useful scholarship is quite apart from the concerns of social movement scholarship. Developed expertise on public policy generally, or specific areas such as antipoverty policy, taxation, education, or nuclear weapons, is a resource for activists. It helps identify goals and buttress both instrumental and normative arguments about goals. This scholarship endorses and encourages activist efforts, but does not examine the questions that animate studies of social movements, specifically the how and why and the outcomes of mobilization. In other words, scholarship on issue areas can shape the ends of activism but gives little guidance on what is to be done. The message of the policy scholars is ultimately vague advice advocating some specific set of alternatives without dealing with how desired reforms might be achieved.

Scholarship That Could Matter

Activists generally spend far more time discussing and debating questions about how to mobilize than about the explicit grievances around which they organize. In my experience, the largest and most disruptive debates within movements are about the effects of particular strategies rather than the intrinsic merits of particular positions on issues. There is little serious debate about the primary issues of concern, that is, the grievances that activism addresses, as the initial decision to attend a meeting, organize an event, or show up at a fund-raiser serves as something of an ideological screen. Environmental justice crusaders don't generally argue about the need for government oversight so much as the best ways to pursue their larger agenda and to mobilize others, including government. In the same way, within social movement organizations, activists are much less likely to argue about the merits of tax policy, the morality of their position on abortion, gay and lesbian rights, the desirability of a higher minimum wage, or the morality of nuclear deterrence than about the best ways to motivate, mobilize, and organize those who agree with them, educate those less aware, and respond to those who oppose them. Absent established answers to the how questions, activists resort to habits and belief, familiar routines, and well-established scripts for action that may not have ever been particularly effective, or—even if optimal at one point—are less adapted to current circumstances. Systematic research and scholarship can help shine some kind of light on such issues. Both activists and scholars want to know, for example, what works in communicating issues to people outside a social movement organization, what tactics of influence are effective and when, how to respond to political defeats or victories, and how to manage alliances with politicians. Without knowing real answers to what are, after all, answerable questions, debates turn on habit, superstition, or personal affiliations. We can all do better. If we as scholars can take the questions that activists engage with as our own, effectively entering into the how and why, we can create a useful social science.

In the sections that follow, I draw questions that come more from my own relatively limited activist experience than from my academic work. My contention is that activist questions can drive important and useful scholarship. Of course, we can find questions by looking beyond our experience to that of other activists and organizers. Teaching and service can provide links that ultimately help create and enliven an activist social sciences.

When and Who to Mobilize for What

One point well established in the scholarly literature on movements is that activists generally agree on far more than their explicitly articulated grievances, which represent the proverbial tip of an ideological and political iceberg, 90 percent of which is submerged and invisible. Indeed, at any given time, organizers try to pick the most promising or urgent issue on which to mobilize and educate from a whole range of other issues. Thus, the American citizen concerned with social justice in the United States might organize for a nuclear test ban in 1963, civil rights for African-Americans in 1964, against military intervention in Vietnam in 1965, for abortion rights in 1970, for an Equal Rights Amendment in 1972, and against nuclear power in 1977. Although scholars have long recognized that individual activists move among distinct issues and campaigns while maintaining the same essential worldview and activist orientation (e.g., Klatch 1999; McAdam 1988), and while others have noted the connections among seemingly distinct movements (della Porta and Rucht 1995; Meyer and Whittier 1994), there is much work to be done to turn this recognition into usable activist knowledge. Indeed, most scholarship recognizes each of those episodes as part of a different movement, and case studies of each will generally do little more than note connections among campaigns without explaining why many activists move from one issue to another over the course of a career.

Organizers want to know which issues are most promising for mobilization at any given time, specifically, the issues on which their efforts are most likely to be successful—to generate attention, support, and influence. To a large extent, organizers operate reactively, rather than strategically, without analytical leverage on why they pick the issues they pick. On one hand, "specialists," that is, people associated with a particular organization, especially those employed by a movement organization, operate with a systematic optimistic bias (Gamson and Meyer 1996), believing that this time this issue will catch the imagination of a larger public. Seizing every chance to press their claims, they develop resilience as most of their efforts to mobilize meet little response. During the odd times when their concerns might line up with larger openings or propensities in mainstream politics and society, they may mistakenly neglect the circumstances beyond activist control that made it so. Thus, crusaders against the death penalty, for example, motivated by moral concerns, may neglect the role that DNA evidence has played in generating a more fertile field for their efforts. They often lack the flexibility to deal with new circumstances and new alliances, and are ill-prepared to control the agenda when opportunities come their way.

Alternatively, and probably more commonly, activists react in the moment to agendas pursued by politicians and government. To some degree, this is understandable, even desirable; activists should respond to changing political situations. At the same time, it is essential to keep a broader agenda in mind while responding to the crisis of the moment. For example, President George W. Bush set the political agenda for a wide range of activist groups by preparing to invade Iraq, and organizers did everything they could to stop that war. The flexibility and focus of activist groups worldwide allowed organizers to build the largest and most global antiwar movement in history. In spite of massive global mobilization against the war, however, the United States led a military attack that fractured the massive international antiwar coalition. Component activist groups moved on to a range of other issues, ill-prepared to make claims or engage in public education efforts on the war even as the occupation of Iraq lent credence to their articulated charges and concerns just months earlier.

The challenge, of course, is to find the issue that allows a window to the public, but to maintain a broader political program at the same time. Either by rigorously adhering to a single program or flexibly responding to every new circumstance, organizers underperform. The rigid specialist will hit the mark on occasion but is more likely to miss, squandering opportunities. The flexible opportunist will be in the news and the public eye more often, but with less force and depth. Further, he may miss the opportunity to be most effective at influencing policy by not building institutional inroads that can be exploited in times of less mobilization. We know, for example, that peace activists do best when the perceived threat of war is greatest. At such times, however, the prospects for effecting change are the lowest, and activist influence may be in preventing an unwelcome change in the status quo rather than in promoting more desirable alternatives (Meyer 2004). Activists are cognizant of these dangers and try to navigate these difficult straits, but do so mostly on instinct. Within social movement coalitions, superstition, ideology, and market forces interact, as activists argue about which issues are most central at what time.

Scholars could help. One strand of research on social movements addresses political opportunities, that is, the constellation of factors outside a social movement that make its claims more or less likely to resonate with a broader public as well as when social movements are likely to affect public policy. Thus far, most research reads political opportunities back through mobilization, but an activist-oriented social science *could* identify sets of factors that activists can track in making strategic decisions about issues, claims, and tactics. Such a social science would look at times when opportunities for mobilization appear (e.g., Sawyers and Meyer 1999) but are unexploited by activists, as well as the reasons that lead organizers to miss such opportunities. The questions, when are peace movements most likely to emerge, for example, and when are they most likely to influence policy, could serve as a research agenda that activists, as well as scholars, could use. By actively monitoring chances, organizers could enhance their prospects for success. Moreover, by discovering when certain claims are most likely to emerge successfully, academics can add substantially to what we now know about political opportunities.

As students of social movements, we can develop the resources to track the histories of protest, politics, and policy reform on a variety of issues over time. We can see when activist organizations flourish or fade, and when certain issues emerge forcefully on a broader public agenda. By rigorously tracking ebbs and flows of activism and reform, we can begin to untangle the complications of political opportunities and find strategies for activism that are more likely to work under particular circumstances. This historical record is long and developed, but not really well-examined in the context of social movement activism. Indeed, analysts of policy, politics, and movements tend to nod to each other only in passing, missing the chances of finding and understanding connections. We can do better by being more inclusive.

Contextual factors, including politics, policy, and personalities, affect the likelihood that organizers will be able to mobilize broad movements at any time; both organizers and scholars have also been concerned with figuring out which individuals will join in their efforts. Scholars have devoted a great deal of effort to understanding the demographic profiles of those more or less likely to engage in certain movements, and even their psychological dispositions. Although it is theoretically possible that such demographic research could provide a useful kind of market research to activists seeking to proffer ideas, it is fairly unlikely to be of much use for a variety of reasons. First, organizers and scholars both know that the single most important variable affecting individual participation is being asked to participate (Rosenstone and Hansen 1993), and that the degree of effort mobilized from any individual over the long and short term is unpredictable. In short, you have to ask. Second, movements based on identity, for example, target their efforts, understandably, at those identities, regardless of these peoples' likelihood of turning out at a demonstration. If we know, for example, that middle-class whites are more likely to participate in politics, that knowledge provides very little useful information for the organizer seeking to mobilize American Indians on tribal autonomy issues. Indeed, even as we know that those middle-class whites are going to be disproportionately involved in movements for environmental protection, it still seems highly unlikely that any environmental activist would abandon efforts at engaging less likely constituencies in the movement. Besides, only a small percentage of people engage in any particular social movement campaign—across all demographic categories.

Such scholarly work raises a more difficult question for activists: concentrate one's efforts on the faithful or reach out to new constituencies and individuals? Most mobilization for campaigns and events takes place among the organized, we know, and most mobilization takes place en bloc, as activists target not disconnected individuals but key leaders in their outreach efforts. The mobilizer calls those associated with groups she knows, organizers she's worked with before, and leaders in established social and political institutions, including churches, clubs, and other political groups. The advantage of this strategy is obvious: people who have organized and mobilized in the past are likely to do so again, if convinced, in the future. At the same time, this means that the unorganized remain unorganized and unmobilized, and the turnout at a demonstration is a familiar one, almost regardless of the issue.

Useful scholarship could examine the inherent trade-offs here, in terms of effort spent organizing, composition of the turnout at an event, and the message it sends. If, as social capital alarmists would have us believe (e.g., Putnam 2000), Americans are less engaged in the civic institutions that compose social life as well as the infrastructure of social protest mobilization, organizers will be targeting a smaller and smaller percentage of the population in their efforts. If, as proponents of a "social movement society" (e.g., Meyer and Tarrow 1998) would have us believe, a greater number of constituencies and causes will resort to social movement tactics, the organized will be increasingly deluged with calls for action. Thus, social movements in the United States will, despite the best efforts of organizers, reflect—and perhaps promote—increased inequality.

Linking Issues

I participated in numerous long and heated meetings during the 1980s, during which peace activists argued about what issues should be linked to the very visible nuclear freeze campaign then sweeping the United States. At one point on the linkage spectrum were so-called freeze fundamentalists who believed that the impact of the movement and its message would be diluted if any additional claims were added to a demand for a bilateral freeze, even if the details of the promised freeze were spelled out to include particular weapons systems. Around them, others argued that in order to be intellectually honest and politically effective, the freeze strength had to be used to press for positions on other issues, including reducing economic inequality in the United States, fighting global capitalism, ending war, increasing development of conventional military forces, stopping deployment of new nuclear missiles in Western Europe, promoting human rights in the Soviet Union, cutting U.S. military spending, ending discrimination against gays and lesbians, stopping the development of nuclear power, ending U.S. military intervention in Latin America and the Middle East, combating racism, ending medical experiments on animals, promoting the election of Democrats to state and national office, ending abortion, and promoting abortion rights. Activists made credible arguments that each of these positions, along with many others, was inextricably linked to a fuller understanding of the forces promoting the nuclear arms race, and that it was morally and politically irresponsible to oversimplify the issues. There was a minority position on every one of these decisions.

Most of the discussions about the inherent linking of those issues took a backseat to discussions about the political expedience of certain links. (Although a few people were sometimes willing to make moral arguments about the necessity of speaking a comprehensive truth to power, majorities in all of the groups I knew were never willing to write off reaching a broader audience as a goal.) Linking issues was a way not only to expand public understanding of the context of nuclear weapons issues, but also to reach and mobilize additional constituencies. Of course, every expansion of the political agenda risked the alienation of core activist constituencies and embracing some kind of political stigma in the larger political arena. To take an obvious example: both feminist and radical Catholic activists were key activist constituencies for the freeze (Meyer and Whittier 1994); any position on abortion would be politically divisive within the freeze coalition. At the same time, the so-called freeze fundamentalism carried a risk of developing very shallow—albeit broad—political support that would be easily co-opted. (To a large extent, this is what happened; see Meyer 1990.) I took positions on each potential linkage, arguing for some and against others, with tremendous urgency and certainty, and absolutely no evidence. In this regard, my participation in the movement was typical.

Such discussions were not peculiar to the nuclear freeze movement. While the freeze campaign generally rejected the link to nuclear power, for example, antinuclear activists had, just a few years earlier, rejected discussion of the nuclear weapons issue as unnecessarily divisive and distracting. Indeed, the same sets of issues and debates, along with others, were recycled within movement coalitions in the recent mobilization against the war in Iraq and are attendant to virtually all social movements in America. The challenge is clear: organizers seek a definition of a problem narrow *enough* to mobilize a large *enough* constituency, yet clear and comprehensive *enough* to be politically meaningful. Of course, the actual definition of "enough" is never explicit, and these debates and discussions take place in an atmosphere in which ideology, habit, and superstition substitute for information. At the same time, to expect organizers to have the time, resources, and skills to find better answers is unfair; scholars could help.

The issues linked and not linked to a growing movement affect several critical elements of a movement's trajectory, including the scope and vitality of a movement coalition, the public reception of movement claims, and the process of political institutionalization. Sharon Kurtz (2002) has shown that discussions about issues reflect conceptions of identity and the day-to-day practices within a movement. Given the clear importance of these issues, surely there are better and worse answers for activists engaged in these sorts of debates, and data would help. Addressing the consequences of various issue linkages is something that scholars could do, and the questions are interesting theoretically as well as important substantively. To my knowledge, such research is largely missing from the scholarly canon, but it need not be. Historical studies of movements that cycle through American political institutions could focus on the choice of defined issues and alliances and trace the consequences of those links, and this would help. Survey research or experimental designs that focus on issue linkages could also inform activist decisions. Pollsters working for candidates for elective office conduct such tests, assessing whether a strong stance on a critical issue helps or hurts their employer's prospects, and smart candidates listen to this research. Most social movement organizations lack the resources to assess the impact of taking a stand on a new issue, but the connections among issues raise questions of substantial theoretical importance to social movement scholars. In short, such research is worth doing, both politically and academically.

Examining the Strategy of Social Protest

More generally, activists want to know what works and how. Within social movement coalitions and organizations, there are heated debates about tactics: whether to emphasize disruption or cooperation with authorities; whether to employ civil disobedience, and if so, how; whether to work with one or both of the major political parties; whether to engage in electoral politics, and if so, how. Most start with a large set of potential tactics off-limits, ranging from political violence to endorsing political candidates, restrictions drawn from organizational charters, state laws, and moral commitments. Most start also with sometimes explicit assumptions about how political change takes place and what tactics are most effective at promoting policy reform, but these beliefs are supported, if at all, by anecdote, rather than systematic research. Here, too, scholars could help by tracing the actual sources of major policy changes and the trajectories of social movements over time.

In this case, Bill Gamson's ([1975] 1990) landmark study, *The Strategy of Social Protest*, offers inspiration rather than concrete answers for activists. Gamson's pioneering effort assessed which challenging organizations got some of what they wanted from political authorities, but strategy referred to some issues well outside the control of activists. If we think about political strategy as making the most of the resources one has by picking claims, tactics, and venues, we can assess the outcomes of different strategies. If we can determine which constituencies are helped by protest, for example, and when, we will actually be providing not only answers to scholars, but information to ongoing activist debates.

We know, for example, that as a cycle of protest passes its peak, some groups or activists try to escalate their tactics, turning increasingly to non-violent civil disobedience or even violent action. At the same time, others try to build inroads into institutional politics or abandon the issue altogether (Tarrow 1989). We know that these tendencies co-occur, but we don't really know how they influence each other. We also don't know what activists can do to maintain linkages between the margins and the mainstream, although it seems clear that these links are what make social movements most powerful. This too is work worth doing.

Conclusion

While activists have provided material for scholars of social movements, scholars have not done much to reciprocate. To be sure, there are some notable exceptions that provide models for the rest of us. For example, Kim Voss and Rachel Sherman's (2000) study of the revitalization of some union chapters identifies factors that allowed some chapters to embrace new strategies, alliances, and issues. They find that organizers who come to labor from other social movements are those most likely to bring new militancy to local organizing and to revitalize activism.

I have argued here that useful scholarship comes from placing activist questions, rather than political commitments, at the center of research projects. I would hold (with Weber) that a scholar's work should not use the apparatus of academia to justify his or her own political beliefs and commitments. Rather, we should to try to answer critical questions where we are animated by a passionate concern for finding truth. Like everyone reading this book, there are some issues on which I am not genuinely open to argument. Both activist and academic positions on, say, abortion or the death penalty, are generally not responsive to data. Scholars should pick questions on which they will be responsive to what they find.

Of course, more can be done. Academics enjoy an institutional space for reflection and an ongoing opportunity to engage with students on issues of concern. In this regard, it is critical to embrace the essentially democratic goal of giving students, activists, and communities the tools to make sense of their lives and politics—even if each outcome and choice is not what we might like. By sharing both the open inquiry and the institutional space with activists, forging alliances with community activists, we can expose our scholarship to real concerns and real data, in effect subjecting our theories and models to a variety of tests: empirical validity, communicative accessibility, and activist utility. By opening that space for activists within the academy, we can afford them a place to reflect on their own efforts and make use of whatever scholarly wisdom is available, writing in language that is accessible to nonspecialists. We can benefit from an approach that treats academic research as a means to answer questions that are important outside the academy. If we do so, we can reasonably assume it will improve not only our scholarship, but also our citizenship.

References

Alinsky, Saul. 1971. *Rules for Radicals: A Practical Primer for Realistic Radicals.* New York: Vintage.

Berlet, Chip, and Matthew N. Lyons. 2000. *Right-Wing Populism in America: Too Close for Comfort.* New York: Guilford.

Blee, Kathleen M. 2002. *Inside Organized Racism: Women in the Hate Movement.* Berkeley: University of California Press.

della Porta, Donatella, and Dieter Rucht. 1995. "Left-Libertarian Movements in Context: A Comparison of Italy and West Germany, 1965–1990." In *The Politics of Social Protest: Comparative Perspectives on States and Social Movements,* ed. J. Craig Jenkins and Bert Klandermans, 229–72. Minneapolis: University of Minnesota Press.

Forsberg, Randall. 1994. *The Arms Production Dilemma: Contraction and Restraint in the World Combat Aircraft Industry.* Cambridge: MIT Press.

Gamson, William A. 1968. *Power and Discontent.* Homewood, IL: Dorsey Press.

———. [1975] 1990. *The Strategy of Social Protest.* Belmont, CA: Wadsworth.

Gamson, William A., Bruce Fireman, and Steven Rytina. 1982. *Encounters with Unjust Authority.* Homewood, IL: Dorsey Press.

Gamson, William A., and David S. Meyer. 1996. "Framing Political Opportunity." In *Comparative Perspectives on Social Movements: Political Opportunities, Mobilizing Structures, and Cultural Framings,* ed. Doug McAdam, John D. McCarthy, and Mayer N. Zald, 275–90. Cambridge: Cambridge University Press.

Jacoby, Russell. 1989. *The Last Intellectuals: American Culture in the Age of Academe.* New York: Noonday Press.

Kaldor, Mary. 2001. *New and Old Wars: Organized Violence in a Global Era.* Stanford, CA: Stanford University Press.

Keniston, Kenneth. 1968. *Young Radicals: Notes on Committed Youth.* New York: Harcourt, Brace, and World.

Klatch, Rebecca. 1999. *A Generation Divided: The New Left, the New Right, and the Sixties.* Berkeley: University of California Press.

Klein, Naomi. 1999. *No Logo: Taking Aim at the Brand Bullies.* New York: Picador.

Kurtz, Sharon. 2002. *Workplace Justice: Organizing Multi-identity Movements.* Minneapolis: University of Minnesota Press.

Lipsky, Michael. 1970. *Protest in City Politics*. Chicago: Rand-McNally.

Lovins, Amory B., and L. Hunter Lovins. 1981. *Energy Policies for Resilience and National Security*. San Francisco: Friends of the Earth.

McAdam, Doug. 1988. *Freedom Summer*. New York: Oxford University Press.

Meyer, David S. 1990. *A Winter of Discontent: The Nuclear Freeze and American Politics*. New York: Praeger.

———. 2004. "Protest and Political Opportunities." *Annual Review of Sociology* 30: 125–45.

Meyer, David S., and Sidney Tarrow. 1998. *The Social Movement Society*. Lanham, MD: Rowman & Littlefield.

Meyer, David S., and Nancy Whittier. 1994. "Social Movement Spillover." *Social Problems* 41, no. 2: 277–98.

Myrdal, Alva. 1982. *The Game of Disarmament*. New York: Pantheon.

Putnam, Robert D. 2000. *Bowling Alone: The Collapse and Revival of American Community*. New York: Touchstone.

Rosenstone, Steven J., and John Mark Hansen. 1993. *Mobilization, Participation, and Democracy in America*. New York: Macmillan.

Ryan, Charlotte. 1991. *Prime Time Activism*. Boston: South End Press.

Sawyers, Traci M., and David S. Meyer. 1999. "Missed Opportunities: Social Movement Abeyance and Public Policy." *Social Problems* 46: 187–206.

Tarrow, Sidney. 1989. *Democracy and Disorder: Protest and Politics in Italy, 1965–1975*. Oxford: Clarendon.

Voss, Kim, and Rachel E. Sherman. 2000. "Breaking the Iron Law of Oligarchy: Union Revitalization in the American Labor Movement." *American Journal of Sociology* 106 (September): 303–49.

Weber, Max. [1919] 1946. "Science as Vocation." In *From Max Weber: Essays in Sociology*, trans. and ed. H. H. Gerth and C. Wright Mills, 129–56. New York: Oxford University Press.

12

Building Bridges, Building Leaders:
Theory, Action, and Lived Experience

Adria D. Goodson

> *I dwell in Possibility—*
> —Emily Dickinson

In many conversations about social movements, the very heart of the movement itself is left out. This chapter recalls the words of the women who, through bringing their experiences into the conversation, gave me a "home." From this emotional and intellectual home I picked up the tools of social movement theory and began to move, to build the theoretical mosaic underpinning my own social justice work. Much like my own racial background—stronger with the melding of both Black and white—the possibilities for social change are stronger with the melding of a Black feminist epistemology and the analytical tools offered in social movement theory.

First, I will engage in a dialogue between Black feminist theory and social movement theory. I will argue that there is a common sensitivity to a view from below and that looking through a Black feminist perspective or an indigenous perspective offers stronger tools for bridging theory to counterhegemonic activism. The second part of the chapter illustrates the power of melding social movement theory explicitly with a social justice perspective rooted in Black feminist theory through my work in philanthropy with a bridging organization, Resource Generation. Through this example I will provide an enriched understanding of bridging as a social movement concept and what it takes to build and sustain bridge leaders and bridging institutions that support social movements.

Melding Theories from Parallel Tracks

The purpose of the first part of this chapter is to revisit the possibilities of social movement theory by giving it its own compass—a compass guided by theories from below. Theory from below, like Aldon Morris's indigenous resource theory and Black feminist theory, acknowledges the capacity of dominated groups, i.e., those operating from below, to generate resources and subsequently to add more resources by uniting allies (bridging). In other words, while dominated peoples exist in a subaltern position, we do not surrender the potential of human agency and personal power.

Several theorists have stated that much of social movement theory is lacking its own moral compass (Ryan, ch. 7 this volume; Flacks 2004; Goodwin and Jasper 2004). These theorists have challenged the purpose of much social movement theory that has been created in the dominant political process paradigm, charging that in the process of paradigm construction and theorizing, the political process model loses much of its heart. Through bridging between Black feminist theory and social movement theory, I hope to connect the heart of critical social theory. Social movement theory and Black feminist theory are the two literatures that provide me with energy that motivates thought and action. By grounding this conversation in the pursuit of social justice, I revive conversations silenced by the overwhelming blizzard of paradigm debate.

Not only the framing of the movement needs to be guided by a sense of injustice as described by William Gamson (1992), but also the theorizing. The efforts of academics, and those in academia who seek to be activists, need to be guided by their own moral compass that is fueled by a desire for justice and possibilities of a different world.

I found my moral compass in Black feminist theory. Black feminist theory could be described as "borning theory," a variation of Bernice Johnson Reagon's titling of the civil rights movement as the "borning movement" of late twentieth-century social movements in the United States—Latino, Asian, women's, gay liberation, environmental justice, and so on (Cluster 1979). Morris's indigenous theory is another example of a borning theory in that it also acknowledges and integrates the role of grassroots activists and indigenous resources (1984, 1992).

It is important to me to retain the "Black" in this title as a tribute to its roots. I do this even while understanding that this races the conversation in a way that the name "intersectional feminist theory" does not. And, I must add, this acknowledges my own heart—it could also be called Brown feminist theory, Chicana feminist theory, Tejana feminist theory. It is rooted in the lived experiences of women who are a variety of shades and colors.

In racing and rooting theorizing, Black feminist and indigenous theorists do not seek to exclude. To the contrary, our intention is to include the marginalized (Sandoval 1991), to incorporate new knowledge and insights into theory and action. Black feminist and indigenous theories open space for theoretical kin and acknowledge related theories that serve and respect those resisting subordination.

At the time I began studying social movement theory, culture was just beginning to be incorporated in the political process social movement theory paradigms. The call for theorizing about the influence of culture, race, gender, and class on social movements brought about a flurry of publications that sought to, among other things, incorporate differences in social location into the preexisting theory. This chapter is not a call for incorporating culture—it is a call for incorporating the insights of Black feminist theory into the very epistemology of social movement theory. How do we know what we know about the possibilities of social movements? How do we ask questions about them? We know about the possibilities of social change from the very core of who we are as people "living in the world" (Reagon 2001, 105).

It is necessary to share a bit about who I am, for that drives not only this chapter, but also my reason for writing it. I am a woman Black/English/Scotch-Irish/Crow corporate professional philanthropic professional social movement student part-time activist triathlete poet sister aunt and bridge worker. None of this is separate. It is a mosaic. It is stated within the epistemology of Black feminist thought, which calls for an integration of all of who I am into the process of theorizing, which recognizes all of me at one time and doesn't seek to break off individual pieces of me (Reagon 1995; Anzaldúa 1987).

In this space, the space of all of me, I can do the work of social moving and theorizing about social moving. For "social moving" I call on the work of Reagon, who reminds us that in the movement something is changed. Reagon states, "Moving was major, tearing, cataclysmic. Changes planned and unplanned, with hope for betterment, were almost always quite disruptive. . . . We Black people needed this new territory to transform our future" (2001, 8–9). It is in the action of moving that I dwell in possibility. And it is as a bridge worker that I span multiple social locations and, in so doing, create possibilities for social justice work.

For those of us who operate at the interstices of historical and hierarchically imposed geopolitical and cultural borders in the pursuit of a more just social structure, it is possible to be paralyzed by these categories and borders. Anzaldúa comments on the experience of being trapped within and between categories and borders: "Petrified, she can't respond, her face caught between los intersticios, the spaces between the different worlds she inhabits" (1987, 20). Or, as Fowlkes and Anzaldúa describe, Anzaldúa can refuse to choose, and in refusing to choose she learns the coping mechanism of "tolerance for ambiguity" (Fowlkes 1997). Fowlkes describes Anzaldúa in the following way, "Because she understands herself as existing where many borders meet or cross simultaneously, she partakes in them all" (ibid.). Through recognizing the simultaneity of imposed categories and mingling across predefined borders, Anzaldúa consciously gathers their effects and prevents them from dividing her within herself and is able to maintain her ability to take action (ibid.).

Black feminist theory calls for the maintenance of the moral center of theory development. To keep "moving" in social movement theory, individuals who are both activists *and* theorists focus on how their actions embody their theories. Social movement theory is one tool that must be used in coalition with others to mount a repeated challenge to social injustice.

Black Feminist Theory and Social Movement Theory: A Dialogue

Some social movement theorists have successfully utilized a Black feminist theoretical perspective as a tool to incorporate an examination of multiple, overlapping structures of power (Buechler 2000; Robnett 1997; Giddings 1984). According to Patricia Hill Collins, Black feminist thought is both critical social theory and specialized/subjugated knowledge. Black feminist theory reflects the interests and standpoint of its creators and its core themes; "work, family, sexual politics, motherhood, and political activism rely on paradigms that emphasize the importance of intersecting oppressions in shaping the U.S. matrix of domination" (Collins 2000, 251). Paradigms encompass interpretative frameworks that can be used to explain social phenomena. Within Black feminist thought, the paradigm of intersecting oppressions also becomes a critical part of the epistemology of the theory. Epistemology "investigates the standards used to assess knowledge or why we believe what we believe to be true. Epistemology points to the ways in which power relations shape who is believed and why" (ibid., 252). Collins goes on to say, "the level of epistemology is important because it determines which questions merit investigation, which interpretative frameworks will be used to analyze findings, and to what use any ensuing knowledge will be put" (ibid.).

In the ongoing debate within academia, the political process model of social movement activism has been critiqued by those identified as "new social movement theorists"—including Black feminist researchers—for emphasizing structure, strategies, and institutions at the expense of cultural elements, social psychological processes, and a more complete understanding of both collective and individual identity (Gamson 1992; Taylor 1995, 2000; Robnett 1997; Melucci and Lyrra 1998; Flacks 2004; Goodwin and Jasper 2004). Simply incorporating the different identifications or culture that inform people's social lives misses out on this underlying epistemology of Black feminist epistemology. According to Richard Flacks, social movements are a search for the latent power available to powerless groups, and the Tilly, McAdam, and Tarrow approach does not do a systematic analysis of the logic of power relations (Flacks 2004). Black feminist theory informs the political process approach by redefining "power" as existing within a matrix of domination and intersecting oppressions of race, class, and gender.

Collins argues that Black feminist theory fosters a fundamental paradigmatic shift in how we think about unjust power relations. By embracing a paradigm of intersecting oppressions of race, class, gender, sexuality, and nation, as well as Black women's individual and collective agency within them, Black feminist thought reconceptualizes the social relations of domination and resistance (Collins 2000, 204–9). Building on earlier efforts, throughout the 1980s and 1990s researchers began to document the role of Black women in the U.S. civil rights movement and beyond (Giddings 1984; Morris 1984; Barnett 1995; Robnett 1997). Working out of a feminist theoretical model and utilizing a Black feminist lens that identifies a matrix of domination, these researchers have provided both theoretical and empirical insights into the dynamics of identity, cultural elements, and social psychological processes (Ward 2004; Kurtz 2002; Ryan, ch. 7 this volume; Collins 2000; Giddings 1984; Robnett 1997). In Robnett's work, for example, she demonstrates that the social location of an individual in relation to society and the movement provides a means of understanding movement mobilization and can lead to routes of inquiry about how movements cultivate collective identities and how this translates into collective action (Robnett 1997).

Robnett utilizes four micromobilization processes that Snow et al. (1986) outline as the social psychological processes central to the recruitment process: frame bridging, frame amplification, frame extension, and frame transformation:

> Frame bridging involves providing those already predisposed to one's cause with information sufficient to induce them to join the movement. Frame amplification rests on the compatibility of the movement's values

and beliefs with those of the potential constituents, emphasizing efforts to convince individuals that their participation is crucial and that the movement's goals can be achieved. Frame extension occurs when movement adherents cast a wider recruitment net, incorporating concerns not originally part of the movement's goals but valuable as a means of expanding support. Frame transformation is the process whereby individually held frames are altered, entirely or in part, to achieve consensus with the movement's goals. (Robnett 1997, 19)

Through these social psychological processes Robnett focuses her study of Black women and their leadership roles during the U.S. civil rights movement. By utilizing these processes with a Black feminist lens that recognizes the social location of the individual, she illuminates new ways of understanding mobilization.

As another example, Buechler (2000) incorporates multiple levels of analysis at the global, regional, and national levels. He utilizes the regional level as an analytical tool to incorporate Collins's concept of the "matrix of oppression" (2000). Referring to Collins, Buechler states, "the most complex aspect of these structures of power involves their interrelations with one another and the simultaneity of all these group affiliations and sources of identity. . . . Although it is possible to isolate each structure for the purpose of analytical discussion, real social actors inhabit multiple, overlapping locations in these structures that make any simple predictions from structure to action impossible" (2000, 106).

Acknowledging and utilizing these structures go beyond analytical discussion when they become a means of making sense of one's own personal multiple locations in preparation for social activism. As an activist and a theorist, as a woman and an academic, as a Black person and a white person, making sense of these structures becomes critical for my own ability to move forward and contribute to both activism and theory. These tools are useful beyond analytical discussion, which in my view is what makes theory useful. As Collins states, "critical social theory constitutes theorizing about the social in defense of economic and social justice. Stated differently, critical social theory encompasses bodies of knowledge and sets of institutional practices that actively grapple with the central questions facing groups of people differently placed in specific political, social and historic contexts characterized by injustice. What makes social theory 'critical' is its commitment to justice, for one's own group and/or for other groups" (1998, xiv). This could be translated into: what makes social movement theory useful is its "commitment to justice, for one's own group and/or for other groups."

Building on this dialogue between Black feminist theory and social movement theory, there are three specific theoretical concepts that are enriched through this coalition: safe spaces, bridge leaders, and building bridging institutions. Safe spaces and bridge leaders are the prerequisites for creating sustainable bridging institutions that can link allies in different social locations and create resources and relationships across traditional divides. In accomplishing this, safe spaces and bridge leaders create possibilities for building something more solid and long-term. The Boston College Media Research and Action Project is an example of a safe space.

Boston College Media Research and Action Project: Borning Possibility in Safe Spaces

As a novice social movement theorist/activist operating at the interstices, the safe space that the Boston College Media Research and Action Project (MRAP) provided was critical. The MRAP provides a home for me from which I can venture out to build coalitions in an effort to participate in and sustain fighting against social inequality and injustice. According to Gamson, "safe spaces are limited access public spaces that permit the development of an oppositional culture" (1996, 31). Gamson (1996) builds on the work of Evans and Boyt in their discussion of "free political space" in which individuals are able to develop new self-respect, a more assertive group identity, and skills and values that enable them to engage in developing collective action frames.

Through having MRAP as a safe space for my own development, I have been able to move between social locations and remain strong and committed to the possibilities and to pick up and effectively use the micromobilization tools that Robnett (1997) speaks of: bridging, amplifying, extending, and transforming. In this fashion, I have been able to embody the role of bridge leader and to engage in the process of trying to build bridging institutions.

I entered MRAP as a new graduate student in sociology at Boston College. MRAP was in essence operating as a halfway house, a term coined by Morris (see Ryan, ch. 7 this volume). A halfway house enables activists to understand theory and theorists to make consistent links to activism (Morris 1984). A halfway house is more than a link, however, especially for those who are still in the process of developing their own perspective, actions, and theories. A halfway house is an incubator of new ideas, which are often fragile and not quite thought out. New ideas are the stuff that activism is made out of—finding new ways to challenge entrenched structures of power takes an inventive mind that has room to move. New ideas also require cross-fertilization, the kind that arises out of cross-disciplinary dialogue as demonstrated in the first part of this chapter. Halfway houses, like MRAP, create safe spaces for theory generation and are the starting points for building sustainable bridges.

Halfway houses also nourish the oppositional consciousness from which counterhegemonic resistance flows. Sandoval argues that "oppositional consciousness depends upon the ability to read the current situation of power . . . self-consciously choosing and adopting the ideological form best suited to push against its configurations, a survival skill well known to oppressed peoples" (1991, 15). Springer comments that the "theory of oppositional consciousness recognizes the multidimensional flow of power and privilege. Incorporating oppositional consciousness into collective identity theory makes identity formation dynamic and defined by those who hold privilege and power within a social movement" (1999, 32). Bridging is one way that subaltern groups navigate this flow; bridging institutions provide support for their actions.

Unlike Robnett and her colleagues, I am defining "bridging" as creating resources, relationships, and ideas amid the "multidimensional flow of power and privilege" represented by the traditional divides. This definition goes beyond individual micromobilization techniques and instead includes bridging activities that build sustainable relationships over time, generate resources, and create bridging institutions rather than individual techniques. Bridging activities such as these create possibilities for sustaining theory generation, relation generation, and resource generation. Networks, unlike bridges, are a series of single lines of relationship, loose connections and affiliations. Bridges, which can be built with rope or stone, must sustain traffic for a period of time and therefore build stronger relationships and richer opportunities for individuals and groups to exchange ideas and resources.

In order to grow and nurture bridge leaders, it is necessary to support and create both safe spaces (Gamson 1996) and bridging institutions. Safe spaces that provide a home as described by Bernice Johnson Reagon (1995) are critical. Once safe spaces are established, bridge leaders can move out from there and be "borned," nurtured, trained, and encouraged through loose networks and efforts funded by philanthropic foundations and allies with access to resources.

Bridge leaders and bridging institutions reach out from these safe spaces to create possibilities for change. In her speech "Coalition Politics: Turning the Century," Reagon states, "That is the nature of coalition. . . . It is not to feed you, you have to feed it. . . . So you better be sure you got your home someplace for you to go to so that you will not become a martyr" (1995, 544). MRAP provides such a home. Striving to develop work that reflects "all of who we are" is what MRAPers seek to do—to explore and develop all of who we are particularly in relation to the pursuit of social justice in all of its forms. It also allows those of us whose identities and personal missions are multiple (this includes everybody, really) to have a home, when in most places we are seeking to build coalitions across varying lines of difference to address social injustice. Safe spaces such as MRAP need to be supported by those who would support social movements dealing with social injustices.

Bridge Leadership

In the end analysis, a dialogue between social movement theory and Black feminist theory does what theory does best—it provides names for the invisible activities of organizing. The concept of bridge leader is a case in point. Barnett (1995) and Robnett (1997) utilize a Black feminist approach to analyze the dynamics of social movements and, through doing so, reconceptualize leadership, organizational dynamics, and repertoires of contention, as well as the intersecting nature of identity. It is on this conceptualization of the individual bridge leader that the concept of a bridging institution is built. For example, Barnett, who has extensively studied women's participation in the U.S. civil rights movement, argues for rethinking the traditional conception of leadership within this context. She argues that the conception of leadership should transform from one that is a formal, public spokesman because it is gender biased and one-dimensional and limits both women's actual opportunities and their recognition as leaders (1995). I would argue that a Black feminist lens guides the conceptualization of things like leadership to a different plane that is multidimensional and interconnected. The social movement organizations exist within the same matrix of domination in which individuals exist. Therefore, utilizing a Black feminist lens to explore the relations of power within a movement, between organizations, and among organizations as they all interact with the state and with each other may provide fruitful ground for activists to develop creative, new strategies of contention within a system where the individuals, the organizations, and the state are all multidimensional.

A Black feminist lens keeps in mind that social location may dictate both an individual's and a collective actor's choices in terms of social movement activity. In her research, Robnett demonstrated that "while it is undoubtedly true, as scholars Charles Tilly and Sidney Tarrow argue, that new contenders adopt, alter and extend upon the 'repertoires of contention' of previous protest groups, it is also true that movement activists may be divided on the issues of which repertoires ought to be used and how. And one's decisions regarding their selection, alteration and implementation rest squarely upon one's social location, both in the movement and in society" (1997, 28).

Robnett's work refers to women holding positions of power, such as grassroots leaders, organizers, and mobilizers, and as "bridge leaders" because they linked the formal power structure of the movement with local community activists and activities (1997). Robnett's conceptualization of bridge leaders comes directly out of a standpoint that examines interconnectedness and dialogue. She defines bridge leaders as those so-called grassroots followers or organizers who "utilized frame bridging, amplification, extension, and transformation to foster ties between the social movement and the community; and between prefigurative strategies and political strategies" (19). She distinguishes between the formal (or primary) leaders and the bridge leaders who were predominantly women because this was the level of leadership that was most open to their participation. The primary leaders focused outside the movement and directed their efforts at the larger, dominant, white society. Bridge leaders focused on linking and relational organizing at the grassroots level (69).

The remainder of this chapter utilizes my experience in philanthropy as a backdrop to explore what is necessary to grow bridge leaders and to build and sustain bridging institutions. It provides an example of the power of melding social movement theory explicitly with a social justice perspective through my work with one such bridging institution, Resource Generation.

Building an Institutional Bridge: An Example

"Those who birth a theory for a movement cannot easily embody the full range of roles necessary to elaborate, sustain, and nurture the theory or the movement. The care and feeding of critical social theory goes hand in hand with the care and feeding of social movements. The work to dwell in possibility to help the whole race (and human race) enter with you by necessity requires collectivity—many people performing mutually respected roles. Black feminist theory, unlike many academic theories, embraces and honors distinct roles" (Ryan, personal communication, 2004).

Currently, I have chosen a distinct role, working in philanthropy. It is a social location that can provide resources (financial, intellectual, and social) in the pursuit of social and economic justice. Through this work, I am perpetually doing the work of coalition building and generating resources across multiple domains. One of the organizations I work with, Resource Generation, is specifically working to organize young individuals with wealth around a progressive social justice agenda.[1] Resource Generation is a philanthropic organization and is seeking to build a bridge from those who

benefit from the current social system to those who don't. At the foundation of Resource Generation's work is the principle stated by Martin Luther
King Jr., "Philanthropy is commendable, but it must not cause the philan-
thropist to overlook the economic injustice that makes philanthropy necessary" (quoted in Tracy and Kohner 2002, 99).

With this underpinning, Resource Generation focuses on growing
and developing social change philanthropists who understand, question,
and challenge social inequality and injustice. As defined by Resource
Generation, "social change philanthropy focuses on the root causes of
social, economic and environmental injustices. It strives to include the
people who are impacted by those injustices as decision makers. It also
aims to make the field of philanthropy and foundations accountable,
transparent and responsive in their grant making. Donors and foundations can act as allies to social justice movements by contributing not only
monetary resources but their time, knowledge, skills and access" (Resource
Generation 2004).

In collaboration with many individuals and groups, Resource Generation built this definition around concepts pulled from the work of activists
and social movement theorists (Ostrander 1995; Jenkins and Halcli 1999).
Their work is a living example of how theory can inform the work of activists and in so doing make each stronger. Resource Generation, which is led
by activists/donors, has purposefully sought theoretical knowledge in con-
junction with activist/experience-based knowledge.

I am a consultant for Resource Generation and over the past three years
have worked with them to develop workshops that provide young people
with the tools to develop their own social change giving plans. Young
people with wealth can play a distinct role in supporting, participating, and
acting as allies for social justice movements. In order for young people with
wealth to engage in social justice movements with integrity, it is necessary
to construct spaces where issues of privilege, power, wealth, and decision
making can be challenged. As a woman of color who does not have inher-
ited wealth, this puts me in the position of working to bridge differences
(race, class, and sometimes gender), find common ground, and work with
other human beings who are at different stages in their own awareness or
interest in creating a more just world. For me, this requires a way of engaging in the world, an epistemology, that is inclusive and challenging at the
same time. The theoretical foundation of Black feminist theory in combination with social movement theory provides both of these elements.

Through this work, I seek to embody the best of the theoretical tools
developed by those who came before me and to operate as a bridge leader

in Robnett's definition of the term. Through this work I am building coalitions with individuals and organizations in an effort to define a possibility for a different way of interacting in the world.

Reaching beyond Safe Spaces and Individual Leaders to Build Sustainable Bridging Institutions

William Gamson posed a question to me in one MRAP session: "If you were the executive director of a new foundation whose mission was to support bridge leaders, what would you fund?" This question has two levels of response. The first is in regard to individual bridge leaders, and the second addresses bridging institutions that can support those individuals. In order to develop individual bridge leaders, I would fund the following:

- Retreats and shared experiences to connect with other bridge leaders and create shared learning (i.e., bridge leader institutes in local social justice foundations that are repeated every quarter to build consistency and trust)
- Mentors who are edge walkers, who connect bridge leaders to power within various social institutions
- Programs that foster cultivating and valuing bridge leaders from an early age (middle school and high school programs that build connections and relationships across traditional boundaries and that reward developing an understanding of social justice issues)
- Specific bridge leader positions within social justice organizations (i.e., community-based organizations, institutional think tanks whose focus is on building relational and institutional resources, institutions that are seeking to organize previously untapped constituencies)
- Training that teaches individual bridge leaders to facilitate learning that challenges people, respects people, and in the end organizes and motivates people to take specific action
- Taking the long-term view that bridge leaders will come in and out of this role as life changes impact possibilities, continuing to support efforts especially when movements are in apparent abeyance

Looking beyond the individual bridge leader, it is important to build sustainable bridging institutions that link individuals and groups across boundaries of historical difference. Bridging institutions require sustainable resource generation for their own activities, not for just those individuals whom the organization connects to each other. In addition to requiring their own resources, bridging institutions create resources for the individuals who move across and through them:

- Safe spaces that provide the necessary institutional support system or infrastructure to enable the work of coalition building and bridge building (these are different concepts)
- Sustainable relationships across social location that become stronger over time rather than through intermittent contact
- Ideas that link shared experiences of alienation and dislocation and empower individuals to envision a different possibility
- Material resources that help challenge existing inequalities and democratize relationships that would otherwise be hampered by inequalities built into their social locations

Concluding Thoughts

At the beginning of this chapter, I entered into a dialogue between Black feminist theory and social movement theory. I argued that in the melding of the two, in the mosaic of these parallel theoretical domains, social movement theory gains a critical moral perspective regarding social injustice that much of social movement theory lacks. Black feminist literature reminded me to keep moving around my own moral center. It provided the grounding, the home, that social movement theory on its own lacked. "Feminist identity politics has an ethical component that gives reason for speaking with and to others, on the way to engaging with them in coalition politics" (Fowlkes 1997). This ethical component is what can encourage social movement theorists to continue to engage in conversations across imposed boundaries of activist/theorist and within and between disciplines. Of course, this is hard. It requires monitoring multiple conversations while navigating multiple identities, systems of reward/success, and means of engaging in the world. But how else will it happen?

As Reagon states about her singing, "I understood early in my performance work that even though I loved to sing, I did not come to the stage for the performance of songs. I came to the stage to sing about and for things I care about as a person living in the world" (2001, 105). I could say the same thing about why I care about social movement theory; even though I love the theoretical (and inherently academic debate), I came to the theory to learn about and encourage movement—action that is built on and/or transformed by the theory. I have found that through becoming a bridge myself and participating in the creation of bridging institutions, I have richer potential, both as a theorist and as an activist.

Notes

This chapter reflects the input of wonderful mentors and editors. In particular, I owe a tremendous debt for the insights of Charlotte Ryan and the encouragement of William Hoynes. Additionally, thoughtful input from William Gamson, Jeff Langstraat, and the MRAP participants guided both the development and the final outcome of this chapter.

1. Thank you to Resource Generation for giving permission to use them as an example.

References

Anzaldúa, Gloria. 1987. *Borderlands = La Frontera: The New Mestiza.* San Francisco: Spinsters/Aunt Lute Press.

Barnett, Bernice McNair. 1995. "Black Women's Collectivist Movement Organizations: Their Struggles during the 'Doldrums.'" In *Feminist Organizations: Harvest of the New Women's Movement,* ed. Myra Marx Ferree and Patricia Yancey Martin, 199–219. Philadelphia: Temple University Press.

Buechler, Steven. 2000. *Social Movements in Advanced Capitalism: The Political and Cultural Construction of Social Activism.* New York: Oxford University Press.

Cluster, Dick. 1979. "The Borning Struggle: The Civil Rights Movement." In *They Should Have Served That Cup of Coffee,* ed. Cluster, 1–38. Boston: South End Press.

Collins, Patricia Hill. 1998. *Fighting Words: Black Women and the Search for Social Justice.* Minneapolis: University of Minnesota Press.

———. 2000. *Black Feminist Thought: Knowledge, Consciousness, and the Politics of Empowerment.* New York: Routledge Press.

Davis, Angela. 1981. *Women, Race, and Class.* New York: Vintage Press.

Dickinson, Emily. 1924. "Poem 657: I Dwell in Possibility—" In *The Complete Poems of Emily Dickenson.* Boston: Little Brown.

Flacks, Richard. 2004. "Knowledge for What? Thoughts on the State of Social Movement Studies." In *Rethinking Social Movements: Structure, Meaning, and Emotion,* ed. Jeff Goodwin and James M. Jasper, 135–53. New York: Rowman and Littlefield.

Fowlkes, Diane L. 1997. "Moving from Feminist Identity Politics to Coalition Politics through a Feminist Materialist Standpoint of Intersubjectivity in Gloria Anzaldúa's *Borderlands = La Frontera: The New Mestiza,* Part 3 of 3." *Hypatia—A Journal of Feminist Philosophy* 12, no. 2: 115–24.

Gamson, William A. 1991. "Commitment and Agency in Social Movements." *Sociological Forum* 6, no. 1: 27–50.

———. 1992. *Talking Politics.* New York: Cambridge University Press.

———. 1996. "Safe Spaces and Social Movements." In *Perspectives on Social Problems,* vol. 8, ed. James A. Holstein and Gail Miller, 27–38. Greenwich, CT: JAI Press.

Giddings, Paula. 1984. *When and Where I Enter: The Impact of Black Women on Race and Sex in America.* New York: Quill, William and Morrow.

Giugni, Marco, Doug McAdam, and Charles Tilly, eds. 1999. *How Social Movements Matter.* Minneapolis: University of Minnesota Press.

Gluck, Sharon Berger. 1998. "Whose Feminism? Whose History?" In *Community Activism and Feminist Politics: Organizing across Race, Class, and Gender,* ed. Nancy Naples, 31–56. New York: Routledge.

Goodwin, Jeff, and James Jasper. 2004. "Caught in a Winding, Snarling Vine: The Structural Bias of Political Process Theory." In *Rethinking Social Movements: Structure, Meaning, and Emotion,* ed. Goodwin and Jasper, 3–30. New York: Rowman and Littlefield.

hooks, bell. 1981. *Ain't I a Woman: Black Women and Feminism.* Boston: South End Press.

Jenkins, Craig, and Abigail Halcli. 1999. "Grassrooting the System? The Development and Impact of Social Movement Philanthropy, 1953–1990." In *Philanthropic Foundations: New Scholarship New Possibilities,* ed. Ellen Condliffe Legamann, 229–56. Bloomington: Indiana University Press.

King, Deborah. 1995. "Multiple Jeopardy, Multiple Consciousness: The Context of a Black Feminist Ideology." In *Words of Fire: An Anthology of African American Feminist Thought,* ed. Beverly Guy-Sheftall, 294–317. New York: New Press.

Kurtz, Sharon. 2002. *Workplace Justice: Organizing Multiple Identity Movements.* Minneapolis: University of Minnesota Press.

McAdam, Doug, John D. McCarthy, and Mayer N. Zald. 1996. Introduction to *Comparative Perspectives on Social Movements: Political Opportunities, Mobilizing Structures, and Cultural Framings,* ed. McAdam, McCarthy, and Zald, 1–20. New York: Cambridge University Press.

Melucci, Alberto, and Timo Lyyra. 1998. "Collective Action, Change, and Democracy." In *From Contention to Democracy,* ed. Marco Guigni, Doug McAdam, and Charles Tilly, 203–27. New York: Rowman and Littlefield.

Morris, Aldon. 1984. *The Origins of the Civil Rights Movement.* New York: Free Press.

———. 1992. "Political Consciousness and Collective Action." In *Frontiers of Social Movement Theory,* ed. Morris and Carol McClurg Mueller, 351–73. New Haven, CT: Yale University Press.

Ostrander, Susan. 1995. *Money for Change: Social Movement Philanthropy at Haymarket People's Fund.* Philadelphia: Temple University Press.

Reagon, Bernice Johnson. 1995. "Coalition Politics: Turning the Century." In *Race, Class, and Gender: An Anthology,* ed. Margaret L. Andersen and Patricia Hill Collins, 540–46. New York: Wadsworth.

———. 2001. *If You Don't Go, Don't Hinder Me.* Lincoln: University of Nebraska Press.

Resource Generation. 2004. "Social Change Giving Notebook." At http://www
.resourcegeneration.org.

Robnett, Belinda. 1997. *How Long? How Long? African-American Women in the Struggle for Civil Rights.* New York: Oxford University Press.

Ryan, Barbara. 1992. *Feminism and the Women's Movement: Dynamics of Change in Social Movement Ideology and Activism.* New York: Routledge.

Sandoval, Chela. 1991. "U.S. Third World Feminism: The Theory and Method of Oppositional Consciousness in the Post Modern World." *Genders* 10 (Spring): 1–24.

Snow, David A., E. Burke Rochford Jr., Steven K. Worden, and Robert D. Benford. 1986. "Frame Alignment Processes, Micromobilization, and Movement Participation." *American Sociological Review* 51: 464–81.

Springer, Kimberly. 1999. "Our Politics Was Black Women: Black Feminist Organizations, 1968–1980." PhD diss., Emory University.

Tarrow, Sydney. 1998. *Power in Movement: Social Movements and Contentious Politics.* New York: Cambridge University Press.

Taylor, Verta. 1989. "Social Movement Continuity: The Women's Movement in Abeyance." *American Sociological Review* 54: 761–75.

———. 1995. "Watching for Vibes: Bringing Emotion into the Study of Feminist Organization." In *Feminist Organizations: Harvest of the New Women's Movement,* ed. Myra Marx Ferree and Patricia Yancey Martin, 223–33. Philadelphia: Temple University Press.

———. 2000. "Mobilizing for Change in a Social Movement Society." *Contemporary Sociology* 29, no. 1: 219–30.

Tilly, Charles. 1978. *From Mobilization to Revolution.* Reading, MA: Addison-Wesley.

Tracy, Gary, and Melissa Kohner. 2002. *Inspired Philanthropy.* San Franciso: Jossey-Bass.

Ward, Jane. 2004. "Not All Differences Are Created Equal." *Gender and Society* 18, no. 1: 82–102.

13

Falling on Deaf Ears: Confronting the Prospect of Nonresonant Frames

David A. Snow and Catherine Corrigall-Brown

One of the significant developments in social movement theorizing and research during the past fifteen to twenty years has been the evolution of the framing perspective on social movements (Benford and Snow 2000; Gamson 1992; McAdam, McCarthy, and Zald 1996; Snow 2004). Its distinctive contribution is that it takes seriously and focuses attention on the signifying work or meaning construction engaged in by social movement activists and participants and other parties (e.g., antagonists, elites, media, countermovements) relevant to the interests of social movements and the challenges they mount. In this context, movements are viewed as signifying agents actively engaged in the production and maintenance of meaning for protagonists, antagonists, and bystanders. Like the media, local governments, the state, and representatives of other authority structures, social movements are regarded as being embroiled in "the politics of signification" (Hall 1982). The verb *framing* is used to conceptualize this signifying work, which is one of the activities that social movement adherents and their leaders engage in on a regular basis. That is, "they frame, or assign meaning to and interpret, relevant events and conditions in ways that are intended to mobilize potential adherents and constituents, to garner bystander support, and to demobilize antagonists" (Snow and Benford 1988, 198). The products of this framing activity within the social movement arena are referred to as collective action frames, which have been conceptualized as "action-oriented sets of beliefs and meanings" that, among other things, "inspire and legitimate the activities and campaigns" of social movement organizations (Benford and Snow 2000, 614; Gamson 1992, 7; Snow and

Benford 1992). Some collective action frames clearly function in this manner, as numerous studies have demonstrated (see Benford and Snow 2000 and Snow 2004 for a listing and summary of these studies). However, this is not always the case, as framing efforts often fail to inspire or direct collective action because audience resonance was never established or because it has withered (Snow et al. 1986, 477; Snow and Benford 1988). In either case, the framing effort is confronted with the problem of nonresonance. That is, the proffered framing falls on deaf ears by failing to generate support among bystanders or potential adherents (what Klandermans [1984] has called "consensus mobilization") or to activate adherents by moving them, metaphorically speaking, from the balcony to the barricades (what Klandermans [ibid.] has called "action mobilization"). In either case, the rhetorical framing efforts of movement activists or leaders do not mobilize intended audiences in the direction or fashion desired.

This problem of nonresonance is of relevance not only to social movement scholars but also to movement practitioners or activists, who often devote a significant portion of their time and energy to mobilizing constituents, converting bystanders, and demobilizing antagonists. Accordingly, in this chapter we seek to advance understanding of nonresonant frames, that is, frames that do not appear to strike a responsive chord with presumed constituents or targets even though they may have done so sometime in the past or its proponents or sponsoring activists think the cause or issue warrants mobilization.

Previously, Benford and Snow (2000, 619–22; Snow and Benford 1988) suggested several interacting factors that hypothetically account for variations in the degree of frame resonance. We take those factors into account but proceed in a less abstract and more pragmatic manner by suggesting four sets of framing problems that confront movements of all stripes and that are relevant to understanding nonresonance: misalignment, scope, exhaustion, and relevance. In elaborating and illustrating these framing problems, we draw on our own research as well as that of others.

Framing Problems

Achieving an understanding of social movements and their activities is partly contingent on understanding the field of action in which they are embedded. This field consists of at least one social movement organization (SMO) and its leadership cadre and activist adherents, as well as other relevant organizations and sets of actors, including potential constituents, targets and antagonists, possible allies, social control agents, the media, and bystanders (see Gamson 2004; Rucht 2004; Snow 2004, 401–4). Discerning the contours and character of these fields of action and the interactions among the relevant sets of actors within the field is fundamental to understanding all aspects of a movement's operation and life history, including its framing activities and their relative success or failure. The framing problems discussed here all represent communication failures of sorts between social movement organizations and their spokespersons and the relevant other sets of actors within their fields of operation. In some instances, for example, the problem may involve a failure to convert crowd bystanders or a segment of the bystander public; in other instances, the problem may entail the failure to activate one's adherents. And sometimes, an SMO's framing efforts may work at cross-purposes, aggravating those targeted for conversion to the cause and turning them into antagonists rather than supporters. We elaborate what we have identified as the major framing problems that sometimes plague movements and their activists and can impede or stall their mobilization efforts.

The Problem of Misalignment

Misalignment cuts to the heart of a framing problem that is sometimes overlooked or insufficiently appreciated by movement activists: the failure to attend closely to the degree of alignment between a particular framing and relevant audiences or targets. It is this mismatch, or failure of correspondence, between the proffered framing and the audience that we conceptualize as the problem of misalignment.

This problem, we think, is particularly endemic with injustice framing, which entails the expression of moral indignation over harm and suffering that has presumably occurred because of the conscious actions or inactions of some designated set of responsible agents (Gamson, Fireman, and Rytina 1982; Gamson 1992; Moore 1978; Piven and Cloward 1979; Turner 1969). Injustice frames have at least two key components that require analytic separation: *victimage* and *perpetration* or responsibility. Accenting victimage establishes the character and extent of harm and suffering incurred, whereas highlighting the perpetrators or responsible agents attributes blame and establishes a target.

Distinguishing between these two components of injustice frames is important because emphasizing one and neglecting the other can have unintended consequences for different audiences or targets. A focus on victimage, for example, is more likely to engender sympathy for a people or cause, whereas a focus on perpetrators is likely to rouse support for action against them—but only if the sympathetic base, and thus victimage, is already established. For this reason, framing that prematurely concentrates attention on the agents presumably responsible for an injustice, before victimage is firmly established, may prove ineffective. In this way, it is clear that a prognostic solution to a problem—for example, action against a perceived set of responsible agents—cannot be legitimately offered if there is not an effective diagnosis of a problem, which involves both the specification of victimage and the designation of a causal or responsible agent. Accenting one and neglecting the other may create a misalignment between movement and audience framing of the situation and, consequently, unintentionally alienate bystanders and potential supporters.

An example of such misalignment is the attempt at reframing engaged in by the New Racist White Separatist (NRWS) movement and one of their framing champions, David Duke. NRWS is a U.S.-based movement that seeks to advance the interests of a new form of racism and white separatism in which both are "redefined as normative and positive, an expression of love and preservation, rather than one of hatred and destruction" (Berbrier 1998, 437). The objective of the movement is to transform the stigma of white supremacy by reframing the movement and its activities in terms of love, pride, heritage preservation, and victimage. This reframing is done through two metatransformative strategies: equivalence and reversal. The reversal strategy attempts to portray whites as victims in the sense of being objects of discrimination or elimination. This framing is evident in former Ku Klux Klansman David Duke's contention that European Americans face "massive discrimination" from the country's rapidly growing population of minorities and that they will soon be "outnumbered and outvoted in [their] country" (Associated Press 2000).

The other strategy used in this reframing is an equivalence strategy, which attempts to portray whites as equivalent to ethnic minority groups by articulating and amplifying claimed commonalities. Duke calls for whites to "band together as a group the same way African Americans do, the same way as other minorities do" (Associated Press 2000). Both of these reframing strategies were used in an attempt to indicate the victimage of white people as a group and to identify the agents responsible for this victimage.

Given that there was no groundswell of support for Duke's framings, it is arguable that they were not particularly resonant because of frame/audience misalignment. As the victimage of white people is not established, this framing risks alienating bystanders and potential supporters in the general public, partially because no responsible agents can be identified and no actions can be viably offered.

Another example of frame/audience misalignment is provided by our observations of an anti-Zionist rally that occurred in mid-May 2002 on the campus of the University of California, Irvine, sponsored by the Muslim Student Association in collaboration with a Muslim student newsmagazine. Many demonstrators carried placards, nearly all of which provided clear-cut perpetrator or responsible agent framings. Some examples follow:

- Only Israel Gets Away With Murder
- Wanted for Crimes Against Humanity [with "Ariel Sharon" at the bottom and his picture in the middle]
- Zionist Equals Nazism

Conspicuously absent were any placards with unambiguous statements of victimage. In fact, the only statement of victimage at this collective action event was displayed by way of a half dozen or so stuffed black garbage bags with the names of allegedly slain Palestinian victims piled together on the ground. When asked, one of the leaders of the Muslim Student Association said that the purpose of the rally was consciousness-raising through increasing public awareness of current events in Israel. This leader was quoted in the campus newspaper: "Our whole purpose here is to make people aware of what's going on. Many people are misinformed through the media and what we are told; [Americans don't] acknowledge the oppression that goes on and are naïve about the issue" (Cheung and Zuetel 2003, 7).

It did not appear, however, that this objective was realized, as the consciousness-raising with respect to victimage was overwhelmed by the concentration on the alleged perpetrators and their character. This focus created little sympathy from the bystanders with whom we spoke. One explained, "All they are doing is making charges against Israelis, but without acknowledging their own involvement in the conflict." Such comments, as well as the general reaction of the bystander observers, who constituted a significant segment of the gathering, suggests that the failure to establish victimage in a compelling manner rendered the emphasis on the responsible agents nonresonant. Thus, due to this frame/audience misalignment, the rally appeared to function more as a commitment-reaffirming or action-mobilization exercise for adherents than as a consciousness-raising rally directed at observers.

As suggested, the issues of victimage and responsible agents tend to overlap rather closely in injustice frames, especially since they are both aspects of the diagnostic component of the framing process. However, in practice they often are uncoupled in ways that may have unintended effects, such as producing a misalignment of message and intended audience, which can lead to less sympathy and, consequently, less support from bystanders and potential supporters.

The practical implication of the prospect of misalignment for activists is that they need to be ever vigilant with regard to the audiences to which any particular faming is directed and what aspect of the proffered frame is accented. If the objective is to win over or convert bystanders to their cause, then victimage must be highlighted rather than assumed or taken for granted. If, on the other hand, the objective is to strengthen the resolve of existing adherents by suggesting various motivational rationales for joining the battle or remaining steadfast, then accenting the presumed perpetrators and action targeted at them makes sense. The point is that there is strategic utility in maintaining awareness of the relationship between the character of a group's framing message, the audiences to which it is directed, and the likelihood of it resonating with those audiences in the way intended.

The Problem of Scope

Social movements must be flexible in their framings in order to be able to adjust their scope in response to changing political or cultural currents. Sometimes, a social movement may benefit from narrow, specific frames; other times, broad, encompassing frames may prove to be more effective. Framing claims can be too broad and general when they do not speak directly to any particular group. Or they can be too specific and narrow, speaking only to a small group. In either case, they are likely to be relatively impotent and unlikely to inspire or mobilize the targeted individuals or groups.

The issue of scope is related to Bernstein's discussion of elaborated and restricted linguistic codes (1970, 1971). Bernstein defines restricted codes as those in which speech is rigidly organized, is highly particularistic in terms of meaning and social structure, and has more predictable consequences for immediate social structure. In contrast, elaborated codes are more flexibly organized, more universalistic in terms of meaning and social structure, and less predictable and reflective of immediate structures. Snow and Benford (1992) have suggested that Bernstein's conception of elaborated and restricted codes can be applied to the concept of framing in that frames exist on a continuum from restricted to elaborated in relation to their level of flexibility and elasticity of scope.

Restricted frames are those that are "exclusive ideational systems that do not so readily lend themselves to amplification or extension" and thus organize a narrow collection of ideas in a tightly interconnected fashion (Snow and Benford 1992). Alternatively, elaborated frames are organized in terms of a wide range of ideas, and their increased flexibility allows for greater extension and amplification. The flexibility of elaborated frames allows many different groups to use the same framing for differing purposes, all other things being equal (Snow and Benford 1992).

While it is clear that the issue of scope is important in the framing process, finding the ideal level of scope is often a problem for activists. Being specific in terms of framing both the problem (diagnostic framing) and the solution (prognostic framing) was often helpful in the case of the homeless movement social organizations studied by Cress and Snow (2000) in eight U.S. cities (Boston, Denver, Detroit, Houston, Minneapolis, Philadelphia, Oakland, and Tucson) from 1989 to 1992. Of the fifteen homeless movements studied, those that were most successful in obtaining their local objectives (at least two of three objectives—representation, rights, and relief) were those whose diagnostic and prognostic claims were clear and concrete in terms of the problems and solutions as opposed to those whose framings were broad and ungrounded. In other words, the most successful homeless movement organizations articulated their diagnostic and prognostic claims in a fashion that accented the abuse or needs of specific subgroups or categories of homeless rather than the homeless in general, and that identified specific lines of action that could be taken in order to remedy the concretized problem. The experience of the Detroit Union of the Homeless (DtUH) is illustrative. It was one of the seven organizations that attained two or more objectives, and was particularly successful in its campaign to get bus service for homeless children to go to school, in large part because its diagnostic and prognostic framing of the issue was specific and concrete. As Cress and Snow explained, its

> diagnostic and prognostic framing activities succeeded on two levels: by targeting children the DtUH focused attention on a population that could not be blamed for its homelessness and that was most likely to be viewed in a sympathetic light; and by targeting education, it focused on an issue that the city was mandated to address. (2000, 1089)

In contrast, movement organizations that were less successful in realizing their objectives tended to have less focused and concrete frames, calling for the city or federal government to attend to the problem of homelessness in general.

There are, of course, trade-offs involved when limiting or expanding the scope of one's frame diagnostically and prognostically. In the above example, there is the danger of suggesting that some homeless individuals, such as children and women, are more deserving of relief than other categories of homeless individuals, such as adult males, thus reproducing the long-standing division of the poor into the "worthy and the unworthy." While such a ploy, even if unintentional, may yield local, group-specific victories, as with the Detroit example, there is the risk of ignoring or sidestepping a segment of the population in need or at risk and thus contributing, albeit unintentionally, to the persistence of the broader problem. To note this trade-off is not to suggest that there is little or no merit to limiting the scope of one's frames, particularly when a subset of the victimized category might be helped. However, it is important to maintain awareness of such a trade-off and to make sure that a group-specific strategy does not become an overarching one that artificially limits the scope of the problem, and thus victimage, both diagnostically and prognostically.

The emergence of the environmental justice movement constitutes an interesting example of an effort to deal with this dilemma of framing the scope of a problem too narrowly. This movement grew out of the environmental racism movement, which surfaced in the 1970s when groups of minorities organized to protest the disproportionate number of waste-producing and polluting industries located in areas where ethnic minorities lived. At the time, the mobilization against environmental racism was viewed as outside the broader environmental movement that had white middle- and upper-class backing. However, in the 1980s the environmental racism movement reorganized and renamed itself the environmental justice movement, which broadened its scope to the equitable distribution of environmental health and risk for all groups, independent of race or ethnicity.

In a relatively short time, the more inclusive environmental justice movement began to receive mainstream political recognition and affirmation. In 1994, for instance, President Clinton signed an executive order that required all federal agencies to address environmental justice issues in their mission statements. In addition, the National Environmental Justice Advisory Council was established in 1993 and the Environmental Justice Small Grants Program was established in 1994 to provide financial assistance to eligible community groups. And in 1997, Edward Rush of the Center for Health, Environment, and Justice argued that

> environmental racism is . . . the result of a power dynamic. The dynamic that causes environmental inequity occurs when people who have power in society choose not to have environmental hazards in their community. This environmental inequity becomes environmental injustice when environmental hazards are placed in a community of disempowered people.

It is apparent from this quote that, by the second half of the 1990s, the broader and more inclusive "disempowered people" frame had replaced the "race frame," thus expanding the conception of victimage associated with certain environmental practices. Presumably the narrower frame of race had been less resonant because it excluded others, most notably poor white communities, who were similarly impacted by environmental hazards. The new, broader injustice frame, which was established under the environmental justice banner, encompassed more potential supporters and thus achieved broader resonance and greater success, as indicated by the policy concessions made in the Clinton administration.

There is no universally successful scope that all frames should attempt to imitate. It is clear from the two foregoing examples that sometimes highly focused and concrete frames are successful, while at other times broader and more inclusive frames are resonant. The problem lies in the fact that some movements remain locked into a particular framing mode rather than adapting to the changing vicissitudes of the context in which they find themselves. Thus, the inflexibility of social movement organizations to respond to their changing environment by increasing or decreasing the scope of their frames as appropriate, without simultaneously "selling out," constitutes an ongoing framing challenge and an important source of framing errors.

The Problem of Exhaustion

Another framing problem often encountered by social movements is tired or exhausted frames, that is, frames that have been overused and perhaps become taken for granted. Social movements have a tendency to frame new events and issues in terms of the ways in which seemingly related events and issues were previously framed. This is logical; if the past framings were successful, a social movement will want to borrow and reuse the resonant frames. However, such borrowing—or what Morris and Staggenborg have called "frame lifting" (2004)—can be problematic in that the social movement may not appreciate the extent to which an old or borrowed frame may need to be revitalized or refurbished because it has been overused and/or become taken for granted. Tired or worn frames can become impotent, in the sense of generating sympathy and/or activating adherents, and may have to be rejuvenated or revitalized in order to engender renewed resonance.

The ways in which the famines in Ethiopia have been framed over the past twenty years, and the different responses to these framings, provide an interesting case for exploring the problem of frame exhaustion. In 1985, the world first became aware of the extreme situation of famine in Ethiopia, which would eventually claim the lives of nearly one million people. The images on the news at the time, showing starving children and families, appeared to be highly resonant, as indicated by the widespread attention the issue received and the dollars it generated. In the United Kingdom, for example, an organization of British musicians called Band Aid was created and recorded a hit song, "Do They Know It's Christmas?" and held two large all-day benefits in London and Philadelphia. U.S. musicians respond-ed similarly by creating USA for Africa and recording the album *We Are the World* as well as performing numerous benefit concerts. These efforts were highly successful and raised over $100 million in the United Kingdom alone, due in part, we suspect, to the resonant nature of the framing of-fered by the musicians. The lyrics of the song "We Are the World" framed the issue of hunger in such a way that individuals in Western nations felt a personal responsibility to help with famine in a country far away: "There's a choice we're making / We're saving our own lives / It's true we'll make a better day / Just you and me." This framing was highly successful in mo-tivational terms, encouraging individuals to donate money and Western governments to commit aid.

In 2000, fifteen years after the first publicized famine in Ethiopia, the country was again experiencing severe problems with food shortages. Aid workers in the country estimated that 8 million people were at risk of star-vation, and called on Western nations to offer aid to the country once more. However, the efforts at mobilizing the Western public were largely unsuc-cessful when compared to the 1984–85 response. The failure of the Western public to respond as before was due to several explanatory factors. Among these were the existence of other events competing for media and public attention and the various sets of factors that affect the "carrying capacity" of a society, or various categories of societal actors, to note and attend to some number of events in a remedial fashion. Included among such influ-ential sets of factors are media attention cycles and institutional rhythms (Hilgartner and Bosk 1988), the cultural patterning of sympathy (Bunis, Yancik, and Snow 1996), so-called compassion fatigue (Moeller 1999), and perhaps public desensitization to, in this case, the erstwhile poignant images of famine and starvation. Undergirding all of these factors in vary-ing degrees, we would argue, was the failure to refurbish and reinvigorate the existing frame or to develop a new one.

Other examples of tired or worn-out and overused frames are plenti-ful. For example, David Duke attempted to reframe the NRWS movement because of the tired nature of the traditional racist framing. The old fram-ing had become nonresonant with group members and the broader public as indicated by the fact that these groups were decreasing in size and their campaigns were proving to be ineffective. The movement's frame suffered from exhaustion, as well as from the misalignment discussed earlier, and

Duke and other leaders felt compelled to refurbish or fine-tune it in order to enhance the prospect of increasing and perhaps broadening the movement's resonance.

Frames can become uninspiring not only because of overuse, but also because the flow of events renders them obsolete or irrelevant, suggesting another problem that can plague movement activists as they go about the business of trying to make a case for their causes.

The Problem of Relevance

It is crucially important for a frame to reflect the cultural understandings of potential adherents as well as to be relevant to the current political context. When frames are not culturally or politically resonant in some fashion or another, they are likely to fall on deaf ears. Snow and Benford (1988; see also Benford and Snow 2000) have suggested that the resonance of a collective action frame is affected by both its credibility and its salience to the targets of mobilization. Empirical credibility, according to Snow and Benford, is the apparent fit between the framing and events in the world. This credibility is based on the extent to which the claims can be empirically verified by indicators in the world at large.

Snow and Benford posit that salience is also an important factor in frame resonance. They discuss three factors that affect salience: centrality, experiential commensurability, and narrative fidelity. Centrality is related to how essential the beliefs, values, and ideas associated with a movement's frame is to the lives of the targets of mobilization. The more central or salient the beliefs, ideas, or values of the movement are to the target of mobilization, the greater the probability that the frame will be resonant. Experiential commensurability is important in that a movement's framing must be congruent with the personal, everyday experiences of the targets of mobilization in order to be felt to be relevant. If they seem too abstract and distant from the experiences of the targets, the frames will lack resonance. Both centrality and experiential commensurability are affected by the cultural and political context, in that what is felt to be a central value or pertinent to an individual's everyday experience interacts with the current context. For example, the issue of terrorism has become an increasingly central concern and ever more relevant to the everyday lives of individuals after the September 11 terrorist attacks. For this reason, movements dealing with issues relating to terrorism or foreign policy must be responsive in their framing to the changing salience of this issue for individuals.

Finally, narrative fidelity is crucial in that the frames must be felt to be culturally resonant. This cultural resonance indicates that the framing strikes a responsive chord and "rings true" with existing cultural narrations (Snow and Benford 1988). It increases the ways in which the individual will feel the frame to be reflective of their overall cultural context and, consequently, increases the frame's salience and resonance. As the cultural context changes over time, then, activists must alter their frames to reflect current cultural understandings. A number of these concepts are particularly pertinent to understanding the problem of relevance.

Recent anti- and pro-war protests with respect to the U.S.-led war on Iraq illustrate not only the connection between the three hypothesized determinants of salience—centrality, experiential commensurability, and narrative fidelity—and frame relevance, but also the highly dynamic character of that relationship. The data we draw on comes from the ethnographic research conducted by one of the authors and a collaborator on a series of antiwar and Support Our Troops (SOT) protest events that occurred over a six-week period in three communities in Southern California in the spring of 2003 (Corrigall-Brown and Oselin 2003). In addition to observing the protest activities of the antiwar and SOT protesters, the signs used by each set of collective actors at the events were recorded. We regard these signs not only as indicators of framing activity engaged in by both sides, but also as snapshot crystallizations of those framing activities. The first noteworthy observation concerns how the signs, which were directed primarily at bystanders and passing automobiles, changed over time as the war developed. On March 8, two examples of signs from the SOT protesters were

- It's God's Job to Forgive Saddam, It's Our Job to Arrange the Meeting
- Bomb the Bastards

It is clear that the framings were very aggressively vilifying Saddam Hussein and his regime. However, by March 29, the framing had shifted dramatically, as indicated by these two examples of signs:

- No Peace for France's Oil
- Free Iraq

At this time, American foreign policy was being criticized for being self-interested. By reframing the issue to highlight the supposed problems with the foreign policies of other countries, the policies of the United States could appear more virtuous. Also, reframing the mission in Iraq from one of deposing a leader to freeing a country created a more positive framing for the SOT movement. By April 12 the framing had shifted yet again. Two signs seen that day were

- Support Our Troops
- We Love America

These signs constitute "trump" frames in that neither the SOT, the antiwar protesters, nor the bystanders or passing cars to which the signs were directed could disagree with the statements they made for fear of being seen as un-American or cold-hearted. These signs resonated with the bystanders as indicated by the high number of thumbs-up gestures and the honking horns of cars as they passed. That there was such indication of deep resonance is not surprising when we consider that the practice of supporting the troops has deep narrative fidelity in American culture and that the association of the war with September 11, 2001, makes the framing experientially commensurate. Thus, these signs show how framings can change with events and underscore the importance of narrative fidelity and experiential commensurability in relation to frame relevance.

These observations are underscored even further by the framings of the antiwar protesters. Consider the following signs that were shown on February 1:

- How Many Children Will We Kill?
- No War
- Only Congress Can Declare War

These signs indicate the desire of the antiwar protesters not to enter the war and highlight the legal or constitutional restrictions on the president's capacity for declaring war. Once the United States entered the war, however, the activists altered their frames to reflect the current situation, as it would not be empirically credible to lobby against entering a war that was already occurring. Thus, on March 8 we noted many American flags at the protest, as well as several signs with a different focus:

- Environmental Suicide
- Support the United Nations

The introduction of American flags can be construed as an intentional attempt to reframe the view of the antiwar movement from being seen as un-American and to associate the movement with patriotism. The use of the "Environmental Suicide" sign can be seen as frame extension, incorporating other values that are posited as being salient to the aims of the antiwar activists. The "Support the United Nations" sign is another attempt to reframe the issue. Instead of asking bystanders not to support the American government, the protesters are positively framing the issue as a request for support for another institution, which is seen to be highly legitimate, at least by some citizens.

Finally, on April 12 the following signs were seen:

- Somebody Lied—No Weapons of Mass Destruction Found
- Peace Is Patriotic
- In Solidarity with Women and Children in Iraq and Syria

These signs continue to place a critical gaze on the past, present, and future policies of the Bush administration. In addition, they persisted in framing the cause of being antiwar as patriotic, despite attempts by the SOT protesters to counterframe this issue.

The analysis of the signs at these war protests shows the importance of understanding the political and cultural contexts in which frames are situated. The flow of current cultural and political events can make old frames irrelevant. For this reason, activists and movements must accomplish the difficult task of accommodating the changes in the cultural and political context into their new framings if they hope to resonate with their audience. By being mindful of the context, frames can be adapted and altered to respond to changing political environments, public sentiments, and other outside pressures. Failure to modify one's framings accordingly can render a movement's framing efforts nonresonant and contribute to a movement's marginality or decline, as it comes to be seen as out-of-step or irrelevant. A movement must be careful, however, not to abandon its original frames totally in an attempt to fit a current context or tide of sentiment. This sort of radical shift in a movement's frame may seem insincere and may alienate adherents and confuse bystanders. Thus, movement activists are often confronted with the tricky dilemma of balancing the need to respond to changing cultural and political contexts while maintaining and expressing allegiance to the core beliefs and principles that undergird and animate the movement.

Conclusion

We have argued throughout this chapter that effective framing is an ongoing challenge for individual activists and social movements as a whole. More concretely, we have suggested that any frame, or framing processes through which it is derived, is vulnerable to four framing problems: misalignment, scope, exhaustion, and relevance. In elaborating these four framing difficulties or errors, we do not presume that they are exhaustive in the sense of capturing all framing errors that might plague the framing efforts of movement activists, wherever they might fall on the right/left continuum. In addition, we want to emphasize that these framing problems are not mutually exclusive, as one frame can encounter several of these problems simultaneously. As noted earlier, for example, the New Racist White Separatist movement experienced the problems of both misalignment and exhaustion.

This discussion of framing problems or vulnerabilities is relevant to the social movement literature more generally in that it provides an extension of evolving work on frame resonance. To this end, this chapter offers a more pragmatic and concrete discussion of framing errors by way of analyses of actual frames and their levels of success and/or failure. Through an analysis of the ways in which frames can fall on deaf ears, social movement theorists may begin to understand better the potential causes of framing errors, and activists may become more sensitive to the array of hazards associated with their framing efforts. This knowledge can increase understanding for both movement scholars and activists of the processes by which frames and audiences or contexts interact to produce resonant frames and, consequently, support for a cause. In addition, increased clarity of the issues surrounding framing problems serves a pragmatic and strategic function for activists.

The prospect of committing the four framing errors discussed in this chapter can be reduced through heightened awareness of their occurrence and the kinds of neglects or oversights that we have cataloged. Even more concretely, movement leaders and activists can work strategically toward minimizing the occurrence of framing errors by attending to such directives as the following:

1. Activists should seek to develop a working understanding among adherents, constituents, and even bystanders of the group's victimage before focusing on the attribution of blame and directing attention to the presumed perpetrators.
2. Activists should remain flexible in the scope of their frames and be responsive to the political context by narrowing or broadening their claims when necessary.
3. Activists should think about refurbishing borrowed or lifted frames to reduce the likelihood of both overextension and exhaustion. Equally important is the need to reinvigorate frames within movements when public attention and interest is low.
4. Activists should aim to have their frames relate to the personal experiences and values of their target audiences and should be sensitive to cultural and political shifts that could reduce the relevance of their frame.

By understanding the ways in which frames can and do fail to appeal to various audiences, social movement activists are more likely to be successful in creating frames with reasonably strong resonance and, consequently, inspire and mobilize other potential activists and the larger public more generally.

References

Associated Press. 2000. "Duke Group Is Pushing White's Rights." At http://www.azstarnet.com/public/dnews/080-5049.html.

Benford, Robert D., and David A. Snow. 2000. "Framing Processes and Social Movements: An Overview and Assessment." *Annual Review of Sociology* 26: 611–39.

Berbrier, Mitch. 1998. "'Half the Battle': Cultural Resonance, Framing Processes, and Ethnic Affectations in Contemporary White Separatist Rhetoric." *Social Problems* 45: 431–50.

Bernstein, Basil B. 1970. "Socio-Linguistic Approach to Socialization." In *Directions in Socio-Linguistics: The Ethnography of Communication,* ed. John J. Gumperz and Dell Hymes, 465–97. New York: Holt, Rinehart, and Winston.

———. 1971. *Class, Codes, and Control.* London: Routledge and K. Paul.

Bunis, William K., Angela Yancik, and David A. Snow. 1996. "The Cultural Patterning of Sympathy toward the Homeless and Other Victims of Misfortune." *Social Problems* 43: 387–402.

Cheung, Mike, and Bryan Zuetal. 2003. "Anti-Zionist Rally Draws Counter-Demonstrators." *New University News,* May 20, 1 and 7.

Corrigall-Brown, Catherine, and Sharon S. Oselin. 2003. "Contested Patriotism: An Analysis of Interactions at War Protests." Unpublished paper. University of California, Irvine.

Cress, Daniel M., and David A. Snow. 2000. "The Outcomes of Homeless Mobilization: The Influence of Organization, Disruption, Political Mediation, and Framing." *American Journal of Sociology* 105: 1063–104.

Delgado, Gary L. 1986. "Ideology and the Clamshell Identity: Organizational Dilemmas in the Anti-Nuclear Power Movement." *Social Problems* 33: 357–73.

Gamson, William A. 1992. *Talking Politics.* Cambridge: Cambridge University Press.

———. 2004. "Bystanders, Public Opinion, and the Media." In *The Blackwell Companion to Social Movements,* ed. David A. Snow, Sarah Soule, and Hanspeter Kriesi, 242–61. Oxford, UK: Blackwell.

Gamson, William A., Bruce Fireman, and Steven Rytina. 1982. *Encounters with Unjust Authority.* Homewood, IL: Dorsey Press.

Hall, Stuart. 1982. "The Rediscovery of Ideology: Return of the Repressed in Media

Studies." In *Culture, Society, and the Media,* ed. M. Gurevitch, T. Bennett, J. Curon, and J. Woollacott, 56–90. New York: Methuen.

Hilgartner, Stephen, and Charles L. Bosk. 1988. "The Rise and Fall of Social Problems: A Public Arena Model." *American Journal of Sociology* 94: 53–78.

Klandermans, Bert. 1984. "Mobilization and Participation: Social-Psychological Expansions of Resource Mobilization Theory." *American Sociological Review* 49: 583–600.

McAdam, Doug, John D. McCarthy, and Mayer N. Zald. 1996. *Comparative Perspectives on Social Movements: Political Opportunities, Mobilizing Structures, and Cultural Framings.* Cambridge: Cambridge University Press.

Moeller, Susan D. 1999. *Compassion Fatigue: How the Media Sell Disease, Famine, War, and Death.* New York: Routledge.

Moore, Barrington. 1978. *Injustice: The Social Bases of Obedience and Revolt.* White Plains, NY: M. E. Sharpe.

Morris, Aldon D., and Suzanne Staggenborg. 2004. "Leadership in Social Movements." In *The Blackwell Companion to Social Movements,* ed. David A. Snow, Sarah Soule, and Hanspeter Kriesi, 171–96. Oxford, UK: Blackwell.

Piven, Frances Fox, and Richard A. Cloward. 1979. *Poor People's Movements: Why They Succeed, How They Fail.* New York: Vintage Books.

Rucht, Dieter. 2004. "Movement Allies, Adversaries, and the Media." In *The Blackwell Companion to Social Movements,* ed. David A. Snow, Sarah Soule, and Hanspeter Kriesi, 197–216. Oxford, UK: Blackwell.

Rush, Edward. 1997. "Environmental Racism: Fact or Fiction?" Falls Church, VA: Center for Health, Environment, and Justice.

Snow, David A. 2004. "Framing Processes, Ideology, and Discursive Fields." In *The Blackwell Companion to Social Movements,* ed. David A. Snow, Sarah Soule, and Hanspeter Kriesi, 380–412. Oxford, UK: Blackwell.

Snow, David A., and Robert D. Benford. 1988. "Ideology, Frame Resonance, and Participant Mobilization." *International Social Movement Research* 1: 197–217.

———. 1992. "Master Frames and Cycles of Protest." In *Frontiers of Social Movement Research,* ed. Aldon Morris and Carol McClurg Mueller, 133–55. New Haven, CT: Yale University Press.

Snow, David A., E. Burke Rochford Jr., and Steven K. Worden. 1986. "Frame Alignment Processes, Micro Mobilization, and Movement Participation." *American Sociological Review* 51: 464–81.

Turner, Ralph H. 1969. "Theme of Contemporary Social Movements." *British Journal of Sociology* 20: 390–405.

14

Crossing Boundaries in Participatory Action Research: Performing Protest with Drag Queens

Verta Taylor and Leila J. Rupp

Our study of drag queen performances at the 801 Cabaret in Key West, Florida, and their connection to the gay, lesbian, bisexual, and transgender movement is a project that, in some ways, found us. One hot summer night, when Verta's Southern Baptist nephew was visiting us in Key West, we took him to a drag show. Sushi, the house queen at the 801 Cabaret, was performing. At some point, talking about gay marriage, she asked who in the bar had been in a relationship the longest. We were then over the twenty-year mark and won hands down, earning a free drink and Sushi's comment, "lesbians, of course." We were entranced with her performance, but what stood out most was the political talk on stage and her frequent references to the gay and lesbian movement.

The next time we were in Key West, we caught an expanded show, and we were hooked. Right before our eyes, gender and sexuality theory were acted out by and for people who most likely knew nothing about such feminist and queer theory concepts as gender as performance, troubling the homo/heterosexual binary, or counterhegemonic gender and sexual meanings (Butler 1990, 1993; Lorber 1999). We could see that the drag shows at the 801 Cabaret were a kind of political theater, deriving their political edge, in part, from the subtle critique of hegemonic masculinity and mainstream heterosexuality staged in the performances. As important, the cabaret was a site where drag was being used to affirm gay identity, where heterosexuals were being exposed to gay life and politics, and where the performers were using drag to cross the boundaries between "us" and "them" (male and female, heterosexual and gay) in order to attract support for the gay, lesbian, bisexual, and transgender cause.

Those fateful nights led us into over three years of field research, from 1998 to 2001. From the beginning, Sushi invited us to come to drag queen meetings and urged us to "tell the truth" about them. The 801 Girls are full-time drag queens who perform different lip-synched shows nightly in the cabaret with audiences ranging from fifty people on an off night to several thousand people during community celebrations when a stage is set up on Duval Street. The audience mixes gay, lesbian, bisexual, transgendered, and heterosexual people, men and women, tourists and locals, first-time attenders and regulars. Our study used a multimethod qualitative and participatory approach that relied on intensive interviews with twelve drag queens (as well as two of their mothers, two boyfriends, and one of the bar owners); attendance at drag queen meetings, rehearsals, special events, and social gatherings; attendance at and taping of over fifty performances; analysis of the coverage of the drag queens in the local media; and focus groups with audience members. The full story of the drag queens can be found in our book *Drag Queens at the 801 Cabaret* (Rupp and Taylor 2003; see also Taylor and Rupp 2004).

One book review described us as "strangers in a strange land," lesbian academics hanging out with "a randy band" of drag queens.[1] The moniker might just as well apply to the straight tourists enjoying the show at the 801 or the drag queens engaging in knowledge production. For us, this project was about crossing all sorts of boundaries, between male and female, masculine and feminine, straight and gay, theory and practice, scholarship and activism. That boundary crossing allowed us to see the value of participatory action research among activist groups in local settings for addressing theoretical questions that have broad significance to the study of social movements. We have written separately and together about the feminist participatory approach we have used in previous research projects (Taylor 1996, 1998; Taylor and Rupp 1991, 1993, 1996). In this chapter, we draw on our research on drag queens and on the literature on participatory research methods to propose a general methodology for producing social movement scholarship that bridges the divide between academic scholars and movement activists.

Only recently have students of social movements begun to reflect on the strengths and weaknesses of the methods used in conducting social movement research and to assess how methods and tools of empirical investigation have shaped theory building and theoretical debates in the field (Staggenborg 1998). The most comprehensive account, Klandermans and Staggenborg's

Methods of Social Movement Research (2002), provides an overview of the qualitative and quantitative techniques used by social movement researchers. Despite this new attention, the emerging body of literature in the United States on research methods in social movements refers only minimally to participatory research models oriented toward breaking down the separation and hierarchy between researchers and activists and educating and empowering oppressed groups for social change.

European approaches to social movements, particularly the work of Alain Touraine (1981) and Alberto Melucci (1989), have a strong preference for methods that rely on participation and collaboration between researchers and actors. Touraine (1981) used the term "sociological intervention" to describe a method that entails observing the activities of social movements and then soliciting participants' feedback of the researcher's analysis as part of the movement's "self-analysis." Melucci's (1989, 1995) influential theoretical model of collective identity construction in social movements derives, to a large extent, from the use of such participatory methods with small groups of activists.

Occasionally U.S. scholars have used participatory methods to develop, extend, and test theories about social movements using empirical data. Stoecker relied on participatory strategies in his study of neighborhood movements struggling for community control of urban redevelopment (1994), and this work has been central to the formulation of participatory action research as a distinct practice of sociological inquiry (Stoecker and Bonacich 1992). There is also a small body of writings by U.S. scholars who aim to bridge the world of activists and scholars by producing academic scholarship that is movement relevant (see Freeman 1975; W. Gamson 1992; Darnovsky, Epstein, and Flacks 1995; Jasper 1997; Flacks 2004; Bevington and Dixon 2004), although these writers have not explicitly connected their research techniques to the larger field of participatory action research.

Scholars of women's movements who subscribe to the tenets of feminist methodology have been more likely to employ participatory methods (for examples, see Mies 1983; Beckwith 1996; Naples 1998; Naples and Clark 1996; Taylor 1996, 1998; Taylor and Rupp 1996; Kurtz 2002; Fonow 2003). In large measure, this is because feminist social scientists have more eagerly embraced the critique of positivism that underlies participatory methods and adopted postmodern sensibilities regarding voice and reflexivity, the necessity of collaborative and nonoppressive relationships between researchers and those studied, and the social responsibility and accountability of the researcher (for overviews of feminist research methods, see Fonow and

Cook 1991; Cancian 1992; Reinharz 1992; Oleson 2000; Naples 2003). Taylor suggests that participatory strategies might be the key to producing movement-relevant research (Taylor 1998; Tayor and Rupp 1996), arguing that feminist participatory techniques allowed her to unpack taken-for-granted ideas in the social movement literature about what constitutes a social movement.

In this chapter we connect the participatory research tradition to the literature on social movements. We outline a methodology and logic of inquiry and theory building for producing academic scholarship that treats the needs of social movement actors as central and simultaneously addresses questions that have larger theoretical relevance for the field of social movements. Our discussion draws on two sets of writings on participant observation. The first is the body of literature on participatory action research as a methodology and epistemology (for an overview, see Whyte 1991; Stoecker and Bonacich 1992; Cancian 1996; and Kemmis and McTaggart 2000). The term "participatory action research" has been used in a variety of ways and in a number of different academic fields to refer to methods that democratize the knowledge process and aim to transform both the theories and practices of the researcher and the theories and practices of actors in local settings. We view participatory research, as does Gaventa (1991, 121–22), as "simultaneously a tool for education and development of consciousness as well as mobilization for action." Following Stoecker, the first and principal feature of participatory action research, as we outline here, is participation, which goes beyond participant observation and involves activist and scholar collaboration in the research process. Participatory action research engages scholars and activists in examining their respective knowledges and interpretive categories and allows both parties to understand and criticize how that knowledge shapes and constrains both their theories and actions. In this model, a scholar takes abstract academic knowledge into a group of activists, then collaborates with them to uncover local knowledge or rich experiential insider understandings with the goal of generating new knowledge and understanding for activists as well as academics. The second feature of participatory action research is an emphasis on social change that empowers both the scholar and the activist by transforming social movement theory and the actions of social movements (e.g., their organizational forms, tactics and strategies, styles of leadership, goals, and ideology). Participation encourages activists to go beyond the specifics of a particular situation and their experiential understandings of it to explore different knowledges, discourses, practices, and theories. In turn, for the researcher, participation involves learning by doing through interaction and becoming immersed in the activists' social world and struggle for change.

Our approach is also indebted to a second body of literature regarding analytical techniques scholars use to construct theory through participant observation (Burawoy 1998; Lichterman 2002). We think that participatory action research is conducive to the kind of critical reflection that allows theory building using Burawoy's extended case method (Burawoy 1998; Burawoy et al. 1991). Here we outline a research method that combines participatory action with the logic of the extended case method to allow researchers to address theoretical questions that go beyond the particular social movement studied. Using the extended case method means that researchers approach subject matters—a network of activists, a social movement tactic, forms of leadership, collective identities, political opportunities—as cases or categories of a previously developed theory (Lichterman 2002) and then use participatory methods to discover features and anomalies of the case in order to improve on existing theories of the phenomenon in question. The extended case method is theory driven, rather than field driven, allowing social movement researchers and participants to start with, build on, and extend existing theory as a result of their collaborative dialogue. Since methods are merely tools or strategies for generating theory, it is our view that participatory action research will only yield lasting theoretical contributions to the study of social movements if the method is combined with a logic of inquiry and conceptualization that treats particular cases as evidence of larger social or cultural processes operative in social movements and other forms of political contention.

We begin with a brief description of the role that drag queens play in the Key West community. Then we turn to a consideration of the way that participatory methods combined with the extended case logic led us to build on and elaborate social movement theory. The heart of the paper uses our research on drag performances at the 801 Cabaret to elaborate the two principal elements of participatory action research that depart from those typically used in social movement studies, illuminating how participation in the performances was a part of our overall commitment to changing the knowledge process and to the gay and lesbian movement's goal of contesting social discrimination and legal restrictions imposed by gender and sexual categories and hierarchies. We conclude by discussing how these strategies allowed us to develop a definition of social movement tactics that overcomes the bifurcation of the political and the cultural found in much of the current scholarship on social movements.

"A Plate of Food and a Drag Show"

David Felstein, aka Margo, "the oldest living drag queen in captivity," in his guise as newspaper columnist for *Celebrate!* Key West's gay newspaper, described benefits in Key West as consisting of "a plate of food and a drag show." Key West is a drag-friendly town, and the 801 Girls play a central role in community life. From their presence every night of the week on Duval Street, where they drum up an audience before the show, to their appearances at holiday events, gay pride celebrations, local festivities, and fund-raisers, they are celebrities in Key West and beyond. But they are also marginal, both economically and socially. They generally earn salaries of less than two hundred dollars a week, and their pooled tips vary wildly from night to night and season to season. And to some extent an unsavory reputation clings to them. "Freaks, we're still considered that," says Milla. It's an odd combination of celebrity and hostility.

Key West is a quirky tropical community almost entirely dependent on tourism, closer to Cuba than Miami, and attached to the rest of the United States by a highway resting tenuously on a chain of tiny islands. The self-proclaimed "Conch Republic," among other things, issues marriage licenses for same-sex couples. Diverse communities coexist in Key West—Cuban, Bahamian, hippie, gay—and the official philosophy calls for tolerance, recognition that we are all "one human family." Key West is a place unto itself, but not unlike other gay tourist destinations. And the drag shows at the 801 Cabaret, although notable for the extent of interaction with the audience, represent a style of drag that can be found throughout the United States and even around the globe.

The 801 Girls are a troupe of full-time drag queens who perform every night of the year. The group has changed and grown in size over time, but during our research consisted of eight regulars. Following their own practice, we switch between male and female pronouns somewhat randomly.

Sushi, whose mother is Japanese and late father was from Texas, has a beautiful, tall, slender body, with thin but muscled arms and dancer's legs. She never really looks much like a man, even when dressed as Gary. In fact, Sushi passed as a woman for a time, including while hooking on the streets of Los Angeles. Sushi is the house queen: she is responsible for hiring and paying the girls and keeping them in line, and, as a talented seamstress, she makes most of the costumes.

Milla is, like Sushi, beautiful. She is the only one in the group we studied who has altered her body in any way, getting black-market silicone injections in the cheeks and forehead, mostly to get rid of the wrinkles they all fear so much. With her olive skin and dark eyes and fondness for Erykah Badu numbers, when onstage Milla is often misidentified as African-American, and she describes herself sometimes as a white gay man trapped in a black woman's body. She also describes herself as "omnisexual," as Milla is attractive to men and women of all sexual identities.

Kylie is Sushi's best friend from high school, as Sushi announces in nearly every show. They began dressing in drag together as a way both to attract attention and to hide behind a costume and makeup. Kylie hosts the Saturday night "Sex Show," where, at the end of the night, she strips to "Queen of the Night," leaving on her wig and makeup. She is a great emcee, using that role to advance the drag performances' political mission.

R. V. Beaumont also engages in a lot of political talk. She wears T-shirts that say "I'm not an alcoholic, I'm a drunk," and she has a penchant for Bette Midler numbers. At the end of her show, she performs "What Makes a Man a Man" while removing her wig, makeup, and dress and transforming herself back into a man.

Margo is a painfully thin sixty-something New Yorker with a deep voice who only began performing drag at the age of fifty-nine. Her commentary in the shows, including talk about Stonewall and gay pride, and David's commentary in his newspaper columns in the local gay paper are consciously political.

Scabola Feces is HIV-positive, is thin, and has large expressive eyes, a raspy smoker's voice, and a big evil-sounding laugh. As Matthew, he is very creative and designs the sets for the shows. Scabby's numbers are clever and outrageous critiques of conventional gender and sexual norms; for example, she performs "Wedding Bell Blues" as Monica Lewinsky clutching a photo of Bill Clinton.

Inga, the "Swedish bombshell," really is Swedish, tall, blond, big, soft, and adorable, with deep dimples. She did the choreography for the troupe before she left the 801 to perform at Divas, a club down the street, but she frequently comes by to visit.

Gugi Gomez joined the troupe when Inga left. She's Puerto Rican, from Chicago, and she performs as Cuban, hosting a show called "A Night in Havana." She moves and dances seductively. Like Sushi and Milla, Gugi lived for a while as a woman.

In Key West, the drag queens at the 801 Cabaret entertain and educate. In their shows and at Key West events, they are central to the life of the community and especially to the gay, lesbian, bisexual, and transgender movement. We came to understand them as activists, and, like many social movement participants engaged in public protest, they wanted us to use both their real and their drag names in our writing.

The Logic of the Extended Case Method

Using the extended case method means using participatory action research to speak back to central questions in social movement theory. In this logic of theory building, the aim is to utilize the specific case to *reconstruct existing theory* so that general theories of social movements accommodate cases and issues that are relevant to activists' experiences and concerns. We began our research with questions derived from gender and social movement theories that consider drag performances as contentious interactions between gays and lesbians and heterosexuals and as sites for identity negotiation, creation, and change. Drag performances have a long history, since at least the 1920s, building same-sex communities and making gay identity visible to heterosexual audiences. Scholars of gender and sexuality, influenced by the writings known as queer theory, advance the theoretical argument that drag performances, cross-dressing, female masculinity, and other forms of in-your-face queer politics function to deconstruct and criticize heteronormativity, which underpins virtually every aspect of contemporary social life, by presenting hybrid and minority genders and sexualities (Butler 1990, 1993; Garber 1992; J. Gamson 1995; Halberstram 1998; Lorber 1999; Muñoz 1999). Social movement theory, following Tilly (1978; Traugott 1995; McAdam, Tarrow, and Tilly 2001), turns our attention to the recurrent and culturally encoded tactics and strategies used in political contention. Drag shows as a style of protest, however, represent an "anomaly" (Burawoy et al. 1991) that existing formulations cannot accommodate because the dominant resource mobilization and political opportunity approaches have, for the most part, ignored the use of cultural performances in political contention. Our preliminary fieldwork at the 801 Cabaret suggested that drag performances, even in commercial venues, promote the collective expression of oppositional ideas and the creation of solidarity and collective identity among participants.

Using the logic of case extension with the goal of elaborating Tilly's concept of repertoires of contention, we started with the view that drag performances in gay venues can be understood as tactical repertoires of the larger gay and lesbian movement (Rupp and Taylor 2003; Taylor and VanDyke 2004). Our data collection, then, was theory driven, embedded in the suppositions of these two literatures, and we sought to challenge and improve on existing conceptions of protest repertoires, not to reject them. Specific questions guided our data analysis. Do the gender and sexual displays staged in the performance reinforce or contest dominant and dichotomous sexual and gender categories? Do the performances intentionally promote interactions between groups with different gender and sexual identities? Is collective identity articulated by the performers and enacted among the participants? We used participatory research methods to explore these questions with the drag queens and their audiences. Although our research was theory driven, listening to and observing the drag queens and their audiences in their own local settings, attending the performances regularly, and talking with members of the Key West community about the drag queens and the shows at the 801 Cabaret gave us a closer view of what Lichterman (2002) refers to as "the everyday meaning of activism" and helped us to clarify and expand on existing conceptions of social movement tactics.

Tilly introduced the concept of "repertoires of contention" (1995; Tarrow 1998) to identify important historical variations in forms of protest and to explain the rise of the national social movement as a form of claims making used by subordinate groups in modern capitalist societies. Collaborating with the drag queens in the analysis of our data and being accountable to community members who reacted to our research, we developed the more delimited concept of *tactical repertoires* based on this case. We define tactical repertoires as interactive episodes that link social movement actors to each other as well as to opponents and authorities for the intended purpose of challenging or resisting change in social identities, groups, organizations, or societies. For participatory research to yield results useful both to scholars and to activists, the researcher must balance theoretical relevance with a style of participation that involves true collaboration; the researcher commits to the activists' hopes and dreams, and in turn the activists allow the researcher to use their lived experiences to address larger theoretical questions about social movements.

Participation

Participatory research offers an epistemology or way of knowing that is subjectively derived—what Kemmis and McTaggart (2000, 575) characterize as an "internal standpoint" as distinct from an objective or "external standpoint." Participation, as the central component of participatory research, involves more than the standard practice of participant-observer. Rather, participation means democratizing the research process through true collaboration between the scholar and the activist. We probably should have been far more worried whether we as women academics could really achieve this with a troupe of gay male drag queens who were different from us in many ways. Most of them have no more than a high school education and live economically precarious lives. The drag queen life involves heavy drink-ing, drug use, and sexual promiscuity. But we developed a collaborative process across the chasms of education and class and lifestyle that allowed us to understand the world of drag queens and to use insights from our work together to produce social movement theory.

From our first meeting with Sushi, we began to move slowly into their world. We interviewed most of the drag queens by inviting them to din-ner at our house, and then we began to go to their parties. We went to the weekly drag queen meetings, hung out at the shows, visited them on the street or in the dressing room, talked in the bar after the shows were over, and appeared on stage to discuss the research. One summer night, when we were almost finished with the research, Sushi announced that we could not really understand drag until she dressed us up as men in drag as women and we performed a number. She had in mind the lesbian duet from *Rent*. We demurred on the number but volunteered to go out on the street and to fetch drinks for them and carry the tip bucket around the bar during the show.

In all of these ways, we applied strategies from participatory research not typically used in mainstream social movement research: immersion and participation in the performance, exchange and reciprocity between ourselves and the drag queens, and collaboration in the research process and production of the published text. These strategies allowed us to con-ceptualize drag as a form of activism and to understand the relationship of culture and politics in a more nuanced way, extending existing conceptions of social movement tactics to encompass cultural performances. In turn, exposure to our theoretical ideas and research findings led the drag queens to recast their performances in more explicitly political terms.

We knew that drag had a long history in same-sex communities as an institution that supported gay identity and pride and that some gay activ-ists dismissed drag as embarrassing, demeaning to women, deviant, and/or frivolous. From the very first show, we saw what we considered the political nature of drag: the way the performances destabilized institutionalized gender and sexual classifications by making visible the social basis of gender and sexuality and presenting hybrid and minority genders and sexualities. In talking with the drag queens, we found out right away that they in-tended these messages and that they wanted us to write this book to affirm that they are making a difference. We also wanted to go beyond the cultural studies approach that analyzes drag as a text (Butler 1990; Garber 1992). And we wanted to consider what conceptualizing drag performances as part of the tactical repertoire of the gay, lesbian, bisexual, and transgender move-ment might mean for distinguishing cultural expressions that are purely entertainment from those that disseminate oppositional ideas and facilitate the formation of collective identities.

That involved *immersion and participation* in the world of the drag queens, on- and offstage. We became friends with the girls, learning things in conversation over dinner or sitting in the dressing room after the show that might never have come up in an interview situation. We were also immersed in the shows as audience members, and it was attending the performances on a regular basis that helped us understand the complexity and the political mission of drag. People at the shows would share their impressions and reactions with us. These ranged from a straight man confiding that he "could do Milla" to two straight Mormon women assuring us that it was all right that we are lesbians and admitting to us that, if they were going to be lesbians, they would choose to be with each other. Audience members play an important role in the shows, and the drag queens' interactions with the people who come to the cabaret, both on the street and during and after the shows, constitute a very important part of the performance of protest. Seeing this repeated night after night brought that point home.

In the middle of the show, for example, the drag queens call for audience volunteers from what they call "each sexual category," meaning a straight man, gay man, straight woman, and lesbian, and sometimes a bisexual or transsexual as well. They play on stereotypes, pointing to "lesbian shoes" or "faggy behavior." Kylie might taunt a straight man who is reluctant to come onstage: "Come on, chicken shit. You're supposed to show us how to be macho." Or, to an audience member who calls out that he's straight and proud of it, Kylie might respond, "Well, get up here, bitch." What we came to see was that, as much as these performances might seem to make concrete and distinct the categories of sexuality and gender, in fact the point is just the opposite. People volunteer outside their actual categories, and they mime sex acts beyond their experience. "Who wants to be a lesbian?" Margo might ask, and a table of gay men volunteer. Kylie drags a woman onstage and pretends to hump her, asks her if she is a lesbian, and when she says "no," Kylie asks, in mock astonishment, "Even after being with me?"

We became something of a fixture at the shows as "the professors of lesbian love," as they were wont to introduce us. Or sometimes they would greet us with the cry, "It's the pussy lickers!" reminding us, along with the rest of the audience, that we might be college professors, but in the end we, just as they, could be defined by our sexuality. Their use of slang terms for body parts and sex acts, like their openness about sexuality, served to blur the boundaries between the vulgar and the respectable. They grab and touch and strip willing audience members, both onstage and off. Their bawdy talk and touching shocks the audience, creating an opening for the introduction of ideas about gender and sexuality that are shocking in a different sense. Through watching this process and being involved in it, we came to understand this part of the show as a political act in that it points out the performativity of gender and undermines the binary categories of male/female and straight/gay.

Then there was the night Sushi put us in drag as Jinxie Dogwood and Blackée Warner. Once in drag, we went out on the street, where for forty-five minutes before the show begins the girls recruit an audience, handing out flyers, calling out to passersby, and inviting everyone to come upstairs. We had already spent a lot of time observing them there, but it wasn't until we joined them that we really understood everything that happens. That night allowed us to experience in the same way that the drag queens do how gender presentation and externally marked categories of difference determine perceptions of what makes a man a man and a woman a woman.

We had quite different reactions that seem to mirror both the positive and negative sides of the experience. Verta felt vulnerable, afraid that men staring at her would come up and touch her, as often happens. People touch the drag queens all the time, in ways that they never would anyone else, and the girls, in turn, grope them back. Occasionally people on the streets will harass them, calling them names such as "faggot" or even throwing things out of cars, and the girls admit to being afraid sometimes. They aren't at all feminine on the street, they are aggressively sexual, which comes off as profoundly masculine in the sense, ironically, that female prostitutes are masculine. So it is not all vulnerability either.

In contrast to Verta, Leila felt powerful disguised as a man dressing as a woman. She felt freed to say and do things she would not ordinarily, and she enjoyed the in-your-face nature of the performance in front of straight tourists. We both came to experience what we had already noted, that drag queens are neither feminine nor masculine in any conventional sense, that they are, in fact, simply drag-queenish. Immersion in their world allowed us to understand both drag queen as a gender category and drag performances as a form of social protest.

Jinxie's and Blackée's night at the 801 was not only the culmination of our immersion in the world of drag, it was also part of our *exchange and reciprocity* with the drag queens, which is another element of the process of participation. Throughout the research, we shared our interpretations of drag with the girls. When we told them what we were learning about the history of drag, and how we saw them fitting into the identity and community-building process, Sushi decided we should do a little segment in the show on drag history. But we are educators, not entertainers, and as hard as we tried to be amusing and light, we still came off sounding like professors. Our first attempt was a flop, but it made us realize how perfectly tailored to the venue their style of political expression is.

A painful kind of exchange came after the book appeared and Sushi's mother moved to Key West from Oregon. Sushi told us that her very traditional Japanese mother wanted to meet us and to talk to us alone. We went across the street from Sushi's apartment to a café, where Mrs. Marion asked us why we had written the book and then proceeded to cry for two hours, telling us we had shamed her entire family. It wasn't that Sushi is gay or even a drag queen that disturbed her, but that we had written about her time as a prostitute on the streets of Los Angeles. We began by trying to share our interpretation of the ways that Sushi and the other girls help to build pride and community among gay people and educate heterosexuals about gay life, but she would have none of it. Ultimately, she told us that the worst thing about Gary (Sushi) is that he isn't ashamed of anything he has done. It was a lesson for us about the burden that Sushi carries, or has shed, and it made us understand her proud insistence on her identity as a drag queen and transgendered person. The reciprocity involved in our ongoing exchanges with the drag queens helped us to think more deeply about drag and other types of cultural expression as social movement tactics.

Finally, the emphasis in participatory research on *collaboration in the research process* and production of the final text was essential to this project. All of the drag queens knew from the beginning that we were writing a book about them. It took some time to gain their trust, more for some than for others, and we never entirely gained the trust of one drag queen who joined the troupe later. We wanted, after all, not only to interview them, but to be a part of their weekly drag queen meetings, where sensitive topics sometimes came up and Sushi sometimes had to talk to them about intensely personal matters. As older, educated, lesbian academics, we were outsiders, but they incorporated us into their world, eventually not hiding anything from us. As they came to trust us, they shared stories and feelings about each other. They were also honest and open about such things as drug use, alcoholism, sexuality, dishonesty, lying, illness, and prostitution.

When we first wrote the book prospectus and sent it to presses, we also shared it with the drag queens. They sat around the bar at a regular Monday meeting and giggled and commented on what we had written. Their reactions were incredibly helpful. Some were worried about any mention of drug use, yet we knew we had to talk about that. They suggested that we not identify a particular time and place that they used drugs, and

R. V. came up with the idea of describing them in the dressing room, "sipping their cocktails and powdering their noses." We showed the first two sections of the book manuscript to all of them and the entire manuscript to Sushi. When the book first came out, Kylie told us she was upset about the discussion of drug use, even though we had "veiled it," but later she assured us that it was all right. There were a few other things that individuals asked us not to mention—such as HIV status—and we honored that, although now Scabola regrets that the book leaves that out. We also tried to avoid making trouble between them by not being precise about who called whom a liar or thief, although when we first gave them the book to read, R. V. hit Kylie over the head with it because of something he had said. Tourists regularly ask them to sign what the drag queens refer to proudly as "our book."

Because of the 801 Girls' involvement in the research process and because of their marginal economic status, we promised to share whatever royalties we earn with them. Sushi's dream is to save for a down payment on a house where they and other drag queens in Key West can live together. Despite Margo's success in her sixties, Sushi knows that one can't be a drag queen forever, and on the money they make, they are not likely to save any. Of course they have no health insurance or pensions, with the exception of Kylie, who can retire from Ralph's, the L.A. supermarket where he worked, when he is old enough. And Key West is very expensive, so they live in single rooms or shared rented apartments (see Ehrenreich 2001 on the difficulty of finding affordable housing in Key West).

They already function as a family—what they sometimes call the "drag mafia" or "queen nation"—taking care of one another when they are sick, celebrating birthdays and holidays together. Sushi takes in drag queens in need. When her mother moved to Key West, Sushi rented a bigger apartment downstairs from where she and Kylie and Desiray (who had joined the show) were living, where Sushi is also taking care of Mama, a Brazilian drag queen with AIDS. When Desiray, who was originally a tourist in one of our focus groups, moved to Key West and was sleeping on a lawn chair behind the bar, Sushi took her in, got her hired as a server at the bar, and eventually gave her a spot in the troupe after her successful debut in drag. Not all the girls are enthusiastic about the idea of a drag queen house, but Sushi is determined and as a result very invested in the book. Sushi once told us with pride, "You love me because I took a group of people nobody cared about and made them into celebrities."

Once the book came out, the drag queens helped to promote it. They organized a book-signing party for us one afternoon at the 801 and made it a smashing success. When we arrived at the bar, they were all in drag. It was the height of the war with Iraq, so Sushi dressed as Saddam Hussein's ex-mistress, Scabby as her bodyguard. We sat under the spotlights and signed books, and the girls sat on the side of the stage and signed and kissed books, leaving their luscious lip prints. They talked to the reporter assigned to cover the story for *Celebrate!* who came in response to the barrage of publicity Sushi arranged to send out. David wrote about the book in his online column, admitting that when they knew the book was finally coming out, they were nervous, realizing, "My God, we told them everything!" (Felstein 2003). In what we took as the ultimate compliment, David wrote in his column, "If by any chance you thought or think that you know us, you don't know us at all until you read this book" (ibid.). They continue to tell audiences about the book, handing out flyers in the bar. A year after the book appeared, we brought Sushi, Kylie, and Gugi to our university, where they performed for and talked with over a thousand students and provoked a weeklong discussion in the student newspaper about the social and political implications of drag performances.

These three aspects of participation—immersion, reciprocity and exchange, and collaboration—made the study possible and pointed us toward new ways of thinking of the drag queen as activists who utilize their performances to reshape moral boundaries and political hierarchies. And that allowed us to use this case to broaden the conceptualization of social movement tactics from the standard and more limited forms of political protest such as marches and sit-ins directed against the state to encompass a wider range of forms of cultural expressions designed to change or oppose change in identities and institutions of social life.

Social Change

In addition to changing the structure of the knowledge process, participatory action research is committed to collective action to produce societal change (Stoecker 1997). Social change in this context takes two forms: transformation of the participants, including the drag queens, researchers, and audience members; and transformation of theory, which results from using activists' local knowledge and everyday meanings to reconstruct preexisting social movement theory in ways that make it more relevant to activists.

Our research on the drag shows at the 801 contributed to the *transformation of participants* that was already occurring through the interactions between the performers and their audiences. Our interviews, immersion in the shows, and focus groups revealed the ways that the performances promote the construction of two levels of collective identity among participants: a sense of "we-ness" among gay men, lesbians, bisexuals, transgendered people, and drag queens; and an audience collective identity that transcends gay and straight and female and male to redefine the meaning of community. The affirmation of marginal identities begins with the drag queens' pride in their own identities. "Did I tell you that I'm a drag queen?" Sushi asks the audience. Another night she explains, "A drag queen is somebody who knows he has a dick and two balls." Moving out from their own identities as drag queens, the performers embrace gay/lesbian identities. Margo performs "I Am What I Am," a gay anthem that concludes with her removing her wig as a sign of pride in her identity as a gay man in drag. Other gay anthems, too, evoke powerful emotions in audience members. R. V. Beaumont's rendition of "What Makes a Man a Man?" a plaintive ballad about the difficult life of a drag queen, takes on great meaning for lesbians as well as gay men. A lesbian got "choked up" because "there was a feeling of acceptance and I was really struggling with acceptance." Another lesbian tourist thought that if straight people really listened to the words, "then maybe they would start thinking about it . . . I think that they could get it."

At the same time that they affirm a collective identity as gay, lesbian, bisexual, or transgendered, the performances also reach out to heterosexual audience members. Margo introduces "I Am What I Am" in a way that makes this explicit: "The next song I'm going to do for you will explain to everyone who, what, and why we are. We are not taxi drivers or hotel clerks or refrigerator repair people. We are drag queens and we are proud of what we do. Whether you are gay or straight, lesbian, bisexual, trisexual, transgender, asexual, or whatever in between, be proud of who you are!"

Through being a part of the audience and holding focus groups with audience members, we came to see that the shows successfully fostered these two levels of collective identity. Over half of our focus group participants described the shows as nurturing a gay/lesbian identity, and for three-quarters, the performances created a collective identity across genders and sexualities. Describing what she took from the show, a lesbian entertainer proclaimed, "I am what I am." A gay male New Yorker broadened the point: "The message really comes across as it doesn't matter who you are; you have to be able to laugh at who you are and enjoy being who you are." At the 801, as one man put it, "Everybody is equally fabulous."

The affirmation of collective identities was already central to the shows, but our participatory methods enhanced the process of the transformation of participants in four ways. We exposed the drag queens to our analysis and to the reactions of audience members, thus allowing the performers to incorporate what they learned into the shows. Our focus groups facilitated interactions and stimulated thought among audience members about the impact of the shows. We as researchers were exposed, through interactions with other participants, to new modes of activism. And our research raised debate in the community of Key West about the political significance of drag performances.

The drag queens were already engaged in challenging hegemonic masculinity and heteronormativity, but as we developed our analysis and shared our findings, they added what they learned about their impact on audience members into their routines, making them even more explicitly political. The girls wanted to know what worked and what didn't, and occasionally they stopped by when we were conducting the focus groups to answer questions. One group asked Kylie about her stripping on Saturday night, and Kylie responded that she performs the way she does because leaving on the wig and makeup "confounds people. It baffles them and it does make them think." After the book came out, Kylie told us that, although they had always intended to challenge the way people think about sexuality and gender and to foster a collective identity, our research had made them realize that they did in fact have an effect on people, that they did make audience members think in a more complex way about gender and sexual categories and about the discrimination that gay, lesbian, bisexual, transgendered people experience in their daily lives.

Increasingly, their public pronouncements and banter during the shows reflected the conviction that their performances had the potential to change people's thinking about gay life and the world of drag. To us, Sushi confided, "I have a platform now to teach the world." Scabby described straight people coming in feeling intimidated, a little shy and scared, and then "nine times out of ten, they stay till the very end because they're having so much fun. And they leave with a little bit more knowledge about being a homosexual, even being a drag performer." R. V. thinks that when straight people leave the bar, "They have a better, more tolerant understanding of what we're all about, what gay people are about. We change their lives." Taking the role of educator even further, the Friday night show is now called "Good Boys Gone Drag," and it features the girls as teachers. Desiray, the emcee, is the homeroom teacher, and she introduces the history teacher to cover the disco era, the school nurse to talk about AIDS, and they all cover the topic of gay sex. In this way, they translate our analysis of the way they are teaching the world into an entertaining drag performance.

Our focus group strategy also had the potential to transform audience members' awareness of the meaning of drag. At times, it was evident that heterosexual couples had never conversed with a gay man or lesbian about the kinds of issues that came up in the discussions. Sometimes focus group participants stated that the shows were purely entertaining but would then describe some significant message indicating that the shows conveyed oppositional ideas and imparted new collective identities. Gay and lesbian focus group members often speculated on the show's impact on straight people in the audience. A group of gay men thought that the performances and the audience interaction would cause straight people to open up a little bit. "They go back home and run across somebody and they find out they're gay, they're going to be a little bit less judgmental." And in fact many audience members concluded that the labels of "gay" and "straight" (or "female" and "male") just don't fit. Almost all of our focus group members made reference to this aspect of the shows. For one gay man, "You leave them at the door." A straight male tourist put it this way: "I think that one of the beauties of attending a show like this is that you do realize that you . . . shouldn't walk out and say 'I only like men,' and you shouldn't say 'I only like women,' and it all kind of blends together a lot more so than maybe what we want to live in our normal daily lives." A young gay man thought, "They're challenging the whole idea of gender and so forth and they're breaking that down." These kinds of responses indicate that focus group participants thought about the political content of drag shows. At the same time, the focus groups confirmed for the drag queens that they were getting their messages across. After the book came out, we ran into a local heterosexual woman realtor who commented on the publicity surrounding our book in the local media. Sounding very much like a focus group member, she provided her analysis of the community-building function of the show: "They bring a gay guy up, then a straight woman, and a straight man, and a lesbian. By the end, you just think, 'what's the difference?'"

If our research process helped the drag queens to articulate their politics more explicitly and encouraged audience members to reflect on their responses to the shows, our participatory methods also exposed us to new forms of political activism. As researchers and academics we adopted drag-queen flamboyance when we talked about the book, speaking openly about sexuality, including our own lesbian identity, and using a lot of the drag queen vocabulary. When Verta was invited to the University of Milan to give a paper in celebration of the legacy of Alberto Melucci, she talked about the drag queen research, prompting her translator to approach her before her session to ask, "Do I have to translate all these words?" Another time, we told a group of administrators at Ohio State about our nickname of "professors of lesbian love" and joked that maybe we would leave whatever money we had to any department that would establish a chair of "lesbian love." The shock on their faces made us realize how much we had learned in our exchanges with the drag queens about the performance of identity and the use of humor and vulgarity to gain the attention of audiences in order to educate them about the restrictions placed on lesbian, gay, and transgendered people by the larger society.

The process of writing and talking about the book served as a way to empower marginal identities and transform the attitudes of people who might not otherwise be exposed to drag culture. By talking about drag queens in venues ranging from the classroom to community groups, to a social movement seminar at Harvard, to Milan ("in the shadow of the Pope," as Verta was fond of pronouncing), our research, like the shows themselves, challenged a variety of people to rethink traditional notions of binary and hierarchical categories of sexuality and gender.

The publication of our book and the attention it attracted in Key West provoked the community itself to engage in debate about the political nature of drag shows. An article in the local gay/lesbian newspaper about the ways the performers challenge gender and sexual boundaries elicited a series of heated responses about what is or is not political (Gilbert 2003; "Mail" 2003). This debate in the community was itself part of the social change emphasis so central to participatory research. The theory we had developed, based on our interactions with the performers and their audiences, had indeed begun to challenge the way people in the community thought about the show at the 801 Cabaret and about the various tactics used by the gay and lesbian movement. Community members, drag queens, audience members, and we as researchers all found ourselves transformed to various degrees by the participatory nature of the research.

The research process also led to the *transformation of theory,* specifically the development of the concept of tactical repertoires and a framework for understanding the political nature of cultural performances and other forms of cultural expression in a social movement context. Participatory methods allowed us to develop a more grounded conceptualization of tactical repertoires as engaged in contestation, intentionality, and collective identity work.

First, tactical repertoires are sites of *contestation* in which bodies, symbols, identities, practices, and discourses are used to pursue or prevent change in institutionalized power relations. Through our extensive involvement in the shows and our interactions with audience members, we were able to see how central the subversion of mainstream heterosexual gender codes is to drag.

Second, following the argument of resource mobilization and political process theorists that strategic decision making is an essential aspect of the social psychology of claims making (McCarthy and Zald 1977; McAdam 1982; Tarrow 1998), we view *intentionality* as the second component of tactical repertoires. Talking at length with the drag queens made it clear that they are intentionally thinking about the ways their performances undermine biological conceptions of sexuality and gender and challenge rigid social definitions of masculinity and femininity. We would never have known this without collaboration in the formulation and dissemination of the research.

Finally, we view protest actions as not only directed to external targets, but also having an internal movement-building dimension. A movement's tactical repertoires represent one of the means by which challenging groups develop an oppositional consciousness or the *collective identity* necessary to recognize common injustices, to oppose those injustices, and to define their shared interests in resisting those injustices (Melucci 1989; W. Gamson 1992; Taylor and Whittier 1992; J. Gamson 1995; Klandermans and de Weerd 2000; Snow and McAdam 2000). Our participatory methods opened our eyes to the ways that drag shows promote the construction of collective identity not only among people with marginalized sexual identities but also across the lines of sexuality and gender.

This model of tactical repertoires, which emerged out of interaction between the theoretical perspectives we brought to this case and the knowledge of the drag queens and their audiences, extends social movement theory by broadening what counts as a social movement tactic. Incorporating the case extension logic with participatory action research allowed us to understand the way the drag queens and their audiences look at activism and to use these local meanings to offer a conceptualization of social movement tactics that enabled us to recognize the varied cultural strategies used by social movements and to evaluate their political significance using the same criteria that define more conventional forms of protest (Taylor, Rupp, and J. Gamson forthcoming; Taylor and Van Dyke 2004). This framework lets us distinguish oppositional performances (such as the drag shows) from rituals of cultural affirmation (for example, some forms of theatrical female impersonation that have no connection to the broader gay, lesbian, bisexual, and transgender movement). Participatory action research has the potential to contribute to social change by transforming all of the participants in the research process, as well as by making social movement theory more reflective of activists' understandings.

Conclusion

We never imagined that that first night at the 801 Cabaret would lead to such an intensive research project. The two basic features of activist research—participation through immersion, exchange and reciprocity, and collaboration; and an emphasis on social change through the transformation of participants and theory—made this project possible. The experience changed our lives, and we think the lives of the drag queens as well, in some important ways. They began talking like professors, at least at some points in the show, and we began talking like drag queens, and we all still do. We realized how profoundly educative and identity building drag is, and the drag queens in turn took what they learned from audience members to enhance those processes. We came to love each other across lines of sex, gender, class, race, and ethnicity, and to appreciate those differences. We came to see how much social movement research could benefit from the practices of participatory research, and how such practices could aid in the development of better social movement theory. We came to realize how much we could learn from drag queen–activists and how we could enhance, as scholar-activists, the drag queens' performance of protest as well as community discussions of the politics of drag.

We have outlined here what we see as the advantages of a participatory action research strategy combined with the case extension logic for activists, for researchers, and for theory building. We think that this method has promise for research on other social movements. Using this approach, we offer a conceptual definition of tactical repertoires—as engaging in contestation, intentionality, and the construction of collective identity—that allows us to get beyond the view that culture and politics are fundamentally different components of social reality, with political action intended and rational and cultural action unintended and nonrational. This is an extension of social movement theory with utility for activists as well. For the relationship of activists and researchers is a symbiotic one in participatory social movement research. Our collaborations with the drag queens were crucial to the development of our theoretical understanding of social movement tactics, and the drag queens' integration of our knowledge of social movements into their shows made them more effective as vehicles of social change.

In talking with the drag queens about writing this piece, Sushi quipped, "You're like modern Oscar Wildes, you descended into a den of iniquity and emerged with a new view of the world." That we did. And ultimately we came to realize that we were not, as lesbian activists and academics, such strangers in a strange land.

Notes

We would like to thank Jennifer Earl, Richard Flacks, Richard Sullivan, and other members of the social movement proseminar at the University of California, Santa Barbara, for helpful comments on this chapter.

1. Review by Richard Labonte, e-mailed from University of Chicago Press, June 2003.

References

Beckwith, Karen. 1996. "Lancashire Women against Pit Closures: Women's Standing in a Men's Movement." *Signs: Journal of Women in Culture and Society* 21: 1034–68.

Bevington, Douglas, and Chris Dixon. "An Emerging Direction in Social Movement Scholarship: Movement-Relevant Theory." Unpublished paper.

Burawoy, Michael. 1998. "The Extended Case Method." *Sociological Theory* 16: 4–33.

Burawoy, Michael, Alice Burton, Ann Arnett Ferguson, Kathryn J. Fox, Joshua Gamson, Leslie Hurst, Nadine G. Julius, et al. 1991. *Ethnography Unbound: Power and Resistance in the Modern Metropolis.* Berkeley: University of California Press.

Butler, Judith. 1990. *Gender Trouble: Feminism and the Subversion of Identity.* New York: Routledge.

———. 1993. *Bodies That Matter: On the Discursive Limits of "Sex."* New York: Routledge.

Cancian, Francesca M. 1992. "Feminist Science: Methodologies That Challenge Inequality." *Gender & Society* 6: 623–42.

———. 1996. "Participatory Research and Alternative Strategies for Activist Sociology." In *Feminism and Social Change: Bridging Theory and Practice,* ed. Heidi Gottfried, 187–205. Urbana: University of Illinois Press.

Darnovsky, Marcy, Barbara Epstein, and Richard Flacks, eds. 1995. *Cultural Politics and Social Movements.* Philadelphia: Temple University Press.

Ehrenreich, Barbara. 2001. *Nickel and Dimed: On (Not) Getting by in America.* New York: Metropolitan Books.

Felstein, David. 2003. "Random Observations." *Pistol & Enema: The Gay E-Zine for the Gay Keys Scene,* April 11.

Flacks, Richard. 2004. "Knowledge for What? Thoughts on the State of Social Movement Studies." In *Rethinking Social Movements,* ed. Jeff Goodwin and James M. Jasper, 135–53. Lanham, MD: Rowman & Littlefield.

Fonow, Mary Margaret. 2003. *Union Women: Forging Feminism in the United Steelworkers of America.* Minneapolis: University of Minnesota Press.

Fonow, Mary Margaret, and Judith A. Cook. 1991. "Back to the Future: A Look at the Second Wave of the Feminist Epistemology and Methodology." In *Beyond Methodology: Feminist Scholarship and Lived Research,* ed. Mary Margaret Fonow and Judith A. Cook, 1–15. Bloomington: University of Indiana Press.

Freeman, Jo. 1975. *Women: A Feminist Perspective.* Palo Alto, CA: Mayfield.

Gamson, Joshua. 1995. "Must Identity Movements Self-Destruct? A Queer Dilemma." *Social Problems* 42: 390–407.

Gamson, William A. 1992. *Talking Politics*. New York: Cambridge University Press.

Garber, Marjorie. 1992. *Vested Interests: Cross-Dressing and Cultural Anxiety*. New York: Routledge.

Gaventa, John. 1991. "Toward a Knowledge Democracy: Viewpoints on Participatory Research in North America." In *Action and Knowledge: Breaking the Monopoly with Participatory Action Research,* ed. Orlando Fals-Borda and Mohammad Anisur Rahman, 121–33. New York: Apex Press.

Gilbert, Constance. 2003. "Teasers Comes to the 801." *Celebrate!* September 4–17, 10.

Halberstam, Judith. 1998. *Female Masculinity*. Durham, NC: Duke University Press.

Jasper, James. 1997. *The Art of Moral Protest: Culture, Biography, and Creativity in Social Movements*. Chicago: University of Chicago Press.

Kemmis, Stephen, and Robin McTaggart. 2000. "Participatory Action Research." In *Handbook of Qualitative Research,* 2nd ed., ed. Norman K. Denzin and Yvonna S. Lincoln, 567–605. Thousand Oaks, CA.

Klandermans, Bert, and Suzanne Staggenborg, eds. 2002. *Methods of Social Movement Research*. Minneapolis: University of Minnesota Press.

Klandermans, Bert, and Marga de Weerd. 2000. "Group Identification and Political Protest." In *Self, Identity, and Social Movements,* ed. Sheldon Stryker, Timothy Owens, and Robert W. White, 68–90. Minneapolis: University of Minnesota Press.

Kurtz, Sharon. 2002. *Workplace Justice: Organizing Multi-identity Movements*. Minneapolis: University of Minnesota Press.

Lichterman, Paul. 2002. "Seeing Structure Happen: Theory-Driven Participant Observation." In *Methods of Social Movement Research,* ed. Bert Klandermans and Suzanne Staggenborg, 118–45. Minneapolis: University of Minnesota Press.

Lorber, Judith. 1999. "Crossing Borders and Erasing Boundaries: Paradoxes of Identity Politics." *Sociological Focus* 32: 355–70.

"Mail." 2003. *Celebrate!* September 18–October 1, 12.

McAdam, Doug. 1982. *Political Process and the Development of Black Insurgency, 1930–1970*. Chicago: University of Chicago Press.

McAdam, Doug, Sidney Tarrow, and Charles Tilly. 2001. *Dynamics of Contention*. Cambridge: Cambridge University Press.

McCarthy, John D., and Mayer N. Zald. 1977. "Resource Mobilization and Social Movements: A Partial Theory," *American Journal of Sociology* 82: 1212–41.

Melucci, Alberto. 1989. *Nomads of the Present: Social Movements and Individual Needs in Contemporary Society*. Philadelphia: Temple University Press.

————. 1995. "The Process of Collective Identity." In *Social Movements and Culture,* ed. Hank Johnston and Bert Klandermans, 41–63. Minneapolis: University of Minnesota Press.

Mies, Maria. 1983. "Women's Research or Feminist Research? The Debate Surrounding Feminist Science and Methodology." In *Beyond Methodology: Feminist Scholarship as Lived Research,* ed. Mary Margaret Fonow and Judith A. Cook, 60–84. Bloomington: Indiana University Press.

Muñoz, José Esteban. 1999. *Disidentifications: Queers of Color and the Performance of Politics.* Minneapolis: University of Minnesota Press.

Naples, Nancy A., ed. 1998. *Community Activism and Feminist Politics.* New York: Routledge.

————. 2003. *Feminism and Method: Ethnography, Discourse Analysis, and Activist Research.* New York: Routledge.

Naples, Nancy, and Emily Clark. 1996. "Feminist Participatory Research and Empowerment: Going Public as Survivors of Childhood Sexual Abuse." In *Feminism and Social Change,* ed. Heidi Gottfried, 160–86. Urbana: University of Illinois Press.

Oleson, Virginia. L. 2000. "Feminisms and Qualitative Research at and into the Millennium." In *Handbook of Qualitative Research,* 2nd ed., ed. Norman K. Denzin and Yvonna S. Lincoln, 215–55. Thousand Oaks, CA.

Reinharz, Shulamit. 1992. *Feminist Methods in Social Research.* New York: Oxford University Press.

Rupp, Leila J., and Verta Taylor. 2003. *Drag Queens at the 801 Cabaret.* Chicago: University of Chicago Press.

Snow, David, and Doug McAdam. 2000. "Identity Work Processes in the Context of Social Movements: Clarifying the Identity/Movement Nexus." In *Self, Identity, and Social Movements,* ed. S. Stryker, T. Owens, and R. White, 41–67. Minneapolis: University of Minnesota Press.

Staggenborg, Suzanne. 1998. *Gender, Family, and Social Movements.* Thousand Oaks, CA: Pine Forge Press.

Stein, Arlene, and Ken Plummer. 1996. "'I Can't Even Think Straight': Queer Theory and the Missing Sexual Revolution in Sociology." In *Queer Theory/Sociology,* ed. Steven Seidman, 129–44. Oxford: Blackwell.

Stoecker, Randy. 1994. *Defending Community: The Struggle for Alternative Redevelopment in Cedar-Riverside.* Philadelphia: Temple University Press.

————. 1997. "The Imperfect Practice of Collaborative Research: The 'Working Group on Neighborhoods' in Toledo, OH." In *Building Community: Social Science in Action,* ed. Philip Nyden, Anne Figert, Mark Shibley, and Darryl Burrows, 219–25. Thousand Oaks, CA: Pine Forge Press.

————. 1999. "Are Academics Irrelevant? Roles for Scholars in Participatory Research." *American Behavioral Scientist* 42: 840–54.

Stoecker, Randy, and Edna Bonacich. 1992. "Why Participatory Research?" *American Sociologist* 23: 5–14.

Tarrow, Sydney. 1998. *Power in Movement: Social Movements and Contentious Politics.* New York: Cambridge University Press.

Taylor, Verta. 1996. *Rock-a-by Baby: Feminism, Self-Help, and Postpartum Depression.* New York: Routledge.

————. 1998. "Feminist Methodology in Social Movements Research." In "Qualitative Methods and Social Movements Research," special issue, *Qualitative Sociology* 21: 357–79.

Taylor, Verta, and Leila J. Rupp. 1991. "Researching the Women's Movement: We Make Our Own History, But Not Just As We Please." In *Beyond Methodology: Feminist Scholarship as Lived Research,* eds. Mary Margaret Fonow and Judith A. Cook, 119–32. Bloomington: Indiana University Press.

————. 1993. "Women's Culture and Lesbian Feminist Activism: A Reconsideration of Cultural Feminism." *Signs: Journal of Women in Culture and Society* 19: 32–61.

————. 1996. "Lesbian Existence and the Women's Movement: Researching the 'Lavender Herring.'" In *Feminism and Social Change: Bridging Theory and Practice,* ed. Heidi Gottfried, 142–59. Urbana: University of Illinois Press.

————. 2004. "Chicks with Dicks, Men in Dresses: What It Means to Be a Drag Queen." *Journal of Homosexuality* 46, no. 3–4: 113–33.

Taylor, Verta, Leila J. Rupp, and Joshua Gamson. Forthcoming. "Performing Identity: Culture as Protest." *Research in Social Movements, Conflict, and Change,* 25.

Taylor, Verta, and Nella Van Dyke. 2004. "'Get Up Stand Up': Tactical Repertoires of Social Movements." In *The Blackwell Companion to Social Movements,* ed. David A. Snow, Sarah A. Soule, and Hanspeter Kriesi, 262–93. Oxford, UK: Blackwell.

Taylor, Verta, and Nancy E. Whittier. 1992. "Collective Identity in Social Movement Communities: Lesbian Feminist Mobilization." In *Frontiers in Social Movement Theory,* ed. Aldon D. Morris and Carole McClurg Mueller, 104–29. New Haven, CT: Yale University Press.

Tilly, Charles. 1978. *From Mobilization to Revolution.* Reading, MA: Addison-Wesley.

————. 1995. "Contentious Repertoires." In *Repertoires and Cycles of Collective Action,* ed. Mark Traugott, 15–42. Durham, NC: Duke University Press.

————. 2001. *Stories, Identities, and Political Change.* Lanham, MD: Rowman and Littlefield.

Touraine, Alain. 1981. *The Voice and the Eye: An Analysis of Social Movements.* New York: Cambridge University Press.

Traugott, Mark, ed. 1995. *Repertoires and Cycles of Collective Action.* Durham, NC: Duke University Press.

Whyte, William Foote, ed. 1991. *Participatory Action Research.* Thousand Oaks, CA: Sage.

Afterword

William A. Gamson

Reading over the essays in *Rhyming Hope and History* stimulated personal memories about recurrent themes in the book and in my life. I offer here a series of autobiographical riffs on several of these, linked to quotes from some of the chapters herein. These themes include:

- The fraught relationship between activists and scholars
- The ups and downs of the university as a locus of action and a site of contest for would-be scholar-activists
- The meaning and centrality of collaboration as the core of any vision of participatory democracy

Dick Flacks says, "The study of social movements ought to provide movement activists with intellectual resources they might not readily obtain otherwise" (ch. 1).[1]

It's the fall of 1962. My wife Zelda and I have just moved to Ann Arbor—returning, actually, since we both had been students at the University of Michigan. I begin to hear about a meeting at nearby Port Huron—an SDS convention with about fifty participants—that had taken place the previous June. Its participants seem to be everywhere around me. One, Bob Ross, is taking an upper-level undergraduate course on mass communications that I am teaching. In the winter term, then SDS president Tom Hayden (pursuing an MA focused on C. Wright Mills) and future SDS president Paul Potter show up in my graduate seminar on political sociology along with several other "new left" participants.

Meanwhile, I am doing research on the Cold War, based at the Center for Research on Conflict Resolution. We are housed in a former National Guard armory, called the "Temporary Classroom Building." We delight at having taken over quarters recently used by the military for drilling future soldiers and, especially, with a large, high-ceilinged room that serves as a marvelous indoor Frisbee court.

The center's director has provided office space for an SDS project—the Peace Research and Education Project (PREP). The lines between PREP and another SDS effort—the Economic Research and Action Project (ERAP)—are fluid. When they are not in the field, ERAPers are often around.[2] In the next couple of years, either through classes, the Center for Research on Conflict Resolution, or movement activities, I get to know many members of the SDS founding generation. It seems that, without consciously seeking it, I am embedded.

As a would-be social movement scholar, am I providing activists with resources that they might not otherwise obtain? It seems more the other way around. In my mass communications course, the conventional wisdom in the field emphasizes the limited effects of the mass media, heaping ridicule on the discredited "hypodermic model." My activist students are incredulous, reinforcing my own skepticism that something important is being missed. Media framing is an idea whose time had not yet come.

In my political sociology seminar, Paul Potter and Tom Hayden write a joint paper on SNCC as a model for movement political organizations that are serious about participatory democracy. Looking at the conventional wisdom on movement organizations, the choices seem to be none at all or the iron law of oligarchy. Could it be that there are alternatives, overlooked by those who study social movements formally?

Dick Flacks says, "The power of the powerless is rooted in their capacity to stop the smooth flow of social life" (ch. 1).

As I wrap up my research on the Cold War, I begin thinking about American social movements and the issues that will become central to *The Strategy of Social Protest* (1990; the first edition was published in 1975). The central idea is contained in the Flacks quote above on the "capacity to stop the smooth flow of social life." My own experience in the civil rights movement seems to confirm it and, as I increasingly discover, so does my research on American social movements between 1800 and 1945.

Professors are not exactly powerless, even nontenured ones, nor are graduate students. "We are people of this generation, bred in at least modest comfort, housed now in universities, looking uncomfortably to the world we inherit," began the Port Huron statement. But as we watched and analyzed the complicity of the large research universities such as Michigan in the Vietnam War, we felt increasingly powerless to change it. The insight about disrupting business as usual seemed increasingly relevant.

The first disruption began in February 1965, and led to the first teach-in against the Vietnam War on March 24, 1965. I have written about this extensively elsewhere (see Gamson 1991) and will not repeat this account here. We emphasized that our target in this action was not the university but the U.S. government, but this turned out to be the beginning of a long series of actions, some of which explicitly did target university policy.

Student deferments for anyone with passing grades had allowed us professors to avoid recognizing that our grades were deciding who would avoid serving in Vietnam. But with increasing demands to provide a large number of replacements for those soldiers being rotated home and with draft avoidance an increasing issue, the selective service announces that it would use class standing—as determined by grade point average—to determine who would receive such deferments. A difference between a B and a C could determine whether a student would be drafted out of college and sent to kill—and perhaps to die—in an unjust war. Our complicity could no longer be denied or rationalized away.

Faculty and graduate students in the ongoing anti–Vietnam War movement gathered to discuss our problem. With the permission of the group, I schedule a meeting with the vice president for academic affairs, a former law school dean. I explain our dilemma and ask for his assistance in finding a solution. "Grading students is part of the requirements of the job," he explains. "When people can't meet the requirements of the job, they quit and find another." End of conversation.

We decide on a plan that includes the following elements:

- We will withhold grades for the courses we teach and place them in escrow, to be released only when they are not being used to decide who is drafted.
- We will hold a weeklong liquid fast with daily public gatherings for a "non-lunch" to publicize what we are doing and why. The fasters will wear black arm bands to identify themselves.

One aspect of the plan provokes an internal conflict in the group. Some of us—including me—are disturbed by the fact that students will pay the price of our resistance. Grades are a currency used for graduate and professional schools that some students feel they need whether they like it or not. Some of us want an escape clause for students: we will turn in grades for individuals if and only if the student requests it in writing. Others in the group deride us as wishy-washy liberals who lack the courage of our convictions. We persuade a majority and the escape clause is included in the plan. As the plan becomes public, the university administration reacts. Withholding grades is a violation of university rules. If no grade is turned in, a grade of F will be recorded on the student's transcript. The situation is unresolved as we carry out our fast and the end of the term approaches. The women who have fasted complain that while the men lost an average of six pounds during the week, the weight loss of the female participants is a small fraction of this.

My department chair calls me into his office. "This is the second time in two years [referring to the earlier teach-in] that you have brought this university to its knees," he tells me, grimly. Who, me? Exaggerated, but flattering nonetheless. We formally ask the faculty senate to respect our conscientious objection in this situation and are rebuked by a large majority who condemn our actions. We, in turn, denounce the university administration for threatening to punish students for our refusal to turn in grades for them.

I don't know whether federal draft officials are aware of the conflict at the University of Michigan, but their next action resolves it. They abandon the existing system and institute a new draft lottery system in its place. Grading is no longer selecting military service, and we are off the hook. The university continues to conduct classified military research on "distant sensing," used for bombing target identification in Vietnam—but this battle lies ahead, and we feel a little less complicit and powerless for the moment.

David Croteau says, "Some scholars aim to use the security, stability, and freedom of a tenured academic position to conduct research and do writing that provides useful assistance to progressive social movement efforts. This elusive goal is based on integrating two very different roles: academic scholar and movement activist. . . . The university as currently constructed is *not* a neutral entity but instead is usually allied with parties that reinforce the status quo rather than promote progressive social change" (ch. 2).

"A century of struggle and an honor roll of committed scholars have failed to fundamentally change the barriers facing scholar-activists in the academy" (ch. 2).

"Brave souls will continue to make the effort to integrate their scholar-activist identity, and no doubt some will succeed. But for many others, being in a university eventually means being forced to decide which side they are on—and being prepared to live with the consequences of that choice" (ch. 2).

Quoting from Bob Ross: "Our profession manages to punish us for all of our virtues" (1991, 201).

Instead of engaging with the pressing issues of the day, in *Knowledge for What?* Lynd argued that social scientists were "hiding behind their precocious beards of 'dispassionate research' and 'scientific objectivity'" (1939, 181).

It is 1952 and I am in my second year at Antioch College. I discover Lynd's *Knowledge for What?* and I'm excited by its message. I tell my mentor, the late Heinz Eulau, about my enthusiasm. "I see you like propaganda," he remarks contemptuously.

It is 1967 and I am circulating a draft of a paper that would later be published under the title "Stable Unrepresentation in American Society" (1968). It contains the seeds of an argument that will later become central to *The Strategy of Social Protest*. I send a copy to one of my dissertation committee members who is now my colleague at Michigan. "Block that ideology," he comments.

Yes, I've tried to follow the scholar-activist path that Croteau describes, and I recognize the tensions that he and others are talking about, but I can't say that I have personally paid any price. It makes me question my authenticity. I haven't had *Eingebläut*—the German New Left word for the bruises left by police batons. I was never arrested, never fired from my job, or even denied regular and generous pay increases. I went to lots of demonstrations and participated in many different collective actions, but I haven't been beaten or even teargassed. Zelda Gamson was at least maced in a May Day demonstration in Washington in the early 1970s with other members of her affinity group, but I was back in Ann Arbor.

If the academy is so inhospitable to people like me, how come I haven't suffered more? Have I been unconsciously holding back, unaware of it? Is it just a matter of the luck of when I was born—a mid-Depression, under-sized cohort—and a rapidly expanding higher education system when I was starting out? In the 1960s when the actions in which I participated created the sharpest conflicts with the university administration, I already had tenure (as did most of the teach-in instigators), and jobs at other schools were going begging. It took less courage to resist or follow any unconventional path then than it does now. I recognize the truth in Croteau's observations about the inherent tension in being an activist in the academy, and I have watched others suffer for the choice they have made. But, for whatever reason, it is not something that I have personally experienced.

Can I draw lessons from my own experience when much of it may have been mainly the luck of my birth cohort? I'm sure it helped that I paid my dues in the currency that counts—publishing in mainstream professional journals, getting funded grants, and gaining academic and disciplinary recognition. For me, it was enough that my activism was, if sometimes unwelcome, at least tolerated, while I was still rewarded for other things that I liked to do anyway. When activism sometimes brought me into conflict with the university administration, tenure and an expansionist higher education industry gave me the luxury of doing what seemed right without having to think a lot about possible personal consequences. The strength of the movements of the day—the civil rights and antiwar movements—provided resources and support for activist engagement inside and outside the university. Our efforts to address broader injustices and inequalities may even have helped democratize academia.

That some of us are able to avoid the inherent tension does not mean that it is not there. David Meyer talks about the "bait and switch" of academic life. It appears to offer the freedom to do activism for those who want skills and training that will be useful in doing better social justice work. But this "doesn't mean that acquiring those tools, along with requisite certifications, . . . is like doing activism" (personal communication).

Richard Healey and Sandra Hinson say: "For the past twenty years or more, most social change organizations have been on the defensive: shoring up past victories and warding off further attacks on progressive gains from past social movements. Since the 1980s, the right has been successful in eroding New Deal reforms as well as gains made in the 1960s and early 1970s on civil rights, environmental protection, women's rights and reproductive health, and so much more" (ch. 4).

Kevin Carragee describes the concept of standing and its relationship to his work as a housing activist in the Alston-Brighton area. His PhD in communication and long list of publications provides him with standing in the academic world but not in the eyes of the housing task force that he describes:

> Standing involves the granting of voice to groups, organizations, and individuals, allowing them to speak in public forums on controversial social and political issues. . . . My lengthy involvement in the neighborhood's civic and political life provided me with a particular standing on the task force, a standing distinct from my identity as an academic who had a particular set of skills that could benefit this group. (ch. 5)

Charlotte Ryan describes bridgework, the building of social relationships between movement scholars and activists: "Bridgework builds ongoing two-way learning relationships that grow from and facilitate the flow of information, language, concepts, practices, systems, services, and resources in the context of an articulated vision or mission" (ch. 7).

Ryan distinguishes bridge workers from edge walkers: "My success as a bridge worker rested on the good will of respected, well-established residents of the disparate social worlds I proposed to bridge. I needed someone to create entry points for me as a bridge worker and for my companions from the other world" (ch. 7).

It is a discouraging time for those of us who have witnessed so many positive changes in the past forty years and felt a part of making them. Ryan once described the MRAP seminar as a "shelter for homeless radicals." I know that for me, the extended MRAP network provides a sense of community and connection—that antidote to despair.

In the world of MRAP, I am an edge walker and Ryan is a bridge worker. Walking the edge sounds like exciting and dangerous work, while bridgeworking sounds safer and tamer, as if one has something to hold on to. With characteristic modesty, Ryan has made her role seem less heroic.

Edge sitter seems a better term for what I do. The bridge I envision is a shaky rope bridge over a canyon. One can easily fall off or end up clinging to it by one hand, waiting to be rescued. Sometimes the edge sitters in academia who are holding the rope for some bridge workers get pulled loose from their institutional anchors into the canyon. But often they are well anchored and protected from such a fate.

For the edge sitters in the activist community, the anchoring organization is often vulnerable and in a precarious state, especially in such a mean season as this. There is a danger that this end of the bridge will collapse into the canyon, dragging the whole organization down with it. Whichever end of the bridge goes, the bridge worker ends up at the bottom of the canyon.

Edge sitters only require standing in one world; bridge workers require standing in both. This is like working two jobs. Bridge workers, it seems, have to do some double edge sitting as well in order to survive.

During one of his recent visiting seminars at Boston College, Michael Burawoy was discussing doing public sociology as "organic intellectuals" (bridge workers) in contrast to those who do it as "traditional intellectuals" (edge sitters). Someone from the audience wisecracked, "Yeh. Those are the ones who get paid." The wisecrack was a reminder of how, even in the mostly favorable and supportive environment of Boston College, it has been extremely difficult to institutionalize the kind of public sociology pursued by Burawoy's organic intellectuals.

Ryan describes her work with the Rhode Island Coalition Against Domestic Violence and their partner SOAR (Sisters Overcoming Abusive Relationships): As one domestic survivor and SOAR member put it, "I went from being talked about to being involved in the talk" (ch. 7).

Myra Ferree, Valerie Sperling, and Barbara Risman say: "A particular insight that we derived from studying these Russian women's movement seminars is that there is a real body of skills that goes into running a social movement organization, particularly doing so in the more engaging manner that develops a sense of ownership and commitment in the participants and enables them to find a political voice in which to express themselves. These skills involve participants both cognitively and emotionally. We have called these organizational skills necessary to construct a democratic process a 'culture of conversation,' and suggest that social movement scholars take such skills for granted—the invisible infrastructure of democratic political cultures that make civil society function—in part because they are often naturalized and devalued as 'women's work'" (ch. 8).

Verta Taylor and Leila Rupp say: "Participation, as the central component of participatory research, involves more than the standard practice of participant-observer. Rather, participation means democratizing the research process through true collaboration between the scholar and the activist" (ch. 14).

Watching Ryan run a workshop is a lesson in collaboration. For a few years, MRAP had a media fellows program with a monthly all-day meeting of the group. The fellows were nominated by and were representing grassroots community organizations. We did considerable collective planning of these sessions, but Ryan would chair them.

It is one of our earliest meetings with the media fellows, and we have given them the assignment of setting up a media committee in their organizations. None of them has succeeded in doing this, and we are trying to understand collectively what the difficulties were. The participants sometimes seem to blame themselves, and the problems they describe are very concrete and situation specific. I sense some of what is not being said but can't articulate it.

Ryan can. One element of collaboration is a very active form of listening—hearing the unsaid and the question behind the apparent question. It seems to come from a deep and unfeigned respect for the speaker and a genuine desire to understand that person's experience. In this case, the problems have to do with underlying issues of power, status, and gender.

The media fellows were younger than typical board members and leaders of the organizations that they represented. Furthermore, they were more likely to be women. Older male leaders in some organizations seemed wary that the media fellows would become the public face of the organization, siphoning off their own status and power. Other leaders of the organization were eager to dump media work on the fellows so that they would not themselves have to worry about it. The fellows found it difficult to answer such apparently simple questions as, why do we need a media committee?

Once Ryan put these unspoken issues on the table, the media fellows responded with a rush of energy. The diagnosis and strategies for dealing with it became very much a collective process with the fellows involved in the talk and the plans for next steps. We concluded that one needed to analyze the power dynamics in the organization before setting up a media committee. The nature of the media committee and the role that the media fellows would need to play in being a catalyst for such a committee had to be understood clearly in order to make it effective.

The same lesson was true for the second problem of dumping media work on the MRAP fellows. For us, this violated a central MRAP principle: that media strategy should be a part of a larger organizational strategy, not divorced from it. But this kind of strategic thinking does not necessarily come naturally to either the media fellows or the potential members of a media committee in their organizations. Thinking strategically was something that the fellows needed to understand well enough to be able to communicate in explaining to people why a media committee was desirable and what it would do. By the end of the session, we decided to make setting up a media committee a goal to be achieved by the end of the year while we worked through the issues together.

What I have learned about collaboration I learned from watching talented women do it. I have been fortunate to have had gifted role models— especially Zelda Gamson whose work on cooperatives and worker-owned enterprises and on collaboration in the workplace and within and among colleges and universities has heavily informed and influenced my own. And I have watched her put the principles she has articulated into effective practice in countless situations. But my luck began very early with my first collaborative paper.

It is my second year at Antioch College and I am taking a course on self and society. My friend Mary Belenky (then Mary Field), a future co-author of *Women's Ways of Knowing* (1986), is taking the course as well. We decide to do a joint paper on children's play as a form of socialization and to identify what is being learned. The paper argues, not surprisingly, that some kinds of play under some kinds of conditions are about learning to collaborate. The insight, in retrospect, seems modest, but the lessons about play and games and collaboration seem to have stuck with me throughout my life.

It is 1956 and I am a graduate student at the University of Michigan. It is that moment when I first recognize that serious and fun are not in tension with each other. My recreational reading at the moment is Stephen Potter's *Gamesmanship* and *One-Upmanship,* and I am still chuckling over some of the examples when I pick up my assigned reading for a seminar that day: Erving Goffman's "On Face Work." Behold an epiphany: sociology can be serious fun.

Taylor and Rupp's ethnography of a group of drag queens at a club in Key West is in this tradition. They have a good time telling their story. They argue that while the performance is clearly intended to be entertainment, it is subversive and political at the same time—in other words, serious fun.

I have managed to make a lot of my professional work a form of play—especially the teaching. My continual involvement with game simulation began in the mid-1960s and continues today. In my mind, this interest is part of what seems to me a pedagogy of democratic participation. The same classroom techniques that engage students in an active and collective way in their learning are the techniques that foster and sustain political engagement in social movements.

It is December 1963, and I am reading over the Michigan student evaluations of an upper-level undergraduate course that I have just finished teaching for the first time. I had been concerned with covering the field and been reasonably satisfied that I had done justice to it. Meanwhile, the evaluations are talking about being bored by lectures delivered in a monotone and without sufficient eye contact. Comments on other aspects of the course bespeak a lack of engagement in the course material. Students praise the parts where there are clear ground rules about how grades are determined.

I had gone to Antioch with its active learning model; I knew what worked for me and I believed it worked for others. I was aware of people around me using active learning techniques through internships and field experiences. Harold Guetzkow and his colleagues had even begun using game simulations to understand the dynamics of international conflict. Teaching, I tell myself, is not about covering the field. I begin working on a sociology game, called SIMSOC, for Simulated Society, as a laboratory component of a more conventional introductory course with weekly lectures and discussions.

Other smaller-scale role plays and simple field experiments based on Harold Garfinkle's work on ethno-methodology soon become a standard part of my teaching repertoire. When I move to Boston College in 1982, my conversion to active learning modes is accelerated. Somewhat less diverse than Michigan undergraduates, Boston College students seem collectively more passive and dutiful. I become a full-fledged convert to the use of learning groups in my undergraduate courses, designing a series of exercises for each course with classes of varying sizes broken down into groups of five to seven students.

Since most of the exercises have a playful quality to them, I look forward to going to class to see how they work and how students will respond. I get to observe and listen a lot and get to play with the exercises to make them more effective next time. And I never have to listen to myself give a lecture that I've given before—perhaps many times. Finally, I have the continual gratification of watching most students fully engaged in a learning task, sometimes even staying after class to put the finishing touches on what they are doing.

Bob Ross quotes the headline in the *New York Times* of March 26, 1911: "141 Men and Girls Die in Waist Factory Fire; Trapped High Up in Washington Place Building; Street Strewn with Bodies; Piles of Dead Inside" (ch. 10).

It is the spring of 2003 and the Triangle Shirtwaist Factory fire is on my mind. I am working on my current project, developing a game simulation on global justice issues as a training tool for activists and a teaching tool for college courses. It involves a series of six cases, and I am reading about sweatshops.

Specifically, I am reading about the May 10, 1993, fire at the Kader Toy Factory in Bangkok, Thailand, in which the official count was 188 dead, 469 injured, but, as Greider (1997, 337) observes, "the actual toll was undoubtedly higher since the four-story buildings had collapsed swiftly in intense heat and many bodies were incinerated." The Triangle Shirtwaist Company fire—up to then the worst industrial fire in history—has been surpassed.

The Triangle Shirtwaist fire "provoked citizen reform movements and energized the labor [movement]," Greider writes (ibid., 338). No such wave of reform followed the fire in Thailand. In fact, I was barely aware of it until reading Greider and soon discovered that when I mentioned it in conversations about my work, most of my friends and colleagues were equally unaware. It was a short-lived story in the U.S. mass media. As Greider puts it, "A fire in Bangkok was like a typhoon in Bangladesh, an earthquake in

Turkey." As I continued my reading, I became increasingly convinced that understanding the political economy of globalization required understanding why the Kader Toy Factory was a nonevent.

It is almost a year later, and we have just completed a test run of "Factory Fire in Fabrikistan," one of the six cases in the global justice game. The scenario in the game focuses on the aftermath of the fire, and its details are based on Kader. Other parts of the scenario are invented—Fabrikistan is a middle-income country in Southeast Asia that is trying to attract international investment but is experiencing a debt crisis and is petitioning the World Bank and International Monetary Fund for relief. The goods are being produced for a company, Chic Duds International (CDI), that produces athletic shoes and apparel aimed at an international youth market.

The participants in the trial run are Boston College undergraduates in a course on globalization issues. They represent their various teams—some of them real and some of them fabricated. They are given a description of their team, a set of indicators or goals by which they can define their success, and a set of action options that they can decide on after a period of selective communication with other teams.

The students play skillfully, and most of them are able to raise their success indicators. And the results are grimly realistic—a toothless sense of Congress resolution is passed and the international financial institutions give Fabrikistan some debt relief but require them to raise taxes by 20 percent as a condition. Meanwhile, the various social action groups in the game custard-pie some Chic Duds officials and break some windows of Chic Duds retail outlets as part of an anticorporate campaign; Fabrikistan factories go ahead with business as usual. The postgame discussion brings out some of the features of the global system that would need changing to produce a different result, and the students and instructors enjoy it and feel it increased their understanding. Some fine-tuning is definitely needed, but I am pleased with the result and energized to move forward on this and the other six cases.

The next day I read the Ross chapter in this volume discussing his frustration that sweatshops in the Third World are privileged as an issue in ways that make similar conditions in the United States virtually invisible. Do we need another Triangle Shirtwaist Fire in New York City to make the case that this is a domestic issue as well?

David Snow and Catherine Corrigall-Brown say: "The framing effort is confronted with the problem of nonresonance. That is, the proffered framing falls on deaf ears by failing either to generate support among bystanders or potential adherents (what Klandermans [1984] has called 'consensus mobilization') or to activate adherents by moving them, metaphorically speaking, from the balcony to the barricades (what Klandermans [ibid.], has called 'action mobilization')" (ch. 13).

It is the late 1970s and I am spending a lot of my time in Ann Arbor at the Center for Research on Social Organization, located in a former elementary school building adjacent to major traffic arteries at the intersection of Packard and Division streets. This building—like the Temporary Classroom Building in an earlier era—has certain unintended spatial benefits. One must pass through public spaces and smaller bays to get to more private spaces; there are always conversations in progress among graduate students and faculty who hang around.

Many of these conversations focus on the wrongs of U.S. policy in Central America, reflecting the emerging Central American solidarity movement. Before long, another spatial advantage of the building comes into play: many of the offices have high-ceilinged, schoolroom windows, excellent for posting signs that can be readily seen by motorists driving by. These windows practically call out, "This space available for framing political messages."

The first signs that appear in these windows say, "U.S. Out of El Salvador." A few weeks after they appear, we hear a rumor that one or more people have called the university administration to complain that the university is "taking a political position." University officials have apparently passed on these complaints and suggested that the signs are a misuse of university property and a violation of university policy. No threats have been made as far as we know, and we are left to decide what to do about the complaints.

This sparks a lively discussion, and two solutions are proposed, to be implemented as each separate set of office users decides. The liberals opt for adding, in tiny letters at the bottom of each window sign, a disclaimer: "Does not necessarily represent the views of the University of Michigan." The radicals take down their signs and put up a new one, of equal size, reframing the issue as: "U.S. out of North America." We hear no more complaints.

We contributors to this volume continue to grapple in our own lives with the themes emphasized here: the tensions between activism and scholarship, the possibilities of the university as a locus of social action, and the critical importance of collaboration in democratic social movements. From different points of entry, we have found different points of engagement. As always, serendipity plays its role.

All of us have spent part of our lives in universities, but roughly half have located in activist settings outside the academy. Several completed advanced degrees in the social sciences with no intention of pursuing academic careers. One has left a tenured job in search of more meaningful political involvement. Those of us still located in academia continue to struggle to make the university a resource for social movements. We envision universities as safe spaces that welcome activists to engage in collaborative reflection on their experiences.

There is no simple formula. We have made different choices based on our strengths, our circumstances, and the opportunities that presented themselves. Looking at the choices of these contributors and reflecting on my own, I see multiple paths linking social movement scholarship and activism in mutually beneficial ways. Collaborations help us to overcome our individual limits and social locations. Our fates as social movement activists and scholars ultimately depend on the fates of social movements themselves.

In the personal anecdotes I have recounted, I see how my options were set by my historical times but also by my personal receptivity to certain opportunities. The world presents us with chances at collaborative relationships that allow us to be of use and to transcend our individual limits. But we have to be attentive and ready to be hopeful or we may miss the moment.

Seamus Heaney writes:

> History says, Don't hope
> On this side of the grave.
> But then, once in a lifetime
> The longed-for tidal wave
> Of justice can rise up,
> And hope and history rhyme.

I write this in the winter of 2004, in the meanest of mean seasons. The current U.S. administration seems like the worst in my lifetime, and from my reading in American history, possibly the worst of all time. I ponder whether this perception reflects reality or is a product of my life stage. Don't people my age always feel that the world is going to hell in a handbasket? When I discuss the problem with my age peers, they all assure me that my perception is real, but they are unreliable witnesses at the same life stage.

But I also believe that in its excesses, the present regime contains the seeds of its own destruction. There will be a future time when hope and history rhyme again. When it comes, I hope to be there in body—but if this is not to be, you can be sure that I will be there in spirit.

Notes

1. Unless otherwise indicated, all quotations are from chapters in this volume.

2. If the "Media Research and Action Project (MRAP)" label for our current project evokes ERAP, it is no mere coincidence, as my old left colleagues would have put it.

References

Belenky, Mary F., Blythe McVicker Clinchy, Nancy R. Goldberger, and Jill M. Tarule. 1986. *Women's Ways of Knowing.* New York: Basic Books.

Gamson, William A. 1968. "Stable Unrepresentation in American Society." *American Behavioral Scientist* 12 (November–December): 15–21.

———. 1990. *The Strategy of Social Protest,* 2nd ed. Belmont, CA: Wadsworth Press.

———. 1991. "Agency and Commitment in Social Movements." *Sociological Forum* 6: 27–50.

Greider, William, 1997. *One World, Ready or Not.* New York: Simon & Schuster/ Touchstone Books.

Lynd, Robert. 1939. *Knowledge for What?* Princeton, NJ: Princeton University Press.

Ross, Robert J. S. 1991. "At the Center and the Edge: Notes on a Life in and out of Sociology and the New Left." In *Radical Sociologists and the Movement,* ed. Martin Oppenheimer, Martin J. Murray, and Rhonda F. Levine, 197–215. Philadelphia: Temple University Press.

Contributors

KEVIN M. CARRAGEE is associate professor in communication and journalism at Suffolk University in Boston. His research focuses on the relationship between news, ideology, and social movements. He has contributed articles to multiple communication journals, including *Journal of Communication, Critical Studies in Mass Communication,* and *Journalism and Mass Communication Monographs.* He is currently editing two books examining communication activism.

CATHERINE CORRIGALL-BROWN is a PhD student in sociology and a fellow in the Center for the Study of Democracy at the University of California, Irvine. She is the author of several pieces on identity, activism, and the antiwar movement. Her dissertation is on disengagement from social movements.

DAVID CROTEAU is the author of *Politics and the Class Divide: Working People and the Middle-Class Left* and the coauthor (with William Hoynes) of several books about the mass media, including *The Business of Media: Corporate Media and the Public Interest* and *Media/Society: Industries, Images, and Audiences.* He has been active in a variety of social movements for twenty-five years and worked for several years in the peace and justice movement. He was associate professor of sociology at Virginia Commonwealth University where he taught for a decade.

MYRA MARX FERREE is professor of sociology at the University of Wisconsin–Madison. She is a longtime student of the women's movements and coauthor of *Shaping Abortion Discourse: Democracy and the Public Sphere in Germany and the United States* and the third edition of *Controversy and Coalition: The New Feminist Movement* (with Beth Hess). Her current projects are studies of transnational feminist networks on the Internet, a book on transformations of German feminism, and continuing analysis of abortion discourses and feminist politics.

RICHARD FLACKS is professor of sociology at the University of California, Santa Barbara. His books include *Making History: The American Left and the American Mind* and *Beyond the Barricades.* He has been active in community, campus, and labor movements for forty years.

WILLIAM A. GAMSON is professor of sociology and codirector, with Charlotte Ryan, of the Media Research and Action Project (MRAP) at Boston College. He is the author of *Talking Politics* and *The Strategy of Social Protest,* among other books and articles on political discourse, the mass media, and social movements. He is a past president of the American Sociological Association and a fellow of the American Academy of Arts and Sciences.

ADRIA D. GOODSON has worked to bridge the differences across race and class for most of her adult life. In Chicago, she worked with antiracism efforts in the Catholic Archdiocese of Chicago and participated in organizing efforts with the Industrial Areas Foundation. She is currently completing her doctorate in sociology at Boston College, focusing on philanthropy, social movements, and federal social policy in the United States.

RICHARD HEALEY is the president and founder of the Grassroots Policy Project. He has more than thirty-five years of experience in social movement politics, serving as a founder of the New America Movement and the Study Circle Resource Center. He served as executive director of the Institute for Policy Studies before founding the Grassroots Policy Project in 1993.

SANDRA HINSON is executive director of the Grassroots Policy Project. She has been active in the labor movement, reproductive rights, peace and justice work, and campaigns for universal health care. She develops strategic planning and training materials for the Grassroots Policy Project in consultation with local, statewide, and regional partners, and she has prepared strategic analyses of health care, taxes, and budget policies.

WILLIAM HOYNES is professor of sociology and director of the program in media studies at Vassar College, where he teaches courses on media, culture, and social theory. He is the author of several books and numerous articles on the contemporary media industry in the United States, including *Public Television for Sale: Media, the Market, and the Public Sphere* and (with David Croteau) *By Invitation Only: How the Media Limit Political Debate* and *The Business of Media: Corporate Media and the Public Interest.*

DAVID S. MEYER is professor of sociology and political science at the University of California, Irvine. He is author or coeditor of four other books on social movements, as well as numerous articles. He is working on several projects that explore the connections among social protest, institutional politics, and public policy.

CYNTHIA PETERS writes for *Z Magazine, ZNet, Dollars and Sense,* and other progresseive magazines. She is the editor of *Collateral Damage: The New World Order at Home and Abroad* and has contributed chapters to a number of edited volumes. Her grassroots organizing includes work with various neighborhood-based groups in Boston as well as with the regional peace and justice coalition United for Justice with Peace. She teaches in the Worker Education Program of the Service Employees International Union, Local 2020.

BARBARA RISMAN is the author of *Gender Vertigo: American Families in Transition.* Her recent work has been published in *Journal of Marriage and the Family* and *Qualitative Sociology,* and she edits the Gender Lens book series, designed to transform the discipline of sociology by mainstreaming research on gender throughout the curriculum. She is Alumni Distinguished Research Professor of Sociology at North Carolina State University and the cochair of Council on Contemporary Families, a national organization dedicated to providing information to the public and the media about the changes currently taking place in families.

ROBERT J. S. ROSS is professor of sociology and adjunct professor of community development and planning at Clark University in Worcester, Massachusetts. He is author of *Slaves to Fashion: Poverty and Abuse in the New Sweatshops.* A former vice president of Students for a Democratic Society, he has published numerous articles on the New Left and, recently, comparing the antisweatshop movement of the 1990s and 2000s to the campus-based movements of the 1960s.

LEILA J. RUPP is professor and chair of women's studies at the University of California, Santa Barbara. A historian by training, her teaching and research focus on sexuality and women's movements. She is coauthor with Verta Taylor of *Drag Queens at the 801 Cabaret* and *Survival in the Doldrums: The American Women's Rights Movement, 1945 to the 1960s*.

CHARLOTTE RYAN codirects the Media Research and Action Project at Boston College. A former labor and community organizer, she studies the interface of communication and movement building. She has collaborated with the Rhode Island Coalition Against Domestic Violence since 1996.

CASSIE SCHWERNER is a program director at the Schott Foundation for Public Education. She has been a research and editorial assistant to author Jonathan Kozol and has a PhD in sociology from Boston College.

DAVID A. SNOW is professor of sociology at the University of California, Irvine. He has authored numerous articles and chapters on collective action and social movements, conversion, framing processes, homelessness, symbolic interaction, and qualitative field methods. He is coauthor of, among other books, *Down on Their Luck: A Study of Homeless Street People* (with Leon Anderson) and coeditor of *The Blackwell Companion to Social Movements* (with Sarah Soule and Hanspeter Kriesi). He is the principal investigator of a comparative study of homelessness in four global cities (Los Angeles, Paris, São Paulo, and Tokyo).

VALERIE SPERLING is associate professor of government and international relations at Clark University in Worcester, Massachusetts. She is author of *Organizing Women in Contemporary Russia: Engendering Transition* and editor of *Building the Russian State: Institutional Crisis and the Quest for Democratic Governance*. She teaches courses on revolution and political violence, mass killing and genocide under communism, transitions to democracy, Russian politics, political science fiction, and feminist theory.

VERTA TAYLOR is professor of sociology and member of the affiliated faculty in women's studies at the University of California, Santa Barbara. She is coauthor of *Drag Queens at the 801 Cabaret* and *Survival in the Doldrums: The American Women's Rights Movement, 1945 to the 1960s*. She has written many articles on women's movements, the gay and lesbian movement, and social movement theory.

Index

academia, 193. *See also* universities

academy: role in social structure, 47. *See also* universities

ACORN, 160

activism: definition of, 46

activist research: debate about, 14; as defined by Francesca Cancian, 27. *See also* research

activist-academic collaboration, xvi–xvii, 57, 240; lessons for social movement scholarship, 74–75, 112–13; limits to, 111–12; post-research dilemmas, 109; risks of, 107–8. *See also* antisweatshop movement; Black feminist theory; Boston College Community Task Force; City Life/Vida Urbana; civic activism seminars; *Dollars and Sense*; drag queens; Fairness and Accuracy In Reporting (FAIR); labor movement; Media Research and Action Project; *Nightline* study; Rhode Island Coalition Against Domestic Violence

activists' use of theory (1960s), 61

Addams, Jane, 21

Alexander, Susan J., 182

Alinksy, Saul, 21, 23, 61, 65

Allen, Klare, 50

Alliance for Quality Education (AQE), 161, 166, 173

Alliance of Boston Neighborhoods, 89, 90

Allston-Brighton: as home to major universities, 81; housing trends in, 81–82, 91, 94; poverty rate in, 81; tension between students and long-term residents, 90–93

Allston-Brighton Community Development Corporation, 81, 89, 90

Allston-Brighton Healthy Boston Coalition, 81

alternative information: as focus of organizing, 42–44. *See also* educational model of organizing

alternative media: as conduit for radical academics, 44–45

American Sociological Association